Crossing the Rubicon

ALSO BY MARK DANNER

The Massacre at El Mozote

The Road to Illegitimacy

The Secret Way to War

Spiral: Trapped in the Forever War

Stripping Bare the Body

Torture and Truth

Crossing the Rubicon

The Betrayal of American Democracy, 2000–2026

MARK DANNER

nyrb New York Review Books New York

This is a New York Review Book

published by The New York Review of Books

207 East 32nd Street, New York, NY 10016

www.nyrb.com

Library of Congress Cataloging-in-Publication Data
Names: Danner, Mark, 1958– author
Title: Crossing the rubicon: the betrayal of American democracy / by Mark Danner.
Description: New York: New York Review Books, [2026] | Includes bibliographical references.
Identifiers: LCCN 2026012265 (print) | LCCN 2026012266 (ebook) | ISBN 9798896230892 paperback | ISBN 9798896230908 ebook
Subjects: LCSH: United States—Politics and government—21st century | Political leadership—United States—History—21st century | Political culture —United States—21st century
Classification: LCC JK275 .D36 2026 (print) | LCC JK275 (ebook)
LC record available at https://lccn.loc.gov/2026012265
LC ebook record available at https://lccn.loc.gov/2026012266

ISBN 979-8-89623-089-2
Available as an electronic book; ISBN 979-8-89623-090-8

The authorized representative in the EU for product safety and compliance is eucomply OÜ, Pärnu mnt 139b-14, 11317 Tallinn, Estonia, hello@eucompliancepartner.com, +33 757690241.

Printed in the United States of America on acid-free paper.
10 9 8 7 6 5 4 3 2

For my parents,
Robert and Rosalyn,
and
for my children,
Grace and Truman

Contents

Introduction

Julius Caesar led his Thirteenth Legion across the Rubicon, a small river north of Rome, on January 11, 49 BC, and in doing so set the Roman Republic on a course that would lead to Caesar's dictatorship and assassination and to the civil conflict that ended the Republic itself. Just before the crossing, according to Suetonius, Caesar uttered the immortal words "*Alea iacta est*": The die is cast. Donald Trump, vowing to tens of thousands of his followers to lead them to the US Capitol on January 6, 2021, exhorted them to "Fight like hell or you won't have a country anymore!" They would march forth to do so, creating images of spectacular violence, but their leader was not among them, electing to watch the struggle on television in a small dining room off the Oval Office. The coup led not to civil war but to Trump's second impeachment and then to his triumphant return to the White House four years later. No president had ever launched a coup against the state and no president had retaken the White House after doing so. In this as in so many other things, Donald Trump is a singular figure in American history.

Would it to be too much to claim the same for the quarter-century span that produced him? Certainly when historians frame their accounts of American politics of these years—a reporter's "first draft" of which you will find in the following pages—they will be met with a striking plenitude of unprecedented incident. The first presidential election decided by the Supreme Court. The first mass-casualty terrorist attack on American soil. The first worldwide "War on Terror." The first Great Recession in which taxpayers bailed out the financial system. The first Black man elected president. And yes, the first presidential coup d'état. Throw in two impeachments, two upside-down elections in which the winner received fewer votes than the loser, and three failed wars of choice, and you have a quarter century crowded with grand and sometimes violent political events for which it is hard to find parallels in the country's history.

Thanks to the accident of birth and the vision of the editors of *The New York Review of Books*, I found myself covering many of these events. I wrote about every presidential election from 2000 to 2024, often using a method perfected during the Florida vote recount. In key states, the candidates would appear for events every day as they barnstormed the battlegrounds in the days before the vote. I would rent a car, preferably a convertible, and find myself happily driving from rally to rally, listening all the while at high volume to the political ads and the talk radio shows and occasionally to the recorded memoirs of the candidates themselves. The backbone of the collection that follows is much of the reporting I did in advance of those elections—and sometimes, as in 2000, after them—during that eventful quarter century. But for a minor alteration here or there in the footnotes, the texts have been left unchanged. They constitute my major writing about American politics from *Bush* v. *Gore* to Donald Trump.[1]

It was the turn of the millennium, of course, that started it all. Perhaps that grand reconfiguration of clocks and calendars was also our political Y2K. On November 7, 2000—the fifty-fourth presidential election in the Enlightenment-born United States of America—the flipped coin landed . . . precisely on its thin edge. The people had spoken, and lo and behold it became a national nightmare to discover what, exactly, they had said, for their voices melded into what was damned near a perfect tie. And so our new millennium began not with clarity but with a brutal thirty-seven days of political warfare, all carried live from Florida. And what grand theater it was: politicians politicking, lawyers lawyering, judges judging. Barely had Florida's senior judges finally begun to recount the ballots when the 800-pound gorilla in Washington—the Supreme Court—stepped in and ordered them to stop. In effect, the court decreed that the winner would be the candidate backed by the majority of justices—a candidate who, notably, had received half a million fewer votes than his opponent. Behind the convoluted opinion the court handed down lay what was in truth a simple formula of raw political power: Five Republican justices equals one Republican president. And so it came to pass.

Bush v. *Gore* was a decision with legal force but little or no legitimacy, and it looms over the next twenty-five years of chaos and

1. My foreign reporting, principally on Haiti, Central America, Bosnia, and Iraq, and my writing on torture and other human rights issues, can be found principally in *Stripping Bare the Body: Politics Violence War* (Nation, 2009), and in other books, including *The Massacre at El Mozote* (Vintage, 1994) and *Spiral: Trapped in the Forever War* (Simon & Schuster, 2016).

confusion. The election eventually took its place within an unprecedented pattern: seven Democratic popular-vote victories in eight presidential contests, during which Republicans twice captured the White House despite receiving fewer votes than their opponents. Such an outcome—made possible by the anachronism of the Electoral College—had occurred only three times before in American history and never so close together. It was yet another unmistakable sign that the political system in which Americans took such pride was badly broken and less and less able to translate reliably voters' desires into political outcomes. A period that featured such Democratic dominance in the popular vote produced a Republican supermajority in the Supreme Court. The national legislature, its numbers already badly skewed by decades of gerrymandering, was distorted by Republican strength in rural and small states together with Democrats' proclivity to "waste" votes in densely populated cities. The counter-majoritarian tendencies that had plagued the system from its beginning were now increasingly exacerbated by population patterns—one party owned the countryside, the other the cities—that the founders could never have anticipated.

The president elevated by the Supreme Court was keenly aware of his legitimacy deficit and fiercely determined to overcome it. His opportunity came just nine months into his term, when Islamic fundamentalist fanatics hijacked commercial jetliners and directed them into the World Trade Center and the Pentagon, killing nearly three thousand people. To what extent the inexperienced president's response was motivated by shame—by the guilty knowledge that had he given the attention to this threat that his predecessor had urged, the attacks might have been thwarted—we'll never know. What is indisputable is that President George W. Bush responded to 9/11 by launching a global "War on Terror" that would become a debacle for the United States.

The War on Terror, so grand in its pronouncements, so unflinching in its ideological certainties, proved to be more than a defeat, though it included many of those. The United States lost the war in Iraq. The United States lost the war in Afghanistan. And it lost them in full color on the world's television screens. But it was the manner of the defeat that proved historic. The wars crippled the "rules-based international order" the United States had so painstakingly built and long claimed, even in the breach, to champion. During the War on Terror, the United States kidnapped civilians and detained them in secret "black site" prisons, tortured prisoners under color of law, and invaded Iraq against the will of the United Nations. In doing so, it undermined, through its crimes and even more through its failures, the already tenuous claims of American exceptionalism as well as the presumed competence of the American elite. Which is to say, it further undermined its own legitimacy. This began a process that was largely completed by Donald Trump. As I write, in the summer of 2026, the shreds of that legitimacy lie strewn all around us.

Contemplating this collapse, future historians will place alongside the War on Terror the bungled response to Hurricane Katrina of 2005 and the Great Recession of 2008–2009, when the entire high-flying, deeply leveraged financial system that had made the United States the model of prosperity around the world came crashing down. It is difficult now to convey the appalled astonishment of those months, as the titans of mighty Wall Street crawled, hats in hand, to the national Treasury, seeking bailouts from taxpayers in the hundreds of billions. And the bailouts came—by the trillions.

What did not come was any sort of justice. No well-heeled bankers were led off in handcuffs. None went to trial. Few even lost their jobs. The result of the vast financial scandal was simple: The government, under a Republican and then a Democratic president, stepped in to make the bankers and the investors whole. No one was forced to "take a haircut" except the taxpayer. It was a high-profile lesson in contemporary American capitalism that no citizen could miss. Forget moral hazard. In the United States, now and henceforth, profit would remain privatized while risk was socialized. Whatever happened, the dumb-as-dirt public would be left holding the bag.

It is fair to say that the public noticed. The first clear sign was the rise of the Tea Party in the 2010 midterms, an early expression of the furious populism that would seize control of the government half a decade later. Beneath the anger and the denunciations of elites of both parties, darker forces were gathering in a country now governed, for the first time in its history, by a Black man. He was moderate in most of his politics but the *fact* of Barack Obama was not moderate at all. It signified, unmistakably, that the country was changing, becoming what it had had the potential to be since the Voting Rights Act of 1965: a multiracial democracy. Since the founding, American politics had turned on the poisoned fulcrum of race. The most retrograde of its political institutions—the Electoral College, the Senate, even the filibuster—stand as evidence. So too does the country's more recent history: After the Civil Rights Act of 1964 was passed, the Democrats' long-established "solid South" became the Republicans' "Southern Strategy." As newly enfranchised Southern Blacks streamed into the Democratic Party, Southern whites streamed out. From Richard Nixon onward, Southern whites increasingly voted Republican. Blacks had finally been admitted into the political game but the game itself remained as racialized as ever. Meanwhile tens of millions of immigrants poured into the country, most from Mexico or points farther south, turning the United States of America ever more brown. The Democrats, the party of multiracial coalition, stood to benefit.

Thus came seven Democratic popular-vote victories in eight presidential elections—mitigated only by the perverse workings of the Electoral College. Still, the Democrats would likely never have nominated for president a Black man with Arabic and African names without the disaster of the Iraq War. In 2003, young Barack Obama sat in the Illinois state senate free to denounce Iraq as a "dumb war" and thus avoid implicating himself in an undertaking that would taint Hillary Clinton and other senior Democrats. As president, he would govern as a moderate, adopting many of his predecessor's War on Terror policies—including the expanded use of drone assassinations—and refusing to hold anyone accountable for torture and other excesses. Even his signature domestic accomplishment, the Affordable Care Act, was an ungainly compromise that had Republican roots and that fell far short of the "Medicare for All" long championed by the party's progressives.

And yet it was the fact of him. The fact of a Black man in the White House was in itself undeniably radical. And to many on the Right the very fact of him showed the stark radicalism of the Democrats as the face of a new multiracial country. The old white power structure was being overtaken by something new and frightening, and whatever exactly that was the president embodied it. It was no accident that birtherism—by which a New York businessman and reality-television star named Donald Trump first gained political attention—denied the legitimacy of Obama's presidency by denying his very citizenship. It was not just that Republicans were focusing on so-called cultural issues. The legitimacy of a Black American president was itself a cultural issue. His existence led to the nationalizing of a political complex that stretched back to Alabama Governor George Wallace and before in the American South, under the broad and enduring banner of white grievance. The first Black president set all the conditions for white grievance to go national.

Trump proved himself a virtuoso of grievance. Did this skill come from his own experience as an outer-borough hick, never taken seriously in the lofty precincts of Manhattan real estate, forever circling a power structure that disdained him? Perhaps. But from the moment he descended Trump Tower's gilded escalator to announce his candidacy, Trump skillfully shaped a politics of resentment and fear around the looming threat of that dark Other: the "illegal alien." It didn't matter that Obama had deported millions of undocumented immigrants, more than any president before him. "When Mexico sends its people," the new candidate declared, "they're not sending their best.... They're bringing drugs. They're bringing crime. They're rapists..." With a few sentences, Trump compressed decades of heavily racialized Republican politics on crime and drugs into a highly threatening politics of immigration. In the tried and true Republican formula, Democrats' dangerously "soft on crime" policies would lead to a Black man high on drugs raping and murdering your daughter. Now it would be the Democrats' "open border" policies that would lead a dusky illegal to do the same—and afterward to take your job as well.

Trump wielded this new politics of fear brilliantly. Its most effective target was what had been since the late 1960s the most sought-after voters in national elections: white men without college degrees.

For these working-class and lower-middle-class voters Trump's appeal was cultural and economic. To vote against "open borders" was to vote against the changing racial face of the country and the globalizing economy that had stolen high-paying factory jobs and shipped them to Mexico and China. Trump's populism decried the elites responsible for these policies—in both parties—as "idiots" and "suckers" in thrall to the corrupt "swamp" in Washington. He claimed he alone knew how to defeat them because he dealt with them every day as a masterful businessman. True, serious business leaders had long since dismissed Donald Trump as a tabloid-obsessed clown. But millions of American voters knew him only as the commanding impresario of *The Apprentice* and *The Celebrity Apprentice*. They knew he was a business genius because he had played one on TV.

Much was made of the fact that he would be the first man elected president with no government or military experience. More telling was that he was the first who was, in his essence, a celebrity. The cameras loved him and rewarded him with incalculable amounts of free media. Not only did Fox run his rallies live, so did CNN. He dominated the news cycle, and the editors and producers, however unsympathetic they might be to his politics, were his willing accomplices. He generated millions of eyeballs and eyeballs had become the currency of the age. Though the candidate himself initially treated his campaign as a branding exercise—he did not expect to win—he worked furiously, campaigning with particular intensity in the Midwest: the Democrats' famous "blue wall" of Michigan, Wisconsin, and Pennsylvania. In the end, he narrowly carried those decisive states, filled as they were with underemployed white men. His opponent, the first woman to be nominated by a major party, won three million more votes. But Donald Trump ascended to the White House.

He denounced, in his first moments as president, "American carnage." He insisted, despite clear evidence to the contrary, that he had drawn the largest inaugural crowd in history. It was only the opening salvo in his war on truth, expertise, competence. *The Washington Post* would eventually count in his first term more than thirty thousand falsehoods. He carried on a "love affair" with the North Korean dictator, threatened to withdraw the United States from NATO, and, during a pandemic that would kill more than a million Americans, urged people to inject bleach into their veins. But nothing would so exemplify his first presidency than the manner of its ending. After losing the 2020 election to Joe Biden, he denounced the result as "the Big Steal" and exhorted his supporters to march on the Capitol and prevent the counting of electoral votes. Thus the first attempted coup in American history unfolded live on national television.

He had led an attack on the state and had done it in public. And yet the state, confronted with this vital danger, refused to act. The Democratic House impeached him, but the Senate refused to convict, its Republican leader noting that there were laws and courts for such matters. But Joe Biden's attorney general proved to be uninterested in bringing charges. By the time he finally appointed a special prosecutor, the next election was approaching and Trump was gaining strength. Though the special prosecutor attempted to bring the case to trial, it was effectively blocked by the Supreme Court, which saw fit to craft out of whole cloth a new doctrine of presidential immunity. For those with long memories, it was the most appalling decision since *Bush* v. *Gore*.

The state's delay in seeking justice for the coup ensured that the story of Trump's comeback and the story of the state's vindictiveness would become one story. Trump recognized this instinctively, perceiving that the state's belated attacks on him drove his supporters. These attacks reaffirmed, in each day's news, the story of corrupt, incompetent, and self-protective "swamp creatures" dominating Washington. For nearly a decade, he had sustained his assault on truth, expertise, and competence, and tens of millions had come to believe him. The authority once exercised by a centralized press had long since fractured into the decentralized chaos of the Internet. Against that landscape, Trump emerged as the country's dominant troll, denouncing the institutions his supporters believed stood between them and the lives they had been promised. The elites, in this telling, had shipped good jobs overseas, entangled the country in costly foreign wars, and seized the spoils for themselves. It was time for a reckoning. "I am your retribution," Trump vowed. "Burn it down!" they screamed. He won every battleground state. He became only the second man to lose the presidency and then win it again. And this time, he won the popular vote.

His second term has proven far more radical than his first. He fired hundreds of thousands of government workers; dismantled institutions, including the U.S. Agency for International Development and the Department of Education; attacked universities and withdrew their funding; struck out at major law firms; seized control of the Kennedy Center and renamed it after himself; and launched a program of mass deportation that has seen successive Democratic-run cities "occupied" by tens of thousands of ICE paramilitaries. He detained upward of sixty thousand and deported hundreds of thousands. He killed hundreds in drone strikes on small boats in the Caribbean, invaded Caracas and seized Venezuela's president, imposed a fuel embargo on Cuba, and attacked Iran in an ongoing war that closed down the Strait of Hormuz. He has shattered the already crippled "rules-based international order" and abandoned any pretense of the custom by which presidents consulted Congress and the nation before taking the country to war. He seems to be completing his destruction of NATO. And his term is only half complete.

What will the next half bring? The Republican Congress is supine. The courts have ruled against the administration hundreds of times, and though it has mostly obeyed, it has sometimes ignored them. Again and again, Trump in his unremitting aggression has exposed what seemed to be hallowed practices as nothing more than norms without legal force and has shattered them without looking back. Even now, the system is unable to cope with the extreme corruption that persists in the full glare of public scrutiny. As I write, the country is gearing up for midterm elections that could put Congress in the hands of the opposition. If it does, will the administration pay that Congress any mind? For now, the shadow of illegitimacy and Trump's brazen misuse of emergency powers has left our supposedly exceptional nation with a hybrid system: a constitutional dictatorship. The United States has seen facsimiles of this before—under Lincoln, under Roosevelt—but never in the absence of a true emergency.

Such a system, whatever it is, is not stable. Nothing Trump touches is. It must advance, mutate, grow. And the president, dominating the news cycle, will push it erratically, inexorably forward. Many dare to hope that, after Trump, a restoration will come, a period of institutional repair and renewal of the sort that followed Watergate.

But we cannot know now what exactly will remain to restore. At what point does the system, undermined, subverted, abused, become irretrievable?

On January 6, as I describe in the pages that follow, Donald Trump led his followers across the Rubicon. Wherever that finally leads, we are unlikely to find a clear path back. The first quarter century of the new millennium exposed an antiquated political system that seems less and less able to translate pressing political claims into clear outcomes, even as the rise of a truly multiracial electorate and an increasingly desperate resistance to it puts the country under stress as never before. During the last decade, political norms put in place over centuries have been swept away. Will the coming years really see a sustained effort to restore them? Or will they see a crusade of retribution, as voters turn from party to party in an unending search for "justice"? Or will there come a purposeful campaign to refashion and modernize the ways we choose our leaders and govern ourselves? For all its ingenuity, our ancient constitutional machine resists reform. To undertake fundamental change at a time of such bitter combat seems unpromising and perilous. But the alternative may be a violent collapse amid relentless accusations of cheating and vote rigging. Thus far we have barely managed to skirt that abyss. As the midterms approach, America's government and elections are under siege, and the cracks in the foundations—plain to see a quarter century ago, where this account begins—are widening. *Alea iacta est.* The die is cast.

Grizzly Peak, Berkeley
July 2026

Scandal and the Road to Deadlock

November 15, 2000

GAZE UPWARD, through the gaseous clouds of rhetoric littering the sky from the campaign that would not end—"I will never let you down," "I will restore honor and dignity to the White House"—and you can spy, casting a shadow on the land like Barthelme's Dead Father, an enormous pair of lips, belonging not to the Vice President or the Texas governor but to a young woman from Beverly Hills who one fateful day delivered a slice of pizza to the President of the United States. Scandal transformed what should have been an election commanded by a competent if boring incumbent seeking to ride unprecedented prosperity at home and peace and tranquillity abroad. The politics of scandal, of revelation, investigation, and prosecution, born of partisan deadlock and a widely excluded electorate, ended by producing the closest election in more than a century—and, inevitably, more scandal in its turn.*

"What happened yesterday," Pat Buchanan declared on November 8 with characteristic swagger, "was the American people voted to convict Bill Clinton." Better say they had chosen to punish his would-be successor for a fatal lack of subtlety. That Americans continue to approve Clinton's performance by historic margins and yet feel obliged to disdain him personally attests to the President's extraordinary suppleness as a politician. His would-be successor faced the obvious challenge of claiming the glittering mantle—the lowest inflation and unemployment in a generation, deficits magically transformed into surpluses, eight years of declining crime, and on and on—without drinking from the poisoned chalice. This trick the lumbering Al Gore never mastered. Clinton managed to "separate himself" from Clinton much more adroitly than Gore ever could.

Condescending in manner, chameleon-like in his relentless attempts to court the undecided, Gore never achieved intimacy with voters, and the calculation evident in his desperate efforts to distance himself from Clinton worsened his own "character problem." Unable to shed Clinton's moral baggage and still lay claim to the administration's accomplishments, Gore ended by relinquishing the vital advantage of the successful incumbent: the appeal to continuity. Running as "my own man," he gave invaluable cover to the inexperienced Governor George W. Bush, who felt free to proclaim, without risk of decisive refutation, "They had their chance. They have not led. We will." Gore's clumsy refusal to let Clinton campaign for him made the President's "shadow" ubiquitous and left the Vice President himself seeming ungrateful and untrustworthy. The smiling Texas governor seized on Gore's predicament, emphasizing the Vice President's proclivity for "flip-flops" and "exaggerations" and intoning solemnly and relentlessly the need to "restore honor and dignity to the White House." Though the Clinton impeachment scandal had been deeply controversial, and voters had punished

Republicans for it in the 1998 congressional elections, leading to the overthrow of Newt Gingrich, Bush could allude to the scandal without fear of backlash, for he knew he was attacking a sitting target. Gore had trapped himself by his refusal even to broach the impeachment and thus could say nothing of the Republicans' highly unpopular record of carrying "partisan bickering" to new depths in Washington. The unexorcised ghost of Clinton, unmentioned but always present, haunted Gore and did him only harm.

Shortly after Clinton's reelection and years before Americans had heard of White House interns, Boyden Gray, Bush *père*'s former White House counsel, predicted that because of continuing Republican-led investigations in Congress, "Clinton will be debilitated." That Gray's prophecy came bitterly true for Al Gore testifies to the current dominance in Washington of "politics by other means." In their book of that name, Benjamin Ginsberg and Martin Shefter describe in detail how, during the last quarter-century,

> elections have become less decisive as mechanisms for resolving conflicts and constituting governments.... Rather than engage in an all-out competition for votes, contending political forces have come to rely upon such weapons of institutional combat as congressional investigations, media revelations, and judicial proceedings to defeat their foes.[1]

1. *Politics by Other Means: Politicians, Prosecutors, and the Press from Watergate to Whitewater* (Norton, revised edition, 1999), p. 16.

Since Watergate, all the ingredients of this "politics of scandal" have been ready to hand: a closely divided government, often with one party controlling Congress and the other the White House; an alienated electorate sharply divided by class, age, gender, and income, in which only one voter in two casts a presidential ballot; and a powerful and omnipresent communications industry complete with twenty-four-hour news channels hungry to sell scandalous "megastories" to eager viewers. John Ehrlichman, Bob Haldeman, Richard Nixon, Jim Wright, Tony Coelho, Oliver North, Samuel Pierce, John Tower, Newt Gingrich, Webb Hubbell, Bill Clinton; Watergate, Iran-contra, the Keating Five, Travelgate, Whitewater, Lewinsky: these names and nicknames have defined American politics for the last quarter-century.

In the hard-fought, down-to-the-wire election of 2000, one eligible voter in two did not vote. The major parties, beneficiaries of a corrupt funding system, spent more than a billion dollars in advertising, almost all of it "targeted" by issue and by television market to those, like the elderly and the suburban middle class, already known to vote in relatively large numbers. Neither party sees an interest in delivering a message that might mobilize the voters who never turn out. Republicans fear that most of them, poorer and less well educated, would be more likely to favor Democrats; Democrat incumbents fear that these millions of "great unwashed" might prefer that others occupy their now safe seats.

Victories at the polls are thus limited, circumscribed; real combat follows the election, when the congressional committees and the special prosecutors begin their work. In this they are greatly aided by a broadcast and print press that is "not liberal-leaning but 'scandal-leaning,'"[2] whose pundits have learned through long practice to combine artfully the lucrative appeal of sex and scandal with the chiding moral disapprobation displayed by Jenny Jones or Jerry Springer "interviewing" a scantily clad stripper.

Deadlock breeds scandal; scandal has now bred deadlock. Only serious reform offers a hope of eventually breaking this cycle. And yet can anyone imagine the incoming government passing effective laws to limit the sway of money in politics, opening up the electoral regime with an eye toward making voting easier, and championing issues that would attract to the polls millions of currently ignored and disaffected voters? To ask the question is to answer it. Born of relentless contention, the new president's "mandate" will be limited and uncertain, much more so than Bill Clinton's was when he arrived at the White House in 1993 after winning only a plurality. Reform will be out of the question. The knives will be out. Soon committees will be organized and prosecutors will be at their work. The press will hover and feed. The politics of scandal will hold sway. Gaze upward: only the spectacles will change.

2. The phrase was used by Paul Begala, the former Clinton adviser and current cable television commentator.

The Road to Illegitimacy

February 22, 2001

1. In the Iron Triangle

AFTER YOU HAVE SPENT some days searching for the secret of political legitimacy in Miami and West Palm Beach, you want to go further. You have witnessed the ritual on the nineteenth floor of the gleaming granite Stephen P. Clark Building in downtown Miami, where, two months after the voters spoke and a month after the Supreme Court handed down its judgment, a journalist from *The Miami Herald* and a man from the BDO Seidman accounting firm sit hunched over a long table, squinting for five hours each day at the perforated punch-card ballots that were intended, on November 7, to express "the will of the people." You have plumbed the intricacies of the hushed ceremony in West Palm Beach's pale adobe Governmental Center, where three journalists, two accountants, three Republican Party volunteers, a lawyer, and assorted hangers-on lean forward in unison to behold and record the mysteries of these punctured cardboard artifacts that were meant to confer legitimacy on our country's leader.

After many days contemplating these strange ceremonies, you would do well to climb into your red convertible, put the radio on and the top down, and head north, and after many hours of working your way through the clotted mess of Interstate 95, past beach communities and retirement homes and golf courses and condominiums, you will turn west and enter Florida's "iron triangle," a land of farming and lumbering now become a land of teeming prisons and the people who guard them, and there you will find, in a red brick courthouse in Lake Butler, the formidable Babs Montpetit—or Miss Babs, as she is known, the elected supervisor of elections of Union County—and, in the flock of padlocked metal "precinct cans" gathered about her feet, Miss Babs's blessed paper ballots.

A man in white shirt and blue-and-white pants, a prison trustee from the nearby North Florida Reception and Medical Center, lugs the battered cans forward and Miss Babs, perfectly coiffed, resplendent in gold earrings and a gold twenty-dollar medallion, extracts from them sheaves of folded sheets of paper. Having spent days contemplating the recording of dimpled chads, I greet these ballots as a blessed sight; for here there is no cardboard—no punch cards; no chads, hanging, dimpled, or otherwise—and indeed no machines of any kind. Here, alone among Florida's sixty-seven counties, there is only paper, with the printed name of each candidate and to the right of each name a printed box meant to receive, in the form of a penciled cross or check or diagonal line, the mark of the voter's clearly stated will. And in the next few moments, as Miss Babs spreads out before me and before the *Miami Herald* reporter and the accountant who accompanies her and the Republican observer looming over the table ballot after ballot from Union County's pile of 258 "no votes," I see quite clearly the obscurities attendant on that seemingly obvious notion of a "clearly stated will."

Miss Babs passes the ballots swiftly over the table, precinct by precinct, presenting you with an eccentric glimpse into a certain segment of Union County. Apart from the handful of "true undervotes," in which the voter made no mark for any presidential candidate—there are only twenty-five of these—one begins to see among the check marks and crosses certain identifiable types: those voters who insisted on choosing two different presidential candidates, often in rather plausible combinations—Gore and Nader, for example, or Bush and Buchanan; those who insisted on voting for three or four or five of the ten presidential candidates; and those sentimental souls who, confronted with the ten hopefuls, could not help offering their support to all of them. Some apparently decided each grouping of president and vice-president offered a separate choice, from which they selected Bush over Cheney, say, then Lieberman over Gore, LaDuke over Nader, and so on. A handful of voters, having checked one candidate from each party, wrote in, in the spot provided for a write-in vote, their true choice. (A number of Al Gores here.) One voter chose to add John McCain for president and Colin Powell for vice-president; another, having marked Bush and several others, wrote in one Dick Goldberg for president and filled out his ticket with Elmer Fudd.

Among these collections of signs, these bits of expression from the lost world of November 7, one could also make out a significant number in which the voter had made a choice, voting for Gore or for Bush in the first column of nine presidential candidates; and then, where the presidential candidates continued in a second column, cast a second vote for Monica Moorehead of the Workers World Party. It seemed possible, I said to Miss Babs and the room at large, that these voters had been misled by the cluttered ballot and thought the candidate in the Workers World and "write-in" categories, over in their separate column to the right, were competing in another race.

"You can't say that! You can't say that! That's intention. It's pure speculation!" This was the Republican observer, Mr. Remzey L. (Paul) Samarrai, the mayor of Micanopy—"The Heart of Old Florida," as his business card had it—who would not be placated by my ready admission that this was, indeed, pure speculation, and that, in any event, nothing could be done about it. These ballots had already been counted by hand—they were only counted by hand—and the sort of mistakes these double votes represented, unlike many of those on the punch cards in Palm Beach and Broward and Duval Counties, presented an ambiguity of intention that no human counter could penetrate; these were the final errors, those that had to be placed squarely on the side of the uncorrectable.

On the other hand, the source of these mistakes—their dependency at least in part on a somewhat confusing ballot—meant that assessing responsibility for them is a more complicated matter. And as to the charge of "intention"—or, more fully, "*divining* the intent of the voter," as James A. Baker III pronounced it with such deadly effect throughout the battle of Florida in November—this was in fact what Florida law had set as the standard in any recount: "the clear intent of the voter." The Republicans, observing the "media recount" in every place *The Miami Herald*, or *The Palm Beach Post*, or *The Orlando Sentinel*, or any of the other papers involved has reporters, were now insisting that only the "Supreme Court standard" be applied. This "standard," which Republicans assert in their daily press release on the count, *Reality Check*, is now "the law of the land," in fact originated in a remark by Justice Sandra Day O'Connor in oral arguments before the Court, when she inquired of David Boies in some irritation: "Well, why isn't the standard the one that voters are instructed to follow, for goodness' sakes? I mean, it couldn't be clearer." To which Boies replied by citing, once more, the law: "Well, Your Honor, because in Florida law since 1917, *Darby* v. *State*, the Florida Supreme Court has held that where a voter's intent can be discerned, even if they don't do what they're told, that's supposed to count."

One can't help feeling, in looking at the great variety of people and experience manifested by the marks on those paper ballots, that the more pointed response to Justice O'Connor's assertion that "it couldn't be clearer" would have been: clearer to whom? It certainly couldn't be clearer to Justice O'Connor, a well-educated white lady from Arizona. But how about, say, Old Enoch, one of Miss Babs's voters in Union County? "Now there was Old Enoch," she said in her sweet-as-caramel lilt, "and Old Enoch, he's a nice black man, you know, and he had a terrible time. He came in here the first time and he marked one ballot but he wasn't happy with that so he threw it away and he wandered off and then he came back again, and he marked another. But he was suffering; he had the pressure on him, you know. And I said, 'Enoch, you can only get one more, you know the law says you can only have but three ballots.' But he was suffering and he had the pressure on him and he wanted to do right but he didn't know what to do."

Had I seen Old Enoch's ballot in the pile of "no votes"? Had he resolved his suffering by voting for both Gore and Bush, or had he chosen one and then perhaps marked a second candidate in the second column, confused, as many seemed to have been, by the superfluity of names in the presidential columns (the same superfluity that led to the notorious "butterfly ballot" in Palm Beach County and the less notorious but perhaps more damaging "caterpillar ballot" in Duval County)? If Old Enoch, armed with his pencil and confronted by a series of boxes to check, had done either of these things, his vote, like those of 180,110 other Floridians, would not have counted.

What could be simpler than a paper with a list of names on it and a pencil to mark it with? Justice O'Connor would have had no problem with it. And yet to a fair number of people in Union County, Florida, the stark instructions—"TO VOTE for a candidate, mark a cross (X) in the blank space at the RIGHT of the name of the candidate for whom you desire to vote"—appeared to have been, in their very simplicity, opaque. No one said not to mark each column. No one said not to mark each party. And so they marked and they marked again, sometimes with a sure and decisive check, sometimes with a faltering unsteady hand that seemed to betray very old age or an unfamiliarity with the pencil. In Florida's only paper-ballot county, where no punch cards or other machines posed a mechanical barrier between a voter's voice and the recording of it, the number of voters who cast ballots that would not be counted was 6.3 percent of all who went to the polls, more than double the rate statewide.

Though there is no way to say whether Old Enoch's vote, the product of so much worry and self-inflicted pain, was among those "no votes," one can say that for many people, even before they confront a punch card or an optical scanner, voting is a strange and exotic activity in which those with certain kinds of knowledge—including, most obviously, the ability to read but also a familiarity with the wider worlds of politics and contemporary events—are favored and those without them are at a disadvantage. This is a fact that Florida judges and the Florida legislature seem to have recognized in setting out "intent of the voter" as the standard for a hand count. And it is why, if Old Enoch had made certain kinds of mistakes—say, putting a check before "Gore" and then writing in "Al Gore" under "Write In Candidate"—in Union County his vote still would have counted. In Union County, uniquely in Florida, they count every vote by hand.

On the other hand, if Old Enoch had done the same in neighboring Lake County, where they use the optical scanning system, his vote would have been recorded as an "overvote" and would not have been revealed until December 18, when counters working by hand discovered 376 ballots on which people had filled in the oval next to Al Gore, then filled in the one next to "Write In" and written in his name. They found 246 ballots on which voters had done the same for George Bush. The state of Florida recorded all of these as overvotes and yet the voter's intent "couldn't be clearer." These 622 votes—in an election officially decided by 537—were discovered not by the state of Florida but by the journalists of *The Orlando Sentinel.*

How you feel about the 2000 election and the political power it eventually conferred on George W. Bush will to some degree depend on how you feel about people like Old Enoch, and where you think his responsibility to make his voice heard ends and that of the state begins. One view of that responsibility is embodied in the Florida law that David Boies cited; a quite different view is to be found in Justice O'Connor's impatient question and in the decision she and four of her colleagues later handed down.

2. A Very Close Election

All through life you have to follow instructions. And if you don't follow instructions...

—THERESA LEPORE, Palm Beach Elections Supervisor

They lean forward, in West Palm, and they rock back. They look, squint, mark their tally sheets. They rock forward in sequence, a wave of faces moving around the table, following the movement of the punch-card ballot as the expressionless election worker holds it before their eyes: first the two Republican observers—front of the ballot, then back—then the *Miami Herald* reporter and the accountant to her right, then the *Palm Beach Post* reporter with his colleague behind him, then the earnest young man from Judicial Watch, the Washington advocacy group. One side, then the other; lean, squint; rock back, mark. No vote. Dimple. No vote. No vote. Dimple. No vote. The silence is total. They arrive at 10 AM, they leave at 3 PM. They "inspect" five or six hundred ballots a day, all of them "undervotes," ballots on which the machines detected no vote for president. At this rate they will be here for weeks. "I said they'd be here till Easter," Theresa LePore tells me. "Now I'm thinking Fourth of July."

It is an exacting effort, this "ballot review," and it is also very sad. When historians look back on 2000—and when they pronounce the word "2000" they will likely mean by it that year's presidential election, which they will class along with those of 1824, 1876, and 1888—they will have to explain how it was that in that particular year the American political system failed to produce a president broadly viewed as legitimate. One answer that will not do is simply that the election happened to be close—extremely, unprecedentedly close—because in fact it was not. The 2000 election was not even the closest in my lifetime:

2000 Gore–Bush 539,947

1968 Nixon–Humphrey 510,314

1960 Kennedy–Nixon 118,574

More than half a million more Americans voted for Gore than for Bush, a greater number than carried Nixon to victory over Humphrey in 1968, and more than four times the number that carried Kennedy over Nixon in 1960.

What distinguished the 2000 election was that it was extraordinarily, almost inconceivably, close in one state; that neither candidate could claim victory in the country without claiming victory in that single state; and that, finally, an uncommonly large percentage of the ballots in that state—almost 3 percent, as against 2 percent nationwide—were thrown out by the counting machines, either because they recorded no vote for president or because they recorded more than one. It was not simply that Bush's lead in Florida was extremely slight but that the problems with the vote itself made it unstable—an instability that was magnified on the day after the election when the mandatory mechanical recount cut Bush's lead from 1,784 votes to 327. This dramatic change, cutting the margin to less than a fifth of what it had been, suggested strongly that there were legitimate votes that had not been counted. For the two leading candidates in the 2000 election, the challenge of claiming both victory and legitimacy came down to the problem of how to confront those 180,110 discarded votes in a way that most supporters of both candidates could accept. Neither candidate achieved this. And thus the counters, sitting today in Palm Beach County and Miami-Dade County and Union County and all across the state, leaning, squinting, marking.

Gore's lead in the vote nationwide amounted to half of 1 percent (0.516 percent); Bush's official lead in Florida, which the Supreme Court's decision fixed at 537 votes, amounts to five thousandths of 1 percent (0.005 percent). (In the next closest state, New Mexico, Gore's margin was more than twelve times greater.) At the same time, the 180,110 ballots that were thrown out in Florida in 2000 not only represented a much higher percentage than those discarded nationwide; they represented a higher percentage than Florida itself had discarded in 1996 (2.93 percent against 2.52).

How was it that in a scant four years the voting skills of Floridians had so deteriorated? Setting aside for the moment the Old Enoch Question—whose responsibility is it?—one can point to some obvious answers. First, Floridians overwhelmingly passed, during the impeachment crisis in 1998, Amendment 11, which made it much easier for "third-party" candidates to secure a listing on the presidential ballot and which, two years later, presented election supervisors with the obvious problem of how to place, legibly, ten presidential candidates on one ballot. (In 1996, Florida had listed four.)

Second, thanks to the great importance accorded Florida by both Democrats and Republicans—and the vast amounts of money both parties poured into the state for advertisements, voter registration, and get-out-the-vote efforts—turnout in 2000 rose dramatically, from 5,437,964 to 6,145,220. Third, many of these voters were coming to the polls for the first time; African-American turnout, for example, is estimated to have risen by an astonishing 65 percent and four in ten of these voters were coming to the polls for the first time. Fourth, these first-time voters, and indeed many of the poorer and less educated ones, are far more likely to live in counties that use the old punch-card ballot systems, which consistently produce a much higher rate of under- and overvotes—in the 2000 election, nearly three times higher—than other voting methods; eight of every ten ballots that were thrown out in Florida in 2000 were thrown out in counties using punch cards. (Since these counties voted overwhelmingly for Gore over Bush—51.8 percent to 46 percent—the error rates of the voting machines proved, this year, to be a critical Republican advantage.)

And so in the fall of 2000 Supervisor of Elections Theresa LePore found herself confronted with a problem: "A member of my staff drew up several versions of the ballot," she tells me in her soft voice. "The one-page version, the print was just too small to read. The facing-page version, we had used it in the late Eighties for amendments. It would let us make the print larger. I thought it would be easier to read; that was my 'ulterior motive.'" She pauses, laughs softly: "I assumed people would read the directions."

In 1996 Palm Beach County discarded 14,868 ballots, or 3.55 percent of the total; in 2000, Palm Beach County discarded 29,702 ballots, or 6.45 percent. In 1996, 0.75 percent of Palm Beach voters recorded more than one vote for president; in 2000, 4.16 percent did. In precincts 66 and 67 in Riviera Beach, a predominantly African-American part of the county, the rate of overvoting ran to more than 15 percent, meaning that one in six of those who came to the polls voted twice for president and thus nullified his or her ballot.

In Duval County, far to the north, Election Supervisor John Stafford—like LePore a soft-spoken, dedicated public servant—solved the ballot problem by placing the presidential candidates on two pages, five on the first, five on the second. In a normal year, Stafford told me, three to four thousand Duval residents punch more than one hole for president; this time, 21,942 did. On election day 26,909 voters had their ballots thrown out, more than three times the 1996 figure of 7,762. More than 40 percent of these were concentrated in four predominantly black council districts of Jacksonville's North Side, where Democrats had mounted an intensive effort to register new voters, telling them to "vote that second place." On page one, the "second place"—second punch-hole down—was Al Gore; on page two it was Patrick Buchanan.

Although the recount in Duval has not yet begun—thus far the county, citing impending lawsuits, has refused to separate out the undervotes from the rest of the ballots—I saw a tally sheet of the discarded ballots in one North Side precinct. As Stafford pointed out to me, about half of these voters had punched the card more than twice, or twice on one page; the other half, though, had followed the published instructions to vote on every page, and in most cases, as you would expect in this precinct, had "punched the second position" for Al Gore.

"There's no way we set out to 'disenfranchise' anybody," said Stafford, a quiet man who, like LePore, has spent much of his working life trying to get people to vote and suddenly found himself the target of a great deal of unaccustomed and painful criticism for throwing out their ballots. "Some people just want to play the race card. But the fact is, we had the same ballot all over town, the same ballot in every precinct." He did not, of course, have the same people all over town. According to a *Washington Post* computer analysis, in the most heavily white precincts of Jacksonville, one ballot in fourteen was thrown out; in largely black precincts more than one in five was; in some black precincts the rate was as high as one in three.

What are we to make of this startling disparity? Though Stafford freely acknowledges that part of the problem was "literacy, I mean you have to have certain skills," he argues, like LePore, that "the voter has to take on some responsibility. I mean, if you punch that stylus through that card, I don't think there's a more accurate system." Stafford is surely sincere, as is Theresa LePore when she says that people must "follow instructions." But where does the responsibility of the state lie when racial and class differences in "error rates" are so stark—and in a place where many people vividly remember literacy tests and other "informal" barriers to voting? "It couldn't be clearer," says Justice O'Connor. As a Democratic lawyer who tried to help angry voters on election day remarked to a colleague of mine, "You try arguing, to someone who says he's confused, 'You're not confused.'"

3. The Media Ballot Review

We say people have the right to vote. We don't say "educated people" or "literate people" or even "smart people." Just people.

—Mark Seibel, *The Miami Herald*

Drive to downtown Miami, take the elevator to the nineteenth floor of the Stephen P. Clark Building—the same nineteenth floor where Republicans staged their "bourgeois riot" on November 22, after which the canvassing board decided not to go ahead with their hand recount—and you will find an intimate scene. Amy Driscoll of *The Miami Herald* sits beside John Cox of BDO Seidman and both face Jesus Arrechea, the election worker, who holds up ballot after ballot. Some are blank, some have a mark or two near the bottom; some are elaborately decorated, with a pattern of punctures that, held up to the Miami skyline, becomes a dancing pattern of light. Unlike the ritual silence of West Palm, here there is a litany:

> "This is number two?"
> "Number two."
> "Can you turn that around?"
> "Would you lean it back?"
> "Okay, lean it that way, bring it back... Yeah, that's it."
> "This three?"
> "Yeah, three..."

They lean forward in unison, then back, reporter and accountant, then pause to inscribe their separate sheets, noting the type of mark, its "position" on the ballot. I watch as Driscoll's tally sheet fills up: No mark, no mark, no mark, dimple (position six), no mark, pinprick (position two), punched cleanly (position seven), no mark, no mark, punched cleanly (position seven), no mark, no mark, punched cleanly (position three), and on and on. Position two on the punch card belongs to Bush-Cheney, position six on the punch card belongs to Gore-Lieberman; position seven on the punch card belongs to no one—although it would have belonged to Gore if the card were badly aligned on the machine, just as position three, also an orphan, would belong to Bush.

The dimples, though they had become a matter of great controversy, might well have been counted as votes had the recount not been interrupted in Miami-Dade; the "clean punches" in position three or position seven, though the voter was doubtless attempting to vote for Bush or Gore, would not have been. In this distinction, clear as it is, lies some of the poignancy I feel as I watch these two people engaged in their strange occupation, leaning and squinting. For all their work, they are confronting only a small subset of the vast number of errors, misperceptions, and general foul-ups in the Florida election. These include the voters who were wrongly purged from the rolls; the people who thought they were registered but because of bureaucratic "miscommunication" between the department of motor vehicles and the department of elections found they were not; the police roadblocks that in at least one instance near Tallahassee seem to have intimidated some voters trying to get to the polls; the decision of the television networks to project a victory for Al Gore in Florida twelve minutes before the polls closed in the state's western panhandle (in the Central time zone), which may have discouraged some voters from going to the polls; the networks' equally fateful decision, a few hours later, to christen George Bush the winner of Florida and the next president of the United States; the ballots that many people found confusing, leading a huge number of them to vote more than once for president, or to vote for a candidate (notably, Patrick Buchanan) they didn't want; the limited ability of some kinds of voting machines, particularly the punch-card machines found in the large urban counties of Miami-Dade, Palm Beach, Broward, and Duval, to detect votes and their tendency to record many attempted punches as "undervotes."

Take all the errors and difficulties and controversies that marred the Florida election, and gather them into a great pile. Now sort them freely into categories: those mistakes that could have been corrected and were; those that could have been corrected and weren't; those that couldn't have been corrected. You will be able to tell much about people's beliefs by where they choose to put what. Republican partisans would place both the dimples and the misaligned cards in that third, irredeemable category; some, like Justice O'Connor of the so-called Supreme Court standard, would have placed every voting error, all 180,110 of them, there. Democratic partisans would have placed at least the dimples in the second, and if they could have found a way, much much more.

Of course, the Democrats had to make just this choice in the hours and days after the election: What could be remedied? What was legally, and politically, possible? Nothing could be done to record the votes of those who had been purged from the rolls, or those who had thought they were registered but weren't, or those who might have been troubled by roadblocks. The only problem that might have been mitigated lay in the great pile of votes that had been discarded, all 180,110 of them. Two out of every three of those were overvotes, recording more than one choice for president. It might have seemed obvious that a man from the North Side of Jacksonville who had been newly registered after Jesse Jackson's great "get-out-the-vote" visit to the city and who had punched a hole next to Al Gore on the first page of his ballot and then punched again on the second page—didn't it say "every page" in the newspaper? Didn't everyone say "vote position two"?—wanted to vote for Gore when he punched a hole next to the second candidate on page two, Patrick Buchanan. But how in the world do you prove it? How do you prove that all those in Palm Beach County who punched holes next to Gore and then next to Buchanan meant to vote for Gore?

How do you prove that many of those 3,411 Palm Beach residents who voted for Patrick Buchanan—more than three times the number than in any other county, even much larger ones—in fact intended to cast their ballots for Al Gore?

The answer, of course, is that you can't prove it. But that doesn't mean that people don't know it, and don't remember it.

"After that sample count," Theresa LePore tells me, "we normally would not have had a recount. But for the public outcry." By which she means, as a legal matter, the machines had not broken, the election workers had done nothing wrong. She is saying, in effect: we conducted the manual recount partly because we had to prove to thousands of angry, disappointed people that the county, and the state, was doing all it could, given all the problems with the election, to ensure that the count that could be made was as accurate as it could possibly be.

Such an attitude, of course, is sensible and it would have been good for everyone had it prevailed statewide. As many have remarked, the obvious "solution" to the controversy in Florida, the obvious path to ensuring the greatest legitimacy for the winner, was to recount all the ballots by hand. Had the Democrats pushed for it from the first moment, and consistently, it may well have happened. But they feared the consequences of seeming to "prolong" the election—no one then dreamed the struggle would last five weeks—and they worried that even their request for recounts in four counties would be criticized as excessive and impractical. Of course, they could be much surer of what they would find in hand-counting the undervotes in those four heavily Democratic counties.

So, of course, could Republicans, and they fought the recounts tooth and nail, seeking, with a good deal of success, to undermine the venerable practice of counting ballots by hand. They held a slim lead; they had seen, during the state-mandated recount, what could happen when punch-card ballots were recounted, and they knew as well as the Democrats did who lived where and what kind of voting methods they used. The Republicans must have been relieved that Al Gore waited for eight days after the election before suggesting a statewide manual recount. For the Republicans, the legitimacy that might have been gained by winning such a recount could never come close to balancing out the very real risk of losing it.

And so we had the heated arguments over chads and "divining the intent of the voter" and the "objectivity" of voting machines. And so we had two of Al Gore's requested recounts (those in Volusia and Broward Counties) finally completed and included in the official count, and two (in Palm Beach and Miami-Dade Counties) not. And so we had the Florida Supreme Court attempt to rescue the situation by imposing a statewide count, conducted by judges. And so finally we had the US Supreme Court, citing alleged violations of equal protection in the lack of a statewide standard, and claiming that time had run out, stop the counting and decide the 2000 election.

4. The End That Did Not End

Legitimacy: A political order's worthiness to be recognized.

—OXFORD COMPANION TO POLITICS

"The question with which we start is," Mark Seibel of the *Herald* tells me, leaning back behind his mountainously cluttered desk,

"Had the US Supreme Court not stayed the Florida Supreme Court in its recount, what would the result have been?"

We are in the command center, Assistant Managing Editor Seibel's *Herald* office. From rooms full of ballots in Miami and West Palm and Union and several score other counties all across the state, a wire leads directly here, to this desk heaped with state maps and schedules and manila envelopes filled with hundreds and hundreds of vote tally sheets. Telephones ring, voices crackle over the speakerphone; Seibel urges on reporters, sweet-talks election supervisors, bargains with lawyers. He's having the time of his life.

And who wouldn't be? Look at the mystery he's chasing: "Did the US Supreme Court halt a process that would have brought a different result in the presidential election?" How could any self-respecting journalist not attempt to solve it? "We would be abdicating our responsibility not to do it," *Herald* executive editor Martin Baron tells me. "We're going to be criticized either way but it's much more serious to be criticized for abdicating our responsibility. There was never any doubt here whether to do it or not."

Can the *Herald* really, in Seibel's phrase, "complete what the Florida Supreme Court said should be completed"? Given the different standards so troubling to the Justices in Washington, how can the count be reproduced? "We've seen no real evidence," he tells me, patting his manila envelopes, "that there were different standards in Broward and Palm Beach. I mean, there was so much smoke around that election the quality of justice was lacking."

He takes a call from the corporation counsel in Duval, John Stafford's county. They fear lawsuits in Duval; the NAACP, Jesse Jackson, Corrine Brown, the local congresswoman—they're all making noise. Those ballots will be "evidentiary material" and the lawyer must be concerned about their "integrity and retrievability given the specter of litigation." Seibel argues, negotiates, promises to call back.

"You know, we had 300 ballots in St. Lucie County where people, instead of filling in that little bubble, they went over and circled the party affiliation. Now those votes weren't counted yet it was clear those people were trying to vote. Why weren't they counted?"

I hear once more the sound of the Old Enoch Question: those people didn't follow instructions, the voter has to have some responsibility...

But Seibel, who for weeks has been looking at nothing but ballots and tally sheets, will have none of it. "What really got undone in Florida," he tells me, "was decades of a very liberal approach to voting rights. The Florida Supreme Court has always held it is illegal to have an arbitrary mechanical standard. I mean, we have a standard: intent of the voter. Instead of putting the onus on the voter, it puts the onus on the canvassing board. Why force people to address the question mechanically if you know what they were trying to say?"

Or, to put it another way, "There was something wrong with the machines, not something wrong with the people." This is Representative Corrine Brown's way of putting it. She, like many people in Duval County, is angry. "I mean, this man prints up a ballot. The one they ran in the paper, it said vote on every page. Now if you followed that instruction your vote would have been void."

When Congress moved to record Florida's electoral votes on January 6, Representative Brown stood up and, alongside other members of the Congressional Black Caucus, lodged a protest; then she and her colleagues walked out. To many watching on television, it was a shocking act; sitting in Duval County, one finds it much more reasonable. "I've had so many people tell me that they were so glad when we did that," she says, "because, you know, we acknowledged the pain we're feeling. I mean, people here were energized. The community was energized and they were voting. And there was a system that disenfranchised them."

Democrats in Duval had mounted an enormous registration and get-out-the-vote drive. Jesse Jackson had come three times to register people; President Clinton had come for a huge rally. And it worked. Turnout among African-Americans, who were angry about Governor Jeb Bush's "One Florida" program, which in effect ended affirmative action in Florida, rose dramatically. And a great many of their votes were thrown out.

Corrine Brown is not much interested in discussing the Old Enoch Question. To her, what happened on November 7 is familiar; it has a history. "The last time this happened, 1876—it was Florida then, too, you know—the last time it happened, they pulled the troops out of the South. People say, well, Rutherford B. Hayes, he wasn't so bad. But that was the end of it, you know, the end of Reconstruction. We didn't have a black in Congress from Florida for 129 years. Jim Crow, lynchings, poll taxes, literacy tests: all that happened because we were unprotected, because we had no vote, nobody speaking for us."

Today there are no poll taxes, of course, and no literacy tests, at least none written into the law, but what echoes here is the principle of exclusion, of being shut out—the specter of losing a voice gained only after great difficulty. "This has sent me for a loop; I'll take it to my grave. My grandmother always says, they're going to do what they're going to do. A lot of people are saying that now, shaking their heads: They're going to do what they're going to do.

"To me, this lets us know that we're not there yet, that all this, all we've won, can be taken from us. And, you know, maybe they've done it: they took the election, in a coup d'état without guns. But it's not over. He's going to be sworn in, but it's not over. The key is, he didn't win! He lost in his brother's state!"

Eventually, they will count in Duval. After the *Herald* counts the undervote, the great "media consortium," led by *The New York Times* and including *The Wall Street Journal* and *The Washington Post* and other papers and television networks, will count and tabulate all the discarded ballots, including the overvotes. Sometime in February or perhaps March we will have numbers from the *Herald*—numbers of dimples, numbers of pinpricks. And we will have numbers from the Republican Party counters as well, using their "Supreme Court standard," numbers that they issue daily in their *Reality Check* newsletter and by which, at last count, Bush had gained several hundred votes. They, too, are concerned about legitimacy. People will read in these numbers what they will. The fact is that because of the way education and class disparities are reflected in Florida's election machinery, Republicans have held a trump card that proved decisive in this election. People know this and they are angry about it.

In Washington, the new president will govern. Had the count in Florida been allowed to go forward—either the judges' count ordered by the Florida Supreme Court or another organized under a "uniform standard"—the presidential contest might well have been decided in the House of Representatives (the so-called nightmare scenario, although the Founders considered such an outcome quite normal). Had this path been followed, depending on the standards used and the decisions taken by elected men and women, the same man might well be occupying the White House. But he would have arrived there through a political solution, and Corrine Brown and her constituents would be directing their anger at politicians and not the system that elects them. At the end of January, watching the counters and their ballots, what seems saddest about election 2000 is that the way it ended meant that it did not end.

Delusions in Baghdad

November 19, 2003

1.

AUTUMN IN BAGHDAD is cloudy and gray. Trapped in rush-hour traffic one October morning, without warning my car bucked up and back, like a horse whose reins had been brutally pulled. For a jolting instant the explosion registered only as the absence of sound, a silent blow to the stomach; and then a beat later, as hearing returned, a faint tinkling chorus: the store windows, all along busy Karrada Street, trembling together in their sashes. They were tinkling still when over the rooftops to the right came the immense eruption of oily black smoke.

Such dark plumes have become the beacons, the lighthouses, of contemporary Baghdad, and we rushed to follow, bumping over the center divider, vaulting the curb, screeching through the honking chaos of Seventies-vintage American cars, trailing the blasting horns and screaming tires for two, three, four heart-pounding moments until, barely three blocks away, at one end of a pleasant residential square, behind a gaggle of blue-shirted Iraqi security men running in panic about the grass, shouting, waving their AK-47s, we came upon two towering conflagrations, rising perhaps a dozen feet in the air, and, perfectly outlined in the bright orange flames, like skeletons preserved in amber, the blackened frames of what moments before had been a van and a four-wheel drive.

Between the two great fires rose a smaller one, eight or nine feet high, enclosing a tangled mass of metal. Pushing past the Iraqis, who shouted angrily, gesturing with their guns, I ran forward, toward the flames: the heat was intense. I saw slabs of smashed wall, hunks of rubble, glass, and sand scattered about, and behind it all an immense curtain of black smoke obscuring everything: the building, part of the International Red Cross compound, that stood there, the wall that had guarded it, the remains of the people who, four minutes before, had lived and worked there.

"Terrorism," the US Army lieutenant colonel had told me ruefully the week before, "is Grand Theater," and, as a mustached security man yanked me roughly by the arm, spinning me away from the flames, I saw that behind me the front rows had quickly filled: photographers with their long lenses, khaki vests, and shoulder bags struggled to push their way through the Iraqi security men, who, growing angrier, shouted and cursed, pushing them back. Swinging their AK-47s, they managed to form a ragged perimeter against what was now a jostling, roiling crowd, while camera crews in the vanguard surged forward. Now a US Army Humvee appeared; four American soldiers leaped out and plunged into the crowd, assault rifles raised, and began to scream, in what I had come to recognize as a characteristic form of address, "GET. THE FUCK. BACK! GET. THE FUCK. BACK!" Very young men in tan camouflage fatigues, armed, red-faced, flustered; facing them, the men and women of the world press, Baghdad division, assembled in their hundreds in less than a quarter of an hour: in the front row, those who, like me, had had the dumb luck to be in the neighborhood; behind them network crews who had received a quick tip from an embassy contact or an Iraqi stringer, or had simply heard or felt the explosion and pounded their way up to the hotel roof, scanning the horizon anxiously, locating the black beacon, and racing off to cover the story—or, as Lieutenant Colonel George Krivo put it bitterly, to "*make* the story. Here, media is the total message: I now have an understanding of McLuhan you wouldn't believe. Kill twenty people here? In front of that lens it's killing twenty thousand."

Behind the flames and the dark smoke, amid the shattered walls and twisted metal, a dozen people lay dead, many of whom had been unlucky enough to find themselves passing the front of the International Red Cross compound when, at half past eight in the morning, a man later claimed to be of Saudi nationality drove an ambulance with Red Cross markings up to the security checkpoint and detonated what must have been several thousand pounds of explosives, collapsing forty feet of the protective wall and sending a huge sandbag barrier cascading forward.[1] The Red Cross compound, with its security wall and sandbags and manned checkpoints, was a "hardened target"—as were, indeed, the three Baghdad police stations that, within the next forty-five minutes, suicide bombers struck, in the neighborhoods of al-Baya'a, al-Shaab, and al-Khadra.

In the rhetoric of security, all of these attacks failed dismally.

1. For the Saudi claim, see Mohammad Bazzi, "Saudis Suspected in 2 Iraq Attacks," *Newsday*, November 11, 2003.

"From what our indications are," Brigadier General Mark Hertling told Fox News that afternoon, "none of those bombers got close to the target." In the rhetoric of politics, however, the attacks were a brilliant coup de théâtre. In less than an hour, four men, by killing forty people, including one American soldier and twenty Iraqi police, had succeeded in dominating news coverage around the world, sending television crews rushing about Baghdad in pursuit of the latest plume of smoke and broadcasting the message, via television screens in a hundred countries, first and foremost the United States, that Baghdad, US official pronouncements notwithstanding, remained a war zone.

Within a week, as members of the Red Cross left Iraq and many of the few remaining international organizations followed close behind, the attackers had set in motion, at the "highest levels" of the Bush administration, a "reevaluation" of American policy. Within two weeks, even as President Bush went on vowing publicly that the United States "would not be intimidated," he abruptly recalled L. Paul Bremer, the American administrator in Iraq, who rushed back to Washington so hurriedly he left the prime minister of Poland, one of America's few major allies in Iraq, waiting forlornly for an appointment that never came.

After two days of intensive consultations, administration officials unveiled a new policy. They decided to discard what had been a carefully planned, multi year process that would gradually transform the authoritarian Iraqi state into a democracy—seven clearly defined steps intended to allow democratic parties, practices, and institutions to take root, develop, and grow, eventually leading to a new constitution written and ratified by the Iraqi people and, finally, a nationwide election and handover of power from American administrators to the elected Iraqi politicians it produced. The administration put in its place a hastily improvised rush to "return power to the Iraqis." In practice, this meant that in seven months the United States would hand over sovereignty to unelected Iraqis (presumably those on the American-appointed Governing Council, many of them former exiles, who had been pressing for such a rapid granting of power since before the war). Elections and a constitution would come later.[2] Despite President Bush's fervent protestations to the contrary, this was clearly a dramatic change in his policy of "bringing democracy to Iraq"—and, by extension, of making Iraq the first step in what he recently described as his "forward strategy of democracy in the Middle East."

If victory in war is defined as accomplishing the political goals for which military means were originally brought to bear, then eight months after it invaded Iraq, the United States remains far from victory. If the political goal of the war in Iraq was to remove Saddam Hussein and his Baathist regime and establish in their place a stable, democratic government—then that goal, during the weeks I spent in Iraq in late October and early November, seemed to be growing ever more distant.

When I arrived in Baghdad, Iraqi insurgents were staging about fifteen attacks a day on American troops; by the time I left the number

2. See Susan Sachs, "US Is Set to Return Power to Iraqis as Early as June," *The New York Times*, November 15, 2003.

of daily attacks had more than doubled, to thirty-five a day. Though military leaders like General Ricardo Sanchez, the overall commander, have repeatedly denigrated the attacks on his troops as "strategically and operationally insignificant," those attacks led the CIA to conclude, in a report leaked in mid-November, that the "US-led drive to rebuild the country as a democracy could collapse unless corrective actions are taken immediately."[3] The United States fields by far the most powerful military in the world, spending more on defense than the rest of the world combined, and as I write a relative handful of armed insurgents, numbering in the tens of thousands or perhaps less, using the classic techniques of guerrilla warfare and suicide terrorism, are well on the way toward defeating it.

"What we have here," Lieutenant Colonel William Darley told me, "is basically a constabulary action. I mean, this is pretty much the Old West here. Peacekeeping. Where are the regiment on regiment, division on division engagements? We've seen almost nothing above the squad level. Basically this is not a real war." I heard this view, in various versions, expressed by American military men all over Iraq, from staff officers to combat commanders to lieutenants on the ground. Most of these men I found deeply impressive: well trained, well schooled, extremely competent. What joined them together, as the war grew steadily worse for American forces, was an inability, or perhaps a reluctance, to recognize what was happening in Iraq *as a war*.

"There's a deep cultural bias in the United States that if a military doesn't resemble ours, it's no good," the military strategist George Friedman of the private intelligence company Stratfor told me. "We

3. See Jonathan S. Landay, "CIA Has a Bleak Analysis of Iraq," *Philadelphia Inquirer*, November 12, 2003.

have the strongest conventional forces in the world. So no one fights us conventionally. They fight us asymmetrically."

In Iraq, asymmetric warfare has meant a combination of guerrilla attacks on US and other coalition forces and terrorist attacks on a variety of prominent nonmilitary targets, including hotels, embassies, and international organizations. Beginning late this spring, the guerrilla attacks were centered in Baghdad and the so-called Sunni Triangle north and west of the capital but, since mid-autumn, they have increasingly spread to the north and, more slowly, the south of the country. Since late summer, highly effective terrorist attacks, including suicide bombings, have grown steadily more audacious and sophisticated, particularly in their use of the international press to multiply their political effect. In responding to both lines of attack, US intelligence—the "center of gravity" in any guerrilla war—has seemed poor or nonexistent.

The guerrilla attacks have built on, and worsened, the American occupation's unpopularity among many Iraqis, capitalizing on, among other things, the US military's failure to provide security during the early weeks of the occupation and the daily humiliations and occasional brutalities that come with the presence of an occupying army. The terrorist attacks have served to consolidate and then worsen the international isolation the Americans have labored under since the catastrophic diplomatic decisions that led up to the war and have succeeded in depriving the coalition of additional military forces and international help in rebuilding the country.

Terrorism is certainly—as the lieutenant colonel put it—Grand Theater. Or to put it a slightly different way, terrorism is a form of talk. To hear what is being said, one must look at the sequence of major bombings in Iraq over the last several months:

August 7, Jordanian Embassy: A suicide car bomber kills nineteen people.

August 19, United Nations Headquarters: A suicide truck bomber kills twenty-three, including the UN's chief envoy in Iraq.

September 22, UN Headquarters: A suicide car bomber kills two and wounds nineteen.

October 9, police station: A suicide car bomber kills ten.

October 12, Baghdad Hotel: A suicide car bomber kills eight and wounds thirty-two.

October 14, Turkish Embassy: A suicide car bomber kills two and wounds thirteen.

October 27, Red Cross Headquarters and four police stations: Car bombers kill about forty and wound two hundred.

November 12, Italian Carabinieri Headquarters, Nasiriya: A truck bomber kills thirty-one.

Behind these attacks—I list only the major ones—one can see a rather methodical intention to sever, one by one, with patience, care, and precision, the fragile lines that still tie the occupation authority to the rest of the world. Suicide bombers struck at the countries that supported the Americans in the war (Jordan), that support the occupation with troops (Italy) or professed a willingness to do so (Turkey). They struck at the heart of an "international community" that could, with increased involvement, help give the occupation both legitimacy (the United Nations) and material help in rebuilding the country (the Red Cross). Finally they repeatedly struck at

Iraqis collaborating with occupation authorities, whether as members of the American-selected Governing Council (several of whom lived in the Baghdad Hotel) or as policemen trained and paid by Americans.

By striking at the Jordanians, the bombers helped to ensure that no Arab country will contribute troops to support the occupation. By striking at the Turks, they helped force them to withdraw their controversial offer to send soldiers. By striking at the United Nations and the Red Cross, they not only forced the members of those two critical institutions to flee the country but led most other nongovernmental organizations, who would have been central to supplying expertise and resources to rebuilding Iraq, to leave as well. And by striking at the homes of several members of the Governing Council (wounding one member and, in a separate incident, assassinating another), they forced those officials to join the Americans behind their isolating wall of security, further separating them from Iraqis and underlining their utter political reliance on the Americans.

"Signs and symbols," the Italian security officer said. "Terrorism is nothing but signs and symbols." He looked at the sandbags and barbed wire, the rows of concrete Jersey barriers and armed guards that surrounded his embassy. "None of this will matter," he told me. "If they want to hit us, they will, and though they won't get to the building, it will still be a victory because it will kill people and make news. Terror," he said, "is quite predictable." What, I asked, did the signs and symbols mean? He spoke matter-of-factly: that anyone who helps the Americans will be a target; that the Americans cannot protect their allies and provide security to Iraqis; that the disorder is growing and that deciding to work with the Americans, who in their isolation are looking like a less-than-dominant and in any event ephemeral presence, is not the most prudent of bets; that the war, whatever fine words President Bush may pronounce from his aircraft carrier, is not over. Terror, he said, has a logic of its own. Two weeks after we spoke a suicide bomber killed nineteen Italians at Nasiriya.

2.

Autumn in Baghdad is sunny and bright. Drive about the bustling city of tan, sun-dried brick and you will hear the noise of honking horns and see crowded markets, the streets overwhelmed by an enormous postwar expansion of traffic, the sidewalks cluttered with satellite disks and other new products flooding into the newly opened Iraqi market. During the last several months, however, a new city has taken root amid these busy streets and avenues, spreading rapidly as it superimposes itself over the old tan brick metropolis: a new grim city of concrete. It is constructed of twelve-foot-high gray concrete barriers, endless roadblocks manned by squads of men with Kalashnikovs, walls of enormous steel-reinforced bags of earth and rubble and mile upon mile of coiled razor wire, and studded here and there with tanks rooted behind sandbags and watchful soldiers in combat fatigues. This city has a vaguely postmodern, apocalyptic feel, "a bit of Belfast here, a bit of Cyprus there, here and there a sprinkling of West Bank," as one network cameraman put it to me.

Many streets, including several of the grand ceremonial avenues of Saddam's capital, are now entirely lined with raw concrete a dozen feet high, giving the driver the impression of advancing down a stone tube. Behind these walls entire chunks of Baghdad have effectively vanished, notably the great park and building complex that had housed Saddam's Republican Palace and now comprises the so-called Green Zone—a four-and-a-half-square-mile concrete bunker that has at its heart the headquarters of the Coalition Provisional Authority.

To enter the palace you must secure, first, an appointment—hard to get, and made immeasurably harder by the fact that most members of the CPA are difficult or impossible to reach by telephone—and then make your way down several hundred yards of sidewalk lined with razor wire. Your journey will be broken by three checkpoints, two military (concrete cordons, sandbags, machine guns) and one civilian. At two of these you present two identifications and submit to full body searches, standing with your legs parted and arms extended and staring straight ahead, in a ritual I found myself repeating, on a busy day in Baghdad, a dozen or more times. Finally, after securing an identification badge, you must wait for a military escort to drive you to the palace, where yet another series of checks and searches will be performed.

Inside Saddam's Republican Palace—his huge likeness in the central atrium is discreetly masked by a large blue cloth—you will find, amid the dark marble floors and sconces and chandeliers, a great many Americans striding purposefully about, some in uniform but many in casual civilian clothing: chinos, jeans, sport shirts. They look bright, crisp, self-assured, and extremely young; they look, in other words, like what they are: junior staffers from Washington, from the Capitol, the departments and various agencies and think tanks. After all the combat fatigues on the city streets ("During my two weeks here," an oil industry contractor told me, "I've not seen one American who wasn't in uniform"), it is a bit of a shock to find this great horde of young American civilians secreted in Saddam's marble-lined hideaway, now become Baghdad's own Emerald City.

I spoke to one young expert from the Governance Department at some length about the Americans' "seven-point plan" to install democracy in Iraq, which was then stalled at point three: writing the constitution. (To summarize very crudely, the Shia, the majority on the Governing Council and in the country, were insisting that the writers of the constitution be chosen in a nationwide election; the others, fearing the Shias' numerical dominance, were pushing for the writers to be "selected" under various methods. This deadlock over the constitution is a precise reflection of the larger "governance problem" in Iraq—beginning with Shia numerical dominance—that would need to be resolved if Iraq is ever to become a working democracy.) I found myself impressed with the young woman's knowledge and commitment. In general, the CPA members seem dedicated and well-meaning—they'd have to be, to come to Baghdad; they are also entirely isolated, traveling twice daily by military-driven bus within the bunkered compound from their places of work in the bunkered palace to their places of rest in the bunkered Rasheed Hotel.

Or rather they made that trip until October 26, when, just before six in the morning, a person or persons unknown towed a small blue two-wheeled trailer—to any observer (including, presumably, the soldier manning the checkpoint a couple hundred yards away), it looked like a generator, a common sight in electricity-starved Iraq—up to the park across from which the Rasheed stood resplendent behind its impressive concrete barriers, quickly opened the trailer's doors, turned it around, and directed it toward the hotel, and ran off, no doubt looking back to gaze in satisfaction a few moments later when a dozen or so converted French-made air-to-surface missiles whooshed out of their tubes and began peppering the rooms in which the Americans running the occupation slept, wounding seventeen people, killing one (a lieutenant colonel), and coming within a few yards of killing the visiting Paul L. Wolfowitz, United States deputy secretary of defense and mastermind of the Iraq war.

My friend in Governance was thrown from her bed and, finding her door jammed shut by the blast damage, and taking "one look at the smoke coming from under that jammed door and realizing if I didn't get out of there I was going to die," she climbed out on the ledge and crept along it, ten floors up, to the room next door and the smoke-filled, chaotic hallway beyond. The Rasheed was evacuated and many of its former occupants found themselves sleeping on quickly assembled cots in Saddam's palace. As for my friend's "seven-point plan," two weeks later President Bush decided to abandon it. Instead of confronting the problem that had blocked the writing of a new Iraqi constitution—the question of how the fact of Shia numerical dominance, and other unresolved conflicts in the Iraqi state, would be integrated into a functioning Iraqi democracy—the President, faced with mounting attacks from Iraqis opposed to the new political dispensation he had declared himself committed to create, decided to abandon the effort.

Security underlies everything in Iraq; it is the fault line running squarely beneath the occupation and the political world that will emerge from it. As I look back, perhaps my most frightening moment in the country came not at the Red Cross bombing, or an ambush on the highway between Fallujah and Ramadi where five civilians were killed, or at various other scenes of violence of one kind or another, but at a press conference the afternoon of the Rasheed attack, when General Martin E. Dempsey, the impressive commander of the 1st Armored Division, characterized the rocket launcher—the cleverly disguised weapon that some unknown persons had used to pierce successfully the huge security perimeter around the Rasheed and thereby kill and wound, under the noses of tens of thousands of US soldiers, the Americans who were supposedly running Iraq, and nearly kill the deputy secretary of defense—as "not very sophisticated . . . a science project, made in a garage with a welder, a battery, and a handful of wire." What frightened me was the possibility that General Dempsey—a sophisticated man who no doubt had read the literature on counterinsurgency and knew well "the lessons" of the British in Malaya and the French in Algeria and the Americans in Vietnam, but who, like almost every other impressive American commander in Iraq, had been trained to fight with, and against, larger armored formations—was aware of the condescension evident in his tone.

"The idea behind these stay-behind insurgent groups is that they're *clandestine*, they use what's *available*—an old drainpipe, whatever," said a private security officer working for an American television network, who, like many of the security professionals in Iraq, was a veteran of Britain's elite Special Air Service. "They don't need to be sophisticated, they need to be *effective*—and that device that hit the Rasheed was very effective." Raymond Bonner, a *New York Times* reporter, made a somewhat broader point: "The good news is it was a science project put together in a garage. The bad news is it was a science project put together in a garage."

Ten days later, when a colleague, a strong advocate of the United States' invasion, declared to me with some impatience, "The United States will not *lose*. The United States has *absolute military superiority in Iraq*!,"[4] I remembered Bonner's comment. In view of the progress of the war against the US coalition—the spreading activities of the opposition, the growing sophistication of their methods, the increasing numbers of Americans being killed—is the fact that the United States has "absolute military superiority" in Iraq good or bad news? All differences aside (and there are a great many differences), people commonly made the same point about Vietnam; but if it is true that "the United States had absolute military superiority in Vietnam," then what exactly do those words mean—and what do they tell us about those who utter them?

3.

Fall in Fallujah is dusty and bright. Here, on an average day in late October, insurgents attacked American soldiers eight times, twice the rate of a month before, according to General Chuck Swannack, commander of the 82nd Airborne Division. The method of choice was IEDs—"improvised explosive devices," in military parlance—planted, presumably, by FRLs, or "former regime loyalists." On the road leading into town, just emerging from the cloverleaf off the main highway, I saw the aftermath of one such attack. Late that

4. Christopher Hitchens made the comment, in a debate with me at the University of California, Berkeley, on November 4. See "Has Bush Made Us Safer? Iraq, Terror and American Power," at https://markdanner.com/2003/11/04/has-bush-made-us-safer-iraq-terror-and-american-power/

afternoon, as an American armored convoy rumbled up the highway into the city, someone set off what the general described as

> a very sophisticated device, three barrels of flammable material rigged to a triggering mechanism, using a remote-controlled trigger. As our squad was clearing the cloverleaf, the individuals set off the device, killed a paratrooper, and then some individuals directed fire at us with AK-47s from the houses.

General Swannack's men dismounted, returned fire, stormed the houses, and arrested several civilians, leading them roughly away in flex cuffs. It was a typical day in Fallujah, with a typical score: one dead American soldier, two dead civilians, several civilians wounded, several arrested, with an indeterminate number of family members, neighbors, and friends of those killed, wounded, and arrested left furious at the Americans and nursing strong grievances, which tribal honor, an especially strong force in Fallujah, now demanded they personally avenge—by killing more Americans. As for the handful of "individuals" who had set off the device and opened fire on the Americans, they managed—as they do in all but a few such ambushes—to get away clean.

As I write, 423 Americans have died in Iraq since the United States invaded in March and more than 2,300 have been wounded there, many grievously; and the rate at which Americans are being killed and wounded is increasing. But while these tolls are having a discernible effect on President Bush's popularity among Americans, the major goal of this kind of warfare is not only to kill and wound Americans but to increase Iraqi recruits, both active and passive, who will oppose the occupation; its major product, that is, is *polit-*

ical. "The point," said General Swannack, "is to get the Americans to fire back and hopefully they'll get some Iraqi casualties out of that and they can publicize that."

After first estimating the guerrilla strength in and around Fallujah at 20,000, the general revised his figure: "Probably about a thousand people out there really want to attack us and kill us and another nineteen thousand or so really really don't like us." Such estimates vary wildly around Iraq, depending on whom you ask. General Sanchez recently put the total number of the opposition nationwide at five thousand. Whatever the numbers, the guerrillas' main business is to make them grow, particularly the number of strong sympathizers; and all evidence suggests that thus far they are succeeding.

Saddam's Iraq was a national security state dominated by the interlocking intelligence services of the government and the elite security units of the army, all of it rooted in the enormous Baath Party, a highly elaborated structure that over a half-century spread and proliferated into every institution in the country and that originally grew from a complex network of conspiratorial cells of three to seven members. Saddam's elite Republican Guard numbered 80,000; his even more select Special Republican Guard numbered 16,000; his Fedayeen Saddam, a paramilitary force—in effect, Saddam's brownshirts—numbered 40,000. The Mukhabarat and the various intelligence services, of which there were perhaps a dozen, numbered thousands more. All of these men were highly trained, well armed, and tested for their political loyalty. Few of them died in the war.

In May, in an astonishing decision that still has not been adequately explained, American administrator L. Paul Bremer vastly increased the number of willing Iraqi foot soldiers by abruptly dissolving the regular Iraqi army, which had been established by King Faisal I in 1921, and thereby sent out into bitter shame and unemployment 350,000 of those young Iraqis who were well trained, well armed, and deeply angry at the Americans. Add to these a million or so tons of weapons and munitions of all sorts, including rockets and missiles, readily available in more than a hundred mostly unguarded arms depots around the country, as well as vast amounts of money stockpiled during thirty-five years in power (notably on March 18, when Saddam sent three tractor-trailers to the Central Bank and relieved it of more than a billion dollars in cash), and you have the makings of a well-manned, well-funded insurgency.

During the months since the fall of Baghdad in April, that insurgency has grown and evolved. Its methods have moved from assassinations of isolated US soldiers, to attacks on convoys with small arms, to increasingly sophisticated and frequent ambushes of convoys with remote-controlled explosives and attacks on helicopters with rocket-propelled grenades and missiles. While there seems to be some regional coordination among groups, it is clear that the opposition is made up of many different organizations, some regionally based, some local; some are explicitly Saddamist, some more broadly Baathist, some Islamist, and some frankly anti-Saddam and nationalist. “I don’t see a vision by these disparate groups of insurgents or partisans,” said Ahmed S. Hashim, a professor at the Naval War College who has closely studied the opposition. “But at this stage they do not need one. They are making our stay uncomfortable, they have affected our calculus and are driving a wedge between us. What I know is the coalition is losing ground among Iraqis.” Within and among these groupings a competitive politics now exists, an armed politics that will evolve and develop, depending on how successful they are in attacking the Americans and forcing them to adjust their policies and, eventually, to leave the country.

By now much evidence exists, including documents apparently prepared by Iraqi intelligence services, to suggest that this insurgency, at least in its broad outlines, was planned before the war and that the plan included looting, sabotage, and assassination of clerics.[5] Particularly damaging was the looting, in which government ministries and other public buildings, including museums, libraries, and universities, were thoroughly ransacked, down to the copper pipes and electrical wiring in the walls, and then burned, and the capital was given over to weeks of utter lawlessness while American soldiers stood by and watched. This was an enormously important political blow against the occupation, undermining any trust or faith Iraqis might have had in their new rulers and destroying any chance the occupiers had to establish their authority. Most of all, the looting created an overwhelming sense of insecurity and trepidation, a sense that the insurgents, with their bombings and attacks, have built on to convince many Iraqis that the Americans have not achieved full control and may well not stay long enough to attain it.

All of this is another way of saying that if security is the fault line running beneath political development in Iraq, then politics is the fault line running beneath security. By now the failures in planning and execution that have dogged the occupation—the lack of military

5. See Michael Hirsh, Rod Nordland, and Mark Hosenball, "About-Face in Iraq," *Newsweek*, November 24, 2003; and Douglas Jehl, "Plan for Guerrilla Action May Have Predated War," *The New York Times*, November 15, 2003.

police, the refusal to provide security in the capital, the dissolution of the Iraqi army—are well known.[6] All have originated in Washington, many born of struggles between the leading departments of government, principally the State Department, the CIA, and the Pentagon, which the White House has never managed to resolve. (The most obvious product of these struggles was the President's decision, barely two months before the invasion, to discard the year of occupation planning by the State Department and shift control to the Pentagon, which proved itself wholly unprepared to take on the task.)

In Iraq, after the Big Bang of the American invasion, a new political universe is slowly being born. Part of this Iraqi political universe is called the Governing Council, and it does its work behind the concrete barriers of the Green Zone. Another part works at the level of nascent local government throughout the country. Still another works in the mosques of the south and among the Shiite religious establishment known as the Hawza. And yet another part—now a rather large and powerful part—is armed and clandestine and is making increasingly sophisticated and effective use of guerrilla warfare and terrorism, hoping to force the Americans from the country and claim its share of power. The Americans seek to define the armed claimants as illegitimate—essentially, as not part of the recognized universe at all. But in order to enforce that definition—to confine the game to the actors they regard as legitimate—the Americans must prove themselves able to make use of their power, both military and political, more effectively.

As I write, on November 19, US military forces in Iraq are con-

6. See Mark Fineman, Robin Wright, and Doyle McManus, "Preparing for War, Stumbling to Peace," *Los Angeles Times*, July 18, 2003; and David Rieff, "Blueprint for a Mess," *The New York Times Magazine*, November 2, 2003

ducting Operation Iron Hammer, striking with warplanes and artillery bases thought to be occupied by Iraqi insurgents. American television broadcasts are filled with dramatic footage of huge explosions illuminating the night sky. In Tikrit, Saddam's political base and a stronghold of the opposition, the Americans staged a military show of force, sending tanks and other armored vehicles rumbling through the main street. "They need to understand," Lieutenant Colonel Steve Russell told ABC News, "it's more than just Humvees we'll be using in these attacks."

The armed opposition in Iraq seems unlikely to be impressed. However many insurgents the Americans manage to kill in bombing runs and artillery barrages, the toll on civilians, in death and disruption, is also likely to be high, as will damage to the fragile sense of normalcy that Americans are struggling to achieve and the opposition forces are determined to destroy. Large-scale armored warfare looks and sounds impressive, inspiring overwhelming fear; but it is not discriminate, which makes it a blunt and ultimately self-defeating instrument to deploy against determined guerrillas. In general, the American military, the finest and most powerful in the world, is not organized and equipped to fight this war, and the part of it that is—the Special Forces—are almost entirely occupied in what seems a never-ending hunt for Saddam. For American leaders, and particularly President Bush, this has become the quest for the Holy Grail: finding Saddam will be an enormous political boon. For the American military, this quest has the feel of a traditional kind of war not wholly suited to what they find in Iraq. "We are a hierarchy and we like to fight hierarchies," says military strategist John Arquilla. "We think if we cut off the head we can end this."

Whatever the political rewards of finding Saddam, they will not likely include putting a definitive end to the insurgency in Iraq.[7] "The Americans need to get out of their tanks, get out from behind their sunglasses," a British military officer, a veteran of Northern Ireland, told me. "They need to get on the ground where they can get to know people and encourage them to tell them where the bad guys are." As I write, operations on the ground seem to be moving in the opposite direction. In any event it is difficult to impress an opponent with a military advance plainly meant to cover a political retreat.

President Bush's audacious project in Iraq was always going to be difficult, perhaps impossible, but without political steadfastness and resilience, it had no chance to succeed. This autumn in Baghdad, a ruthless insurgency, growing but still in its infancy, has managed to make the President retreat from his project, and has worked, with growing success, to divide Iraqis from the Americans who claim to govern them. These insurgents cannot win, but by seizing on Washington's mistakes and working relentlessly to widen the fault lines in occupied Iraq, they threaten to prevent what President Bush sent the US military to achieve: a stable, democratic, and peaceful Iraq, at the heart of a stable and democratic Middle East.

7. See Ahmed S. Hashim, "The Sunni Insurgency in Iraq," Middle East Institute Policy Brief, August 15,2003, who notes that the "elimination of Saddam and his dynasty may demoralize pro-regime insurgents but may actually embolden anti-regime and anti-US insurgents who may have held back in the past... because of the barely submerged fears that the regime could come back."

The Election and America's Future

November 4, 2004

IT HAS BEEN CLEAR for several months that the United States is losing its war in Iraq. What remains to be seen is whether Americans will come to realize this fact before the election or after it. The answer may well determine who sits in the White House in late January 2005. But whoever wins on November 2 will be confronted by the stark fact that in a bitter, fragmented country the United States has engaged itself in a guerrilla war that no more admits of a clear and easy resolution than did the war in Vietnam in 1968. And in Iraq, a country not far from the Strait of Hormuz—the "chokepoint" through which more than half of the world's oil passes, making it the jugular of the industrialized world—the strategic stakes are much greater.

They are greater still because the Bush administration has succeeded in making the Iraq war a recruiting poster for Osama bin Laden's region-wide cause of Islamic jihad, a rallying point for the Islamic fundamentalist movement that serves as a source of heroic televised images, stirring propaganda, and vital on-the-ground training—serves, that is, roughly the same function that the jihadist struggle against the Soviets in Afghanistan did in the 1980s. It was the Afghan struggle that produced Osama bin Laden and al-Qaeda. And now, during eighteen months of a war that should never have been fought, the Bush administration has managed to create out of Iraq the new Afghanistan.

Among the many reasons that the Bush administration has given for attacking and occupying Iraq—the need to eliminate Saddam Hussein's weapons of mass destruction, the need to remove a "dangerous dictator" from power, the need to transform Iraq into a "shining example of democracy" in the Middle East—we seldom find the one historians may well settle on as closest to the truth: the need for an administration that believed fervently in the unilateral power and world dominance of the United States to act, following a humbling attack on its territory, to reassert that power and dominance. It will be an increasingly obvious irony that the United States acted in Iraq in a way that not only gave the world the specter, for the first time, of what an untrammeled American unilateralism would look like but that demonstrated, at the same time, the stark limits of American power. For the expedition in Iraq has revealed once again an America that is a strange hybrid—a military giant yoked uncomfortably to a political dwarf.

For many in the Bush administration, the conquest of Iraq was a cherished goal long before the attacks of September 11. But when the time came—after the attacks offered them a "window" in which to carry out their war, restoring to Republicans the traditional political advantage in managing national security that had vanished with the cold war—these officials chose to minimize the difficulties of the war and refused to build the political support necessary to fight it with sufficient troops, money, and determination. They clung to a war of the imagination, one fought with high-tech weapons, few troops, and little cost, in which democracy would magically emerge from the Iraqi streets. The lack of troops in particular, and the characteristic stubbornness that has made the administration singularly unwilling to admit a mistake and—much more seriously—unable to correct one, created, in the first weeks of looting and chaos, a fault line under the Iraq occupation that has grown steadily deeper and broader, and undermined every effort to construct a stable order there. Worse—and it is this that the next president will be forced to confront—that political cowardice has created a vulnerability precisely in the spot that the Iraqi insurgents, and ultimately Osama bin Laden, expected to find it: in the American will.

The next president will confront an American public grown tired of a war whose rationale has disappeared along with the weapons of mass destruction their leaders warned them so urgently about, and whose ending has receded into an ever more cloudy future. It is no surprise that the fundamentalist George Bush responded to the cataclysm of September 11 by rallying Americans to a threat he found in the realm not of politics or strategy but of metaphysics. Terrorists were "evildoers" and as such called forth a religious war in which other nations were "either with us or with the terrorists." Such rhetoric falls easily on American ears and it is no mystery why this land's leaders have had recourse to it again and again, from the "City on the Hill" of John Winthrop, to the "evil empire" of Ronald Reagan, and, in between, the starkly divided world set out in the Manichaean divisions of the Truman Doctrine of April 1947. The call to arms against "the evildoers," the beseeching of the country to rise up and defend itself against "the axis of evil"—presidents use such terms because they are simple, universally understood, and persuasive: Who, after all, could object to the need to fight Evil?

The danger has always been that the urge toward metaphysical simplicity eventually obliterates the careful weighing of interests and risks that must guide a great power in its foreign policy. Osama bin Laden, in turning his sights from the "near enemies" ruling in Cairo and Riyadh to the "far enemy" symbolized by New York's mighty towers, had wanted nothing more than an ideological war; he had the great good luck to choose to attack a born-again president and advocate of "moral clarity" who not only was more than willing to give him one but to subsume under its banner a bloody diversion in a complicated, divided country that had up to then been irrelevant to the jihadist cause.

For better or worse, President Bush has now set the terms of the debate, and the political contest now underway, animated by a kind of fear and political anxiety not seen since the darkest days of the cold war, seems fated to be conducted according to those terms. When the rhetoric of crusade dominates public discourse, political leaders find themselves trapped, like characters in a mythological drama that long predates and powerfully overshadows them; Lyndon Johnson, unable to withdraw from and thus "lose" Vietnam the way his Democratic predecessor had "lost" China, came to understand this; John Kerry, if he manages to gain his place in the White House, may well find himself struggling to escape the same trap, caught in the metaphysical prison his predecessor constructed for him and hemmed in by ideologically fierce political opponents determined to make him suffer for any attempt he might make to break free.

The war in Iraq, launched in the glamorous cause of ideological transformation, has now settled down into something bloody, murderous, and crude, fought on behalf of a people who are increasingly weary of its costs and bewildered by its stakes. There is no safe or easy way out, and the winner of this election, like the winner in 1968, will find his administration dogged by it from first day to last.

How Bush Really Won

December 15, 2004

1.

I have won what I call political capital and now I intend to spend it.

—George W. Bush, November 3, 2004

Driving north from Tampa on Florida's Route 75 on November 1, as the battle over who would hold political power in America was reaching a climax but the struggle over what that battle meant had yet to begin, I put down the top of my rented green convertible, turned the talk radio voices up to blaring, and commenced reading the roadside. Beside me billboards flew past, one hard upon another, as if some errant giant had cut a great deck of cards and fanned them out along each shoulder. Hour by hour, as the booming salesman's voice of proud Floridian Rush Limbaugh rumbled from the radio, warning gravely of the dangers of "voting for bin Laden" ("Haven't you noticed that bin Laden is using *Democratic talking points*?"), and other ominous voices reminded listeners of the "hundreds of votes" Senator Kerry cast "against our national defense" ("In a time of terror, when our enemies are gathering... *can we afford to take that risk*?"),

I watched rush by, interspersed with the blaring offers of FLORIDA CITRUS! ONE BAG $1! and NEED HELP WITH SINKHOLES?, a series of perhaps fifty garish signs announcing an approaching ADULT TOY CAFÉ! and ADULT TOY EXTRAVAGANZA! and then WE BARE ALL! and finally, the capper, ALL NUDE—GOOD FOOD—TRUCKERS WELCOME!

It wasn't long before this billboard parade had acquired its stark spiritual counterpoint—JESUS IS STILL THE ANSWER!—and by the time I reached the promised "extravaganza"—a sad and windowless two-room shack just off the highway, smaller than most of the signs advertising it—I found, standing just down the road from the pathetic little house of sin, a resplendent white church more than twice its size. In the world of American hucksterism, the sin may be the draw but the payoff's always in redemption.

This was perhaps thirty-six hours before an army of self-interested commentators, self-appointed spiritual leaders, and television pundits hot for a simple storyline had seized on the answers to a clumsily posed exit poll question—more than one respondent in five, offered seven choices, had selected "moral values" as their "most important issue"—and used those answers to transform the results of the 2004 election into a rousing statement of Americans' disgust with abortion, promiscuity, R-rated movies, gay marriage, late-night television, and other "Hollywood-type" moral laxity. Some, like the Reverend Bob Jones III, president of Bob Jones University, wrote the President with admirable directness to remind him what the election meant, and what he now owed:

> In your re-election, God has graciously granted America—though she doesn't deserve it—a reprieve from the agenda of paganism. You

> have been given a mandate.... Don't equivocate. Put your agenda on the front burner and let it boil. You owe the liberals nothing. They despise you because they despise your Christ....
>
> Undoubtedly, you will have opportunity to appoint many conservative judges and exercise forceful leadership with the Congress in passing legislation that is defined by biblical norm regarding the family, sexuality, sanctity of life, religious freedom, freedom of speech, and limited government. You have four years—a brief time only—to leave an imprint for righteousness upon this nation that brings with it the blessings of Almighty God....
>
> If you have weaklings around you who do not share your biblical values, shed yourself of them.

And yet the voters of Union County, Florida's smallest, whom I found crowding the election supervisor's office in tiny Lake Butler, seemed unaware that they had been impelled to vote by a newfound quest for redemption. In Lake Butler, turnout was higher than anyone could remember; in Union County, voter registration had risen by 25 percent over 2000, when I had last visited. But none of the voters who spoke to me there volunteered a word about "moral values." Their answers tended to be much more concrete. "It's because of 9/11—you know, because of the terrorism," said Babs Montpetit—a.k.a. Miss Babs, election supervisor of Union County since 1985. "Because of the terrorism people are afraid *not* to vote." Through the window behind her I could see Lake Butler's main street, with its scattering of stores and bars—a tiny, isolated place, with barely seven thousand registered voters, far from any major city. Why should its citizens worry about terrorism? "Why, who could have expected that would happen, that business in New York?"

Miss Babs asked me in return, leaning forward and lowering her voice. "You just *don't know*."

Back in the car, I turned on the radio to find the Florida news feed, which led with this story:

> A suspicious package that seemed to be vibrating forced the closing of the State Board of Elections today. The parcel, it turned out, was an ordinary package that happened to have been placed next to an air conditioner, the breeze from which accounted for the apparent vibrating action. . . .

This embarrassing incident, which in other times might have been treated as a humorous item about the haplessness of government officials, was reported in dead seriousness: a dark dispatch from the front lines. As I left Lake Butler, stepping on the accelerator, I turned the radio up and the air around me filled again with the booming voice of Rush Limbaugh, in full and impressive rant:

> Osama bin Laden cannot launch an attack on the United States of America. Osama bin Laden can only deliver a tape, and on that tape, bin Laden appeals to the very appeasers in this country who would allow him to gain strength by agreeing with what he says and voting for the man who is being quoted by bin Laden. John Kerry, as much as Michael Moore, was quoted by Osama bin Laden in that video that we all saw. . . . Michael Moore is not on the ballot; John Kerry is. Osama bin Laden parroting John Kerry in his tape on Friday.

We have a unique responsibility to lead the world in confronting and defeating this evil threat....

Returning to the days of appeasement, trying to meet a "global test" of world opinion, ignoring threats from hostile nations and groups is a deadly mistake we simply can't afford to make.... The Democrat Party in this country is eager to point to the things bin Laden said and suggest that he is right—a man who happily murdered three thousand Americans and is eager to do so over and over and over again! You say, "Rush, I haven't heard the Democrats say that." Oh, you can find it on their Web sites. You can find people who are going to vote for John Kerry who have said this. You can find people on various Democrat Web sites who are excited bin Laden said what he said. They're hoping for an Osama smackdown of Bush, if I may quote one of the things I saw.

Interspersed with Limbaugh's extraordinarily fluid and persuasively deceptive tirade—heard, according to his home station in Sacramento, by "nearly 20 million people over 600 stations"—came the political advertisements, one after another, which turned skillfully around a concentrated version of the same plotline: First, the threat America faces today is as great as any in the country's history. Second, that threat makes this election "the most important in history," because if Americans make "the wrong choice" they could make themselves and their families more vulnerable. Third, therefore, Americans must vote, and must make "the right choice." Fear is joined skillfully to risk: a risk that is personal and looming, and—most important—that could very well increase if the election goes the wrong way.

The script of the famous "Wolves" television ad, with its simple image of a pack of ravenous, circling carnivores readying for the attack, embodied this plotline in perhaps its purest form:

> In an increasingly dangerous world.... Even after the first terrorist attack on America... John Kerry and the liberals in Congress voted to slash America's intelligence operations. By six billion dollars.... Cuts so deep they would have weakened America's defenses. And weakness attracts those who are waiting to do America harm.

A vote for Bush is a vote to stave off that weakness. More important, a failure to vote could make way for that "weakening of America's defenses." As I headed to Jacksonville, grave voices from the radio warned again and again of what was at stake:

> John Kerry. The most liberal man in the Senate. The most liberal person to ever run for president. He voted to cut our military.... To severely cut our intelligence agencies.... He voted for higher taxes 350 times.... And now he wants to be our President.... We live in a dangerous world that requires strong and steady leadership. John Kerry is a risky choice for America... a risk we cannot take.

This rhetoric of risk carries forward a narrative that Republicans began shaping soon after the attacks of September 11, 2001, and that came boldly to the fore as a political strategy the following May, when Vice President Cheney declared that the statements of several Democratic senators, who had rather timidly questioned some of the decisions made in conducting the war in Afghanistan, were "unworthy of national leaders in a time of war." Though this bold shot across the bow essentially put an end to any overt Democratic criticism of the administration on the conduct of the war on terror, Republicans clearly realized that when it came to terrorism and national security, as Karl Rove observed during a speech to the Republican National Committee in January 2002, they could "go to the country on this issue, because [Americans] trust the Republican Party to do a better job of protecting and strengthening America's military might and thereby protecting America."

That autumn Republicans triumphed in the midterm elections, largely because they effectively exploited Americans' apparent willingness to believe that the Republicans could better protect the country. This strategy was displayed most dramatically in Saxby Chambliss's victory over the incumbent Max Cleland in the Senate race in Georgia, in which the challenger portrayed Cleland, a highly decorated veteran who had lost three limbs in Vietnam, as an ally of bin Laden. Though the claims were obviously trumped up—they rested on the fact that Cleland had not instantly voted for the creation of the Department of Homeland Security—the images of Cleland's and bin Laden's faces side by side in effect doomed the incumbent.

The attacks of September 11 restored to Republicans their traditional political advantage in matters of "national security" and "national defense"—an advantage the party had lost with the end of the cold war—and Republicans capitalized on that advantage, not only by running President Bush as "a war president," as he repeatedly identified himself, but by presenting a vote for John Kerry—whom the Republicans succeeded in defining (with a good deal of help from the Swift Boat Veterans, and from Kerry himself) as indecisive, opportunistic, and untrustworthy—as a vote that was inherently, dangerously risky. The emphasis placed on Bush's much-promoted personal strengths—decisiveness, determination, reliability, transparency—served to base his candidacy at once on "moral values" and on "national security," in effect making possession of the first essential to protect the second. Bush's decisiveness was put forward as the flip side of Kerry's dangerous vacillation, the answer to the threat of weakness Kerry was alleged to pose. This equation was dramatized, perfected, and repeated, with much discipline and persistence, in thousands of advertisements, speeches, and "talking heads" discussion programs on conservative networks, especially Fox. (In Lake Butler, Miss Babs's husband, she told me, "watches only Fox News. He believes all the other channels are propaganda.") Despite all the talk about "moral values," the 2004 election turned on a fulcrum of fear.

2.

Famously, as I have mentioned, more than one in five Americans—22 percent—who spoke to pollsters as they left the voting places said, when presented with seven choices, that their "most important issue" had been "moral values," and of these four out of five cast their votes for George Bush. On the other hand, 19 percent selected "terrorism" and another 15 percent chose "Iraq," meaning that more than one in three voters said the war—the Iraq war or the "war on terror"—was their most important issue. In fact, the most striking single result of the exit polls was Bush's much stronger appeal to women—many of them, apparently, the much-discussed "security moms," who were thought to be especially concerned about protecting their families. All of these numbers and conclusions, needless to say, bear further scrutiny.

Using an exit poll to draw precise conclusions from a national election is like using a very blurry magnifying glass to analyze the brushstrokes in a huge and complicated pointillist painting. Our tools for judging what elections "mean" are quite crude, depending as they do on the willingness of voters to speak to pollsters, on their ability to speak honestly about the choices they made, and on their particular talents for understanding and expressing their own motives. As we saw this year—when faulty exit polls that suggested an overwhelming Kerry victory significantly distorted election-day press coverage—they can often produce downright wrong conclusions. Despite the "scientific" feel that numbers lend to any analysis, there is more art to it than science and, despite the impression that election and analysis are starkly separate, much analysis, as the Reverend Jones's letter to President Bush suggests, simply carries forward beyond the election a self-interested political narrative that preceded it.

If one stands back a bit and lets the drifting smoke of the pundits and the preachers and the exit poll analysts begin to clear, three interesting facts about the 2004 election stand out. The first is that the election was very close—historically close, in fact. The table on the following page shows the margins of victory, in percentage of the popular vote and in electoral votes, of sitting Republican presidents who have won reelection during the last hundred years.

MARGINS OF VICTORY *Republican Presidents Reelected During the Last Hundred Years*			
	President	*Popular Vote*	*Electoral Vote*
1904	Theodore Roosevelt	17%	196
1956	Dwight D. Eisenhower	16%	384
1972	Richard M. Nixon	23%	503
1984	Ronald Reagan	18%	512
2004	George Bush	2%	35

As these numbers show, incumbency is a huge advantage; nonetheless, Bush's reelection was a squeaker, the closest for a Republican in more than a century.[1] Four years after the historically close election of 2000, and after a hard-fought eight-month campaign in which the candidates, the parties, and so-called independent groups spent more than a billion dollars to woo voters, the electoral map

1. In 1996 Bill Clinton, the last president to win reelection, won by 8.5 percent and 220 electoral votes; in 1964 Lyndon Johnson—who like Theodore Roosevelt had not been elected but took office after the death of an incumbent—won by 22 percent and 434 electoral votes. To find an elected incumbent who won by nearly as narrow a margin as George W. Bush, one must look back nine decades, to 1916, when Democrat Woodrow Wilson won by 3.2 percent and 23 electoral votes.

hardly changed. Only three small states switched sides: the Democrats picked up New Hampshire (four electoral votes) and the Republicans very narrowly won Iowa (eight) and New Mexico (five). Bush had a net gain of only nine electoral votes, which, added to the seven that the Republicans gained through reapportionment, gave him his narrow margin of victory.[2]

Had fewer than 60,000 Ohio voters decided to cast their ballots for the Democrat rather than the Republican (and according to the exit polls one voter in twenty decided whom to vote for on election day), John Kerry would have won Ohio's twenty electoral votes and with them the presidency—and would have entered the White House in January 2005, as George W. Bush had done in January 2001, having won the votes of fewer Americans than the man he defeated. About 2,991,437 fewer, which, as I write, is George W. Bush's margin of victory, out of 122,124,783 votes cast for president.

Which leads to the second interesting fact about the 2004 election: a great many more people turned out to vote, nearly seventeen million more, than turned out four years ago. Nearly 60 percent of those Americans eligible cast ballots in 2004, an increase in turnout of almost 6 percent.[3] In the so-called battleground states, where

2. Because of population gains recorded in the 2000 Census, some states, like Arizona, Florida, and Georgia, were accorded more electoral votes in 2004, while others, like New York, Pennsylvania, and Wisconsin, were accorded fewer. This process favored the Republicans, with their base in the growing states of the South and Southwest; the same states they had won in 2000 were worth seven more votes in 2004.

3. These figures are drawn from Michael McDonald of George Mason University and the United States Election Project. His turnout figures represent the percentage of people eligible to vote (VEP)—thus eliminating noncitizens, felons, etc.—rather than the more common, but less accurate, percentage of people of voting age (VAP). See election.lab.ufl.edu/voter-turnout/.

vast sums were spent on advertising and one could not escape the barrage of political messages blaring from television and radio and pouring out of the telephone and the mailbox, the increase in turnout was even greater. A million and a half more Floridians cast ballots than had four years before: in 2000—itself an intensely fought election in which turnout substantially increased—fewer than 56 percent of eligible Floridians voted; in 2004 more than 65 percent did.

This leads, finally, to the third interesting fact about the election, which is that in the days leading up to it many of the "indicators" which political professionals have traditionally taken to suggest whether or not an incumbent will win were running distinctly against President Bush. Most notably, more Americans (55 percent) said they thought the country was "headed in the wrong direction" than those who said it was headed in the right one, and fewer than half of Americans polled (49 percent) said that they approved of the President's performance in office. More disapproved than approved of the President's handling of foreign policy (49 percent to 45 percent) and of the economy (51 percent to 43 percent). Finally more Americans disapproved than approved of the President's handling of Iraq (50 percent to 45 percent), his most important foreign policy, and, perhaps most strikingly, more than two Americans in three told pollsters that Mr. Bush's tax cuts—his signal domestic accomplishment—had either been bad for the economy (17 percent) or had not made much difference (51 percent).[4]

4. These numbers are all drawn from *The New York Times*/CBS News Poll, taken in mid- to late- October, with most, though not all, of the polling done between October 28 and 30.

The President went into the election, then, with Americans mildly pessimistic about the direction of the country and broadly disapproving of his performance and his policies. Most polls showed the race "too close to call," and many of the major indicators, "historically" speaking, suggested the incumbent would lose. Small wonder that so many experts, including apparently the President's own political team, were willing to believe the election-day exit polls that into the early evening showed their man losing by a considerable margin. (The widely circulated numbers from the respected polling firm Zogby International, for example, showed Mr. Kerry winning 311 electoral votes.) The fact was that though President Bush was personally popular, many of his major policies were not. The problem for the Bush campaign was how to turn attention away from policies voters didn't like—particularly the President's decisions on Iraq and his conduct of the war there—toward policies they approved of—particularly his conduct of "the war on terror" (into which Iraq would be "folded")—and toward his personal qualities.

3.

If your babies were left all alone in the dead of night, who would you rather have setting there on the porch—John Kerry and his snowboard or George W. with his shotgun?

—SEAN MICHAELS, professional wrestler, warming up the crowd, Tinker Field, October 30, 2004

On a beautiful October evening three days before the election, Orlando's Tinker Field had become an enormous bowl filled with

17,000 screaming, chanting Bush partisans floating in a sea of red, white, and blue. On the stadium wall hung a great fifty-foot-high sign proclaiming that George W. Bush was MOVING AMERICA FORWARD! Inside, flanking the stage in letters that dwarfed it, and echoed by smaller signs bobbing up and down everywhere in the crowd, was the terse slogan AMERICA: SAFER STRONGER BETTER! And then, precisely placed around the stadium in enormous letters, were the words on which the campaign was built: STRENGTH! LEADERSHIP! CHARACTER! INTEGRITY! Disciplined, organized, relentless, the Bush campaign would never be accused of subtlety.

"Well . . . , I'm just so proud of the way he handled 9/11—I mean, that was . . . *amazing*!" Dot Richardson-Pinto told me as we sat together near the podium. When I'd asked why she supported the President, she had had to search a moment for an answer, and not entirely because she couldn't understand how it could be that anyone wouldn't. She'd had to think for a moment, I came to realize, because her ardor had so much more to do with who he was than with what he did. And who he was could be summarized by those four giant words looming over the stage.

"It doesn't matter if the man can talk," Ms. Richardson-Pinto told me. "Sometimes, when someone's real articulate you can't trust what he says, you know?" As the security helicopters circled overhead, and the crowd launched into yet one more chant of "*Kerry is scary!*" I was struck again by how precisely the campaign had managed to define Bush's strengths in perfect contradistinction to what they had defined as Kerry's weaknesses, and then to devote all its resources to emphasizing both. Every repetition of what Bush was—and the repetitions were unending, and intricately varied—was crafted to be a perfect reminder of what his opponent was not. Practically every word emitted by the campaign, whether through the thousands and thousands of television and radio commercials, or the words of the campaign spokesmen, or the speeches of the candidate himself, moved in gorgeously disciplined lockstep to drive home to voters not only who George W. Bush was but who his opponent was not. As Bush became more and more Bush (STRENGTH! LEADERSHIP! CHARACTER! INTEGRITY!), Kerry, little-known, chilly, distant, was turned into the anti-Bush, a weak, shallow, flip-flopping shillyshallyer whose every word was an attempt to deceive Americans about who he really was.

In blue shirt and black slacks the President strode into the stadium, flanked by his wife and brother Jeb, and raised his hands to the rock-star reception. When the thunderous chants—"*Viva Bush! Viva Bush!*"—had finally dropped off to a scattering of shouts, he launched into a speech whose terms I knew well but whose effectiveness, with Ms. Richardson-Pinto sitting beside me, I only now understood. George W. Bush seemed to be speaking directly to her, to be bringing her into his family:

> Sometimes I'm a little too blunt—I get that from my mother. [*Huge cheers*] Sometimes I mangle the English language—I get that from my dad. [*Laughter and cheers*]
>
> But you always know where I stand. You can't say that for my opponent. . . .
>
> The fact is that *all* progress on other issues depends on the safety of our citizens. The most solemn duty of the American president is to protect the American people. [*Loud cheers. Chants of "Four More Years! Four More Years! Four More Years!"*]

> The president must make tough decisions and stand behind them. Especially in time of war mixed signals only confuse our friends and embolden our enemies.
>
> If America shows uncertainty or weakness in these troubling times the world will drift toward tragedy—*and this will not happen on my watch!*

In a few blunt lines Bush had subsumed everything else beneath the preeminent shining banner of the war on terror, and subsumed that war beneath his own reputation for forthrightness, decisiveness, and strength. And he had identified uncertainty, hesitation, vacillation—even the sort of nit-picking that would seek to separate the war in Iraq from the war on terror—as not simply mistaken or foolish but dangerous. "Relentless"…"Steadfast"…"Determined": these words came fast and strong, again and again. And then the climactic line: "*We will fight the terrorists across the globe so we do not have to fight them here at home!*" It drew a huge response and after the applause and chanting had finally died down he followed up with his most important words about the current shooting war:

> I will use every asset at our disposal to protect the American people and one of the best assets we have is *freedom*! Freedom is *powerful*!
>
> Freedom is not America's gift to the world, it is the Almighty's gift to everyone.… Iraq is still dangerous but Iraq will have free elections in January—think how far that country has come!
>
> On good days and bad days, whether the polls are up or the polls are down, I am determined to protect the American people!

The Iraq war was not only irrevocably part of the war on terror—who could think, gazing at the car bombs and beheadings every night on television, that they were any different?—it had become a leading part of the ideological response to the threat of terror: a first step in the expansion of the holy cause of freedom. As Reagan had dared to go beyond staunch anticommunism and imagine a world after communism's collapse, so Bush looked beyond the present chaotic world of terror to see a blessed land of freedom.[6] ("In this election, my opponent has spent a lot of time talking about a day that is gone. I'm talking about the day that is coming.") It was a striking vision, clear and absolutely simple to understand. And it linked, firmly and directly, the so-called moral values of justice, fairness, and the Almighty to the cause of national security, and specifically to the war on terror that the Bush people kept relentlessly at the campaign's heart. "Terror," "Iraq," and "moral values," supposedly separate "important issues," had been seamlessly joined.

Of course whatever its virtues as a campaign theme, the picture the President offered was not especially "fact-dependent." Many well-known facts—on which Kerry, in his campaign, had laid such stress—were either irrelevant to it (the missing weapons of mass destruction, which went unmentioned) or directly contradicted by it (the failure to demonstrate connections between Iraq and the attacks of September 11). But the facts did not matter—not necessarily because those in the stadium were ignorant of them, though some certainly were, but because the President was offering in their place a worldview that was whole, complete, comprehensible, and thus impermeable to statements of fact that clearly contradicted it. The thousands cheering around me in that Orlando stadium, and the many others who would come to support Bush on election day, faced a stark choice: either discard the facts, or give up the clear and comforting worldview that they contradicted. They chose to disregard the facts.

Two weeks before the election, after the Senate Intelligence Committee report on Iraqi weapons of mass destruction and the Duelfer Report, and after intensive news coverage of the administration's failure to find such weapons in Iraq, nearly three Bush supporters in four told pollsters they believed Iraq had either had weapons of mass destruction (47 percent) or had had a "major program" to develop them (26 percent). Nearly three in five said they believed that the widely publicized Duelfer Report, which directly contradicted this, had in fact confirmed it. Three in four believed that Iraq had either been directly involved in the September 11 attacks (20 percent) or had given al-Qaeda "substantial support" (55 percent), and nearly three in ten wrongly believed that the 9/11 Commission had confirmed that they had. Similar majorities believed that the President and his administration still publicly supported these positions.

Many of the Bush supporters I spoke to were educated, well-informed people. They watched the news and took pleasure in debating politics. And yet they clung to views about important matters of fact that were demonstrably wrong. Steven Kull, the public opinion expert at the University of Maryland who authored the study from which these numbers are drawn, acknowledges that although one reason they "cling so tightly to beliefs that have been so visibly refuted... is that they continue to hear the Bush administration confirming these beliefs," the prevalence, and persistence, of these misperceptions is "probably not due to a simple failure to pay attention to the news." Rather, Kull writes, "Bush supporters cling to these beliefs because they are necessary for their support for the decision to go to war with Iraq":

> Asked whether the US should have gone to war with Iraq if US intelligence had concluded that Iraq was not making WMD or providing support to al-Qaeda, 58 percent of Bush supporters said the US should not have, and 61 percent assume that in this case the president would not have. To support the president and to accept that he took the US to war based on mistaken assumptions is difficult to bear, especially in light of the continuing costs in terms of lives and money. Apparently, to avoid this cognitive dissonance, Bush supporters suppress awareness of unsettling information.[5]

This analysis suggests the difficulties Kerry faced in pressing home his highly "fact-dependent" argument that the Iraq war was separate from the war on terror and thus a mistaken distraction from it. Not only did accepting the point require a good deal of sophistication and knowledge, not only did it seem to contradict the evidence on Americans' television screens each night, which often showed vivid depictions of terrorism in Iraq; it also seemed to imply to some voters that they should take what must have seemed an unpatriotic position. For if they accepted the false pretenses on which the war had been based, how could they go on supporting it, as Kerry, somewhat illogically and even dishonestly, seemed to be asking them to do?

5. See Steven Kull et al., *The Separate Realities of Bush and Kerry Supporters* (PIPA/Knowledge Networks, October 21, 2004), p. 13.

Those running the Bush campaign clearly counted on the talent and influence of impressive propagandists like Limbaugh, and the help they received from an often acquiescent mainstream press. More, they counted on the President's reputation for forthrightness, together with the political folk wisdom that many people, particularly "during wartime," believe "the man, not the fact." When Bush, in full rhetorical flower in Tinker Field, declared to his delirious audience that "Americans need a president who doesn't think terrorism is 'a nuisance,'" my neighbor Ms. Richardson-Pinto nudged me with her elbow and shouted over the laughter and cheers, "Do you *believe* Kerry said that?" Actually, I shouted into her ear, Kerry hadn't said that, and then I paraphrased for her the actual quotation:

> We have to get back to the place we were, where terrorists are not the focus of our lives, but they're a nuisance. As a former law enforcement person, I know we're never going to end prostitution . . . [and] illegal gambling. But we're going to reduce it, organized crime, to a level where . . . it's something that you continue to fight, but it's not threatening the fabric of your life.[6]

Hardly exceptional; indeed, Bush himself had only weeks before said something very similar. Ms. Richardson-Pinto, a well-educated, worldly woman—a doctor, and a two-time Olympic gold medalist in women's softball—listened to me intently, nodded politely, began to form a question, and then, thinking better of it, looked at me for

6. See Matt Bai, "Kerry's Undeclared War," *The New York Times Magazine*, October 10, 2004.

a moment longer before turning back to the President. She'd had a choice what—or rather whom—to believe; and she'd made it.

4.

Saddam would never have disarmed.

—GEORGE W. BUSH, first presidential debate, September 30, 2004

Seven o'clock on the evening of election day and the office of the election supervisor in downtown Jacksonville was mobbed, encircled by a raggedy line of hundreds and hundreds of late voters. In the street in front an enormous crowd of Democrats chanted, cheered, and sang, filling every inch of space and spilling out into the streets. Car after car, horns blaring, made its way carefully through the crowd, the drivers leaning out to administer high fives and to cheer, and cheer again. When word of the early exit-poll numbers seeming to confirm an overwhelming Kerry victory swept through the crowd, hundreds broke into song, to the tune of the old civil rights classic, "Ain't Gonna Let Nobody Turn Me 'Round":

> Ain't gonna let nobody steal my vote
> Steal my vote, steal my vote
> Ain't gonna let nobody steal my vote....

It had been Jacksonville where in 2000 the infamous "caterpillar ballot" had led officials to discard tens of thousands of votes, votes cast overwhelmingly by African-Americans. As I stood watching the dancing and the celebration—"We gonna *elect* one, not *select* one!"—the sense people had of justice finally being done was vivid. I had felt it all day as I went from polling place to polling place in the downtown neighborhoods of the city—they were overwhelmed with voters, and overwhelmed with a sense that a wrong would be righted.

What I didn't find was any sense of strong support for John Kerry as a politician or a leader, or even a feeling of familiarity with him. The personality of Bush seemed vivid among voters, whether they admired him or hated him; the personality of Kerry was faint, indistinct, and where I found its mark most strongly was among those Bush voters who saw the Massachusetts senator, or the depiction of him that the Bush campaign had succeeded in creating, as a threat to their security. To counteract this Kerry would have had to become a known quality, trusted, *familiar*; but even after the hundreds of millions spent on advertising and his strong performance in the debates, for most voters he seemed a distant figure. He never entered that great stock company of celebrities—the "Oprah touring company"—that ordinary Americans welcome into their living rooms and believe they have somehow come to know. Love him or hate him, the President had long since taken his place as a recognizable, powerful personality in that company; John Kerry never did.

I had seen Kerry speak two nights before in Tampa, before a crowd fully as delirious as the one that had greeted George W. Bush the night before. Though the Kerry crowd was recognizably younger and, for lack of a better word, "hipper," most of those present would not have seemed out of place at either event. Partly hidden behind a forest of yellow TWO MORE DAYS! signs, Kerry, by far the tallest person on stage, stretched and shifted as he was introduced, raising and lowering himself on the balls of his feet: he was plainly exhausted. Nonetheless he gave a powerful, well-crafted speech, though built around the uninspired phrases "a fresh start" and "first we must choose." And then he turned to Iraq:

> The President tells us that in Iraq, his "strategy is succeeding...." But every day on our TV screens, we see the hard truths. We see the consequences of this President's decision to rush to war without a plan to win the peace: the loss of over 1,100 of our brave men and women in uniform. A cost of $225 billion with billions more on the way. Entire regions controlled by insurgents and terrorists. By pushing our allies aside, George Bush's catastrophic mismanagement of this war has left America to bear almost 90 percent of the costs and 90 percent of the coalition casualties. We relied on Afghan warlords instead of American troops to hunt down Osama bin Laden, and the man responsible for murdering more than three thousand Americans walked away.... On Tuesday, we have the opportunity to set a new course in Iraq...open up a new chapter in our relationship with the rest of the world...and do whatever it takes to defend America and keep our troops safe.... When I'm president, I will bring other nations to our side and train Iraqis so that we can succeed and bring our troops home. As president, I will fight a tougher, smarter, more effective war on terror. We will hunt down, capture, and kill the terrorists wherever they are. I defended this country as a young man and I will defend it as president.

Kerry's indictment of Bush's stewardship of the war was strong, but he offered little by way of an alternative; his "new course in Iraq" amounted to bringing "other nations to our side" to train Iraqis. He would "do whatever it takes to defend America"—a broad, empty assertion that depended entirely on the trust a prospective voter was willing to grant him. And though Kerry struggled to separate Iraq and the war on terror, not just the imagery of the war—the descent of Iraq into a kind of terrorism that, ironically enough, seemed to confirm the President's insistence that it was in fact "the central front of the war on terror"—but Kerry's own discussion of Iraq and terrorism only seemed to bring them together.

For Kerry, this proved fatal. If Bush had succeeded in joining Iraq and terrorism and then wrestling to the very center of the election his chosen question—whom do you trust to protect you and your family from terrorism?—he had also succeeded, for too many of those famous "swing voters," in providing the answer. The exit polls make this clear: nearly six in ten voters said they trusted Bush to "handle terrorism." Nearly six in ten said they did not trust Kerry to do the same.

Of course it is easy to say, as many have, that Kerry's policy on Iraq and terrorism was inadequate or incoherent. It is much harder to say what that policy should have been. Kerry, it is true, did not prove himself a very creative or resourceful candidate, and the Bush campaign was ruthless and brilliant in seizing on his missteps—his mention of a "global test" for United States intervention abroad, for example, and his unfortunate statement that "I actually voted for the $87 billion before I voted against it"—and using them to color in vivid tones the picture they wanted to paint of the senator.[7] Kerry gave them a good deal of help, particularly by focusing on Vietnam, and attempting to make his heroic service as a naval officer there a central part of his campaign while avoiding discussion of his more controversial leadership in the antiwar movement after he returned. The so-called Swift Boat Veterans for Truth, incensed by the antiwar Kerry, did great damage to the reputation of heroic warrior Kerry, and thereby did much to bolster the point that the Bush campaign, with the help of tens of millions of dollars in television and radio ads, had sought to drive home to American voters: that Kerry was inauthentic, untrustworthy, and "unfit to lead."

But Kerry's mistakes, however costly, in fact concealed a deeper problem, which was that Democrats themselves, haunted by the traditional charge of "weakness on national security" (which of course helped lead to Kerry's nomination), were deeply divided on what should be done about the Iraq war, with as many favoring withdrawal as not.[8] This is not surprising: the war itself, a costly, tangled, unending mess, admits of no obvious solution. The war may well be President Bush's greatest wound; but for candidate Bush the ability to depict Iraq as "the central front of the war on terror" and trumpet his willingness to confront the war and "stay the course"

7. See especially "How He Did It," *Newsweek*, November 15, 2004, p. 70, for an excellent account of the Bush campaign's handling of the $87 billion gaffe.

8. See, among others, Ronald Brownstein, "Kerry Feels Squeeze on Iraq Policy," *Los Angeles Times*, May 27, 2004. As Brownstein points out, polls had shown nearly half of Democratic voters favoring immediate withdrawal, a position that, if adopted, would likely have doomed Kerry's candidacy.

to victory was an audacious and astonishing act of political legerdemain. He took what looked to be his greatest weakness and made it his opponent's.

Kerry might have done better to declare early on that Iraq and the war on terror could no longer be separated, and to argue, forcefully and consistently, that Bush had conducted both incompetently—so incompetently, in fact, that four more years of his leadership would put Americans at ever greater risk. But to have been convincing, such a strategy, at least implicitly, would have meant accepting the necessity of going to war in Iraq—a position that many committed Democratic voters strongly disputed and that Kerry's own past statements tended to contradict. And it would have meant demonstrating the kind of single-mindedness, relentlessness, and rigor that the Bush campaign managed but the Kerry forces never did. Either way, as long as Bush was able to succeed in melding Iraq and the war on terror and placing them firmly at the center of the campaign, Kerry faced an incumbent "war president" who, whatever his missteps, Americans would be hesitant to abandon—without a very good reason for doing so. Kerry never produced that reason.

At about half past eight, as I stood amid the roiling sea of jubilant Democrats outside that election supervisor's office in downtown Jacksonville, I began to hear, through the civil rights songs and the laughter and cheers, a distant, booming, amplified chant. One by one people in the crowd before me heard it, and began turning to look down the street whence the chanting came, and then to look at one another. The voices grew louder and louder, and finally we saw their source: a group of twenty or so young men—they looked like football players—led by a beefy fellow holding high a blue Bush/Cheney sign, and chanting through a megaphone in a deep baritone:

> Bush Won the State! Bush Won the State! Bush Won the State!

The dream of a Democratic victory had been fueled by the enormous turnout and by a handful of faulty exit polls. Everyone had believed it, even those distinctly downcast Republicans I'd visited at their Jacksonville headquarters earlier that afternoon. But the dream had ended.

The Democrats had come remarkably close. They had matched the Republicans in fund-raising dollar for dollar and had mounted an unprecedented "ground game." On election day they managed the impressive feat of bringing eight million more voters to the polls than they had four years before. But the Republicans managed to bring in eleven million additional voters. George W. Bush, having gained half a million fewer votes than Al Gore in 2000, defeated John Kerry by three million votes.[9]

Still, the victory was "narrow but clear," as William Kristol described it, with candor rare among Republicans after the election. For all the talk of "moral values," had 60,000 Ohioans made a different

9. Half of those votes came from the President's loyal supporters in the "deep red" states—especially Texas, Georgia, Alabama, and Tennessee— and a third from stronger support for Bush in the "deep blue" states, especially New York and New Jersey. The remainder came from the so-called "purple states," and half of these from Florida—where the President, with a spectacular effort to register new voters in the outer suburbs, increased his margin from 537 to more than 370,000.

choice on election day, we would now be discussing the unpopularity of the Iraq war and the President's failed economic policies. After his narrow but clear victory, George W. Bush remained a popular leader promoting unpopular policies. And though he managed to convince enough Americans that Iraq was "the central front in the war on terror," the truth remains that he has saddled himself and the country he leads with a worsening, increasingly unpopular shooting war that offers no obvious means of escape.

Now he faces a newly emboldened set of claimants. Though several million more evangelical voters turned out in 2004, and thus were critical to Bush's victory, they do not seem to have formed a higher percentage of Republican voters than they had four years before.[10] Still, having accounted, in their increased numbers, for a third of Bush's margin of victory, the evangelicals unquestionably form the Republican Party's most reliable and aggressive base of supporters. Their leaders have been quick and aggressive in claiming full credit for the triumph and the press has been happy to play

10. Much less noticed, and in many ways more dramatic, was the upsurge in Catholics voting for Bush, which was a true shift from four years ago. Kerry, a Catholic, received 5 percent fewer Catholic votes than Al Gore, a Southern Baptist, and these votes were critical in several swing states, especially Ohio, where 55 percent of Catholic voters cast their ballots for Bush. According to Sidney Blumenthal, who reported these figures, the reason can be traced to the aggressive position that many in the Catholic hierarchy took against John Kerry. With the Catholic Church in America "in crisis," writes Blumenthal, "electing a liberal Catholic as president would have been a severe blow" to the Church and its conservative leadership. Because of this, Kerry faced aggressive opposition from many in the hierarchy, including some bishops who openly denounced the candidate and threatened to deny him communion or even to excommunicate him. See Sidney Blumenthal, "The Lowest Ignorance Takes Charge," *The Guardian*, November 11, 2004.

along. As so often in politics, the appearance, through repetition, becomes its own reality.

Leaders like thc unabashedly direct Reverend Bob Jones III now demand, in the name of moral values and the political redemption they claim to have brought the President, that Bush pass legislation "defined by biblical norm" and that he "leave an imprint for righteousness upon this nation that brings with it the blessings of Almighty God." This is a tall order, and one fraught, like the war, with considerable political peril—from moderate voters, who, for example, support outlawing "partial-birth abortion" but oppose outlawing abortion itself; and even, perhaps, from Democrats who may one day come to focus on what they have gained in this election rather than what they have lost. After all the recriminations and all the analyses of how the party must change, the fact remains that the Democrats came very close to bringing off an almost unprecedented achievement: turning out an incumbent president in a time of war. They failed, but not entirely; they now confront a narrowly reelected president, encumbered with a grim and intractable war, constrained by a huge deficit of his own creation, and faced with increasingly extreme demands that will be satisfied only at great political cost.

Frozen Scandal

December 4, 2008

1.

Scandal is our growth industry. Revelation of wrongdoing leads not to definitive investigation, punishment, and expiation but to more scandal. Permanent scandal. Frozen scandal. The weapons of mass destruction that turned out not to exist. The torture of detainees who remain forever detained. The firing of prosecutors which is forever investigated. These and other frozen scandals metastasize, ramify, self-replicate, clogging the cable news shows and the blogosphere and the bookstores. The titillating story that never ends, the pundit gabfest that never ceases, the gift that never stops giving: what is indestructible, irresolvable, unexpiatable is too valuable not to be made into a source of profit. Scandal, unpurged and unresolved, transcends political reality to become commercial fact.

We remember, many of us, a different time. However cynically we look to our political past, it is there that we find our political Eden: Vietnam and its domestic denouement, Watergate—the climax of a different time of scandal that ended a war and brought down a president. In retrospect those events unfold with the clear logic of utopian dream. First, revelation: intrepid journalists exposing the gaudy, interlocking crimes of the Nixon administration. Then, investigation: not just by the press—for that was but precursor, the necessary condition—but by Congress and the courts. Investigation, that is, by the polity, working through its institutions to construct a story of grim truth that citizens can in common accept. And finally expiation: the handing down of sentences, the politicians in shackles led off to jail, the orgy of public repentance. The exorcism of shame, the purging of the political system, and the return to a state, however imperfect, of societal grace.

It is a myth, of course, but a lovely one. It relies on images of power, the press, and the people that fit our collective longing—for justice, for heroism, and for ultimate goodness residing in a people who, once alerted to wrongdoing, insist on its rectification. The obstacle to this natural self-cleansing of our political life can only be the people's ignorance. For if they know, and the corruption and scandals persist—well, how can the people be good? No, what must be missing then—so the myth implies—is clarity, revelation. What is missing is the gatekeepers of our ignorance whose duty it is to draw the curtain back from scandal and show the people everything, thereby starting the polity on the road to inexorable justice. Information is all. Information, together with the people's natural sense of the good and the right, leads to expiation and society's inevitable cleansing.

However tenaciously the mythmakers of our society—and especially journalists, who are after all the stars of this idealized drama—cling to this happy scenario, recent history has not been kind to it. For it rests on an image of journalists and journalism that has become, to put it charitably, outdated. Journalists as the self-abnegating seekers after truth, defenders of society's conscience: had this happy description ever been true, even during Watergate, it now bears little resemblance to the scandal-mongering world of cable news shows and gabfests, for which scandal, the gaudier the better, provides the vast and complicated narratives that are the lifeblood of the twenty-four-hour news cycles. As the first Persian Gulf War begot CNN so did Monica Lewinsky's pouty lips beget Fox News.

Scandals, the more complicated and richer the plotlines the better, have above all to endure. Scandals provide the fodder for on-air confrontation, the verbal slash and parry—which is what television, a terrible medium for conveying information of any complexity, does best, and does most cheaply. Scandals provide subplots and minor characters and spin-offs. They offer, to the post-Watergate, high-profile, well-coiffed, colleague-of-the-powerful journalist hero of today—could anything be further from the deeply irreverent working stiff cracking wise in Howard Hawks's *His Girl Friday* (1940)?—the true venue for the highest practice of his art, the television studio.

That art relies on, or anyway thrives on, scandal. Scandal denotes success. Scandal shows he is doing his job. Scandal means pay dirt. And scandal represents that media-age dream, the perpetual story. Scandal can be rehashed, debated, photographed, from initial leak, to perp walk, to hearing, to trial, to appeal. Scandal offers an endless stream of what the business is after all supposed to be about: news.

As in: what is new. Scandal brings the heart-pumping, breath-gulping surge of stop-the-presses excitement, letting us know that into our fallen world the Gods of Great Events have finally come down from on high to intervene. Scandal represents movement, the audible cracking of the ice. And yet it is all an illusion, for beneath the rapidly moving train of gaudily hyped "breaking news," beneath all the grave and breathless stand-ups before the inevitable pillars of public buildings, beneath the swirling, gyrating phantasmagoria of scandal lies a kind of dystopian stasis. Everything changes and nothing does.

2.

It is not information, it is politics. If we have learned anything this past decade it is that "the people," that vaunted repository of public good—"the people always find out"—the people are willing and able to live with quite a lot. They read, watch television, grunt a pox on all their houses, and turn back to their dinners. Thanks to the efficiency of our age of scandal we now know as never before what the public is willing to live with. "Now you have shown independence, commendable independence," Barack Obama said to John McCain in the third debate, "on some key issues—like torture, for example." Torture has metamorphosed, these past few years, from an execrable war crime to a "key issue." From something forbidden by international treaty and condemned by domestic law to . . . something to be debated. Something one can stand on either side of. Something we can live with.

The story of how this happened is long and elaborate but one thing is clear: it has not happened for lack of revelation. The Abu Ghraib scandal broke in the spring of 2004. The images of Hooded Man, Leashed Man, Man Menaced by Dog—all quickly became "iconic," the stuff of end-of-the-year news tableaux and faded murals on the walls of minor cities in the Middle East. This first and last occasion when torture became vivid, fertile scandal—when torture emerged, thanks to the photographs, as that most valuable of products: televisual scandal—came and went in the spring and summer of 2004, leaving a harvest of rapidly aging images and leaked documents. Those documents—many hundreds of pages, which told in great and precise detail the story of how United States officials, from the President on down, came in the wake of the September 11 attacks to order Americans to torture—were quickly published by journalists and writers, myself included, who no doubt expected that the investigative committees, the televised hearings, and the prison sentences would quickly follow.[1]

In the event, the investigations did come, a dozen or more of them, and their very proliferation was the means by which the story was converted from shocking crime into perpetual news, then minor story, and then, at last, "key issue." But for a handful of hapless soldiers—the smallest of small fish —there were no real prosecutions,

1. See Mark Danner, *Torture and Truth: America, Abu Ghraib, and the War on Terror* (New York Review Books, 2004). See also, for a more compendious collection, *The Torture Papers: The Road to Abu Ghraib*, edited by Karen J. Greenberg and Joshua L. Dratel (Cambridge University Press, 2005).

no images of high officials in handcuffs. The leakers, who had risked their careers to make the documents public, must have been profoundly disappointed. For it was they, as it happened, who had committed one of the era's signal crimes: unguarded idealism. At Guantánamo, at the "dark sites," at various venues around the world, known and unknown, torture continued, even as it was studied and passed by due legislative oversight into the law of the land. Only the courts seemed, intermittently, to have a different idea. And all the while the torture story was well reported, mostly in the newspapers—for after that initial rush of photographs, which quickly became cliché, there followed nothing juicy enough to raise the story to the golden level of the televisual—and it continued to be reported even as it made its way through the complicated and mysterious transformational process by which a war crime becomes a "key issue."

All the while, it must be said, the public, that repository of right, showed relatively little interest. Neither, following the lead of their constituents, did the politicians. John Kerry, running for president in the immediate wake of Abu Ghraib—and perhaps remembering his own unrecompensed temerity in calling attention, as a young returning vet, to war crimes in Vietnam—hardly mentioned it. (In this sense Barack Obama's acknowledging of the "key issue," however offhand, represents a distinct advance.)

Indeed, one might argue that the most visible effect America's use of official torture had on the public consciousness during this era was the smashing success of the Fox television series *24*, each episode of which, in its heyday, was juiced with at least one and frequently many instances of lurid, explicit, and government-sponsored torture, during which heroic super-agent Jack Bauer, acting to save the country from imminent disaster, does what needs to be done. My personal favorite is the scene in which the President orders his National Security Agency director, whom he suspects of disloyalty, to be tortured by his chief Secret Service agent, using (note the American can-do spirit of this) a handy defibrillator, while the commander in chief watches the proceedings on closed-circuit television hookup. Perhaps this enthusiasm should not surprise us: we have known at least since the success of Clint Eastwood's iconic *Dirty Harry* (1971) about the reassuring effect on the public of the image of untrammeled power. But Harry was a rogue cop, raging against "the system" of the early Seventies; Jack Bauer, as we are endlessly reminded, works directly for the President.

3.

What notes on scandal could be complete without mention of the presiding master-scandal of our age, The War. One uses capitals to denote not a set of discrete events—a set of particular people being cut down or blown apart by particular violent actions at particular times—but a state of mind. Threat becomes not only a political shield but what is in the end much more dangerous: a source of bottomless self-justification. What is dangerous is not only that our leaders have endlessly maintained that they are right but that they believe they are. George Bush, as he declared to the world in a proudly emphatic phrase, had been reborn as a "war president."

George Orwell has long since surveyed this ground, most famously in *1984*, in his perpetual war between Eastasia, Eurasia, and Oceania, a never-ending, shape-shifting struggle that,

> if we judge it by the standards of previous wars, is merely an imposture. It is like the battles between certain ruminant animals whose horns are set at such an angle that they are incapable of hurting one another. But though it is unreal it is not meaningless.... It helps to preserve the special mental atmosphere that a hierarchical society needs.

Wars are immensely valuable to those who sit atop "hierarchical societies" because they supply an overarching rationale for power and its expansion while choking off questions, not least by increasingly limiting the information on which those questions must be based. The War on Terror, of course, has been far from bloodless, embodying itself in at least two "real" wars—one of which, in Afghanistan, was launched to respond directly to attack; the other, in Iraq, to achieve less specific, more grandiose goals—as well as in a great number of secret operations of varying ambition carried out "on the dark side." Still, unbounded as it is in space and time, serving as it has as a handy and near-inexhaustible rationale for accruing centralized power, the War on Terror has approached as close as we have yet come in reality to Orwell's imagined perpetual war, accruing to those in control the increased power that comes with war but without the endless costs. Or it would have, had the war not brought in its train its own frozen scandal.

4.

How will history choose to explain a war launched in the cause of ridding the world of weapons of mass destruction that turned out not to exist? It is a tantalizing question. Will the Iraq War take its place as a historical curiosity, alongside the Guano War of the nineteenth century or the Soccer War of the twentieth? And how interested will our descendants be in the response of our democratic polity: the investigations that, like dinosaurs slowly rousing themselves from the mudhole, ever so slowly got under way and then, after years of lumbering effort—hundreds of hours of testimony, thousands of documents examined—finally discovered . . . what? In the end, there was, alas, no "smoking gun."

Another legacy of Watergate, that image, made for a simpler time, when as devious a man as Richard Nixon could insouciantly tape-record every word he uttered. In our own less happy day, we can pore over the ever so explicit Downing Street Memo and scores of similar documents leaked fast and furiously from within the bureaucracy but find them, according to the rules of the scandal game, all too large and obvious to be taken to mean what to any normal person they precisely do mean, which is that those in power—wanting war, not diplomacy, and working hard to "wrong-foot Saddam" into war, as the Downing Street memoranda make explicitly clear—lied us into war. And now they have got us a war that has managed to be at once unnecessary and unending.

Of course the Law of the Smoking Gun tells us that this case, however evident the truth of it is to all, can never (failing the discovery of a tape recording in which the American president or the British prime minister can be heard chortling demonically about the grand charade they are about to perpetrate on their respective publics) be taken as definitively proved. The Law of Frozen Scandal means the case must remain forever open. Forever "alleged." Fodder still for a thousand investigative reports and a thousand revelations that reveal only what is already known. Can you not hear the wheels of scandal spinning? It is the music of our age.

Rumsfeld's War and Its Consequences Now

December 19, 2013

1.

A BARE TWO WEEKS after the attacks of September 11, at the end of a long and emotional day at the White House, a sixty-nine-year-old politician and businessman—a Midwesterner, born of modest means but grown wealthy and prominent and powerful—returned to his enormous suite of offices on the seventh floor of the flood-lit and wounded Pentagon and, as was his habit, scrawled out a memorandum on his calendar:

> Interesting day—
> NSC mtg. with President—
> As [it] ended he asked to see me alone...
> After the meeting ended I went to Oval Office—He was alone
> He was at his desk—
> He talked about the meet
> Then he said I want you to develop a plan to invade Ir[aq]. Do it

outside the normal channels. Do it creatively so we don't have to take so much cover [?]

Then he said Dick [Cheney] told me about your son—I broke down and cried. I couldn't speak—
said I love him so much
He said I can't imagine the burden you are carrying for the country and your son—
He said much more.
Stood and hugged me
An amazing day—
He is a fine human being—
I am so grateful he is President.
I am proud to be working for him.

It is a touching and fateful scene, this trading of confidences between the recovering alcoholic president and the defense secretary whose son is struggling with drug addiction, and shows the intimacy that can be forged amid danger and turmoil and stress. Trust brings trust, confidence builds on confidence: the young inexperienced president, days before American bombs begin falling on Afghanistan, wants a "creative" plan to invade Iraq, developed "outside the normal channels"; the old veteran defense secretary, in a rare moment of weakness, craves human comfort and understanding.

And yet they'd hardly known one another, these two, before George W. Bush chose him for his secretary of defense nine months before. To George W., Donald Henry Rumsfeld had been little more than a political enemy of the Bush family. It was Rumsfeld, as President Gerald Ford's ambitious young chief of staff, who had been instrumental in the so-called Halloween Massacre in 1975 that—so the legend goes—had helped clear the way for his own presidential ambitions by shunting George H. W. Bush, the wealthy eastern born-with-a-silver-spoon-in-his-mouth preppie who was the scrappy Illinois-born wrestler's main rival, off to be CIA director. This was a job for which Bush could gain Senate confirmation only by agreeing not to accept the vice-presidential nomination in 1976—even as Rumsfeld, as he tells us in his memoir, "for the third time in three years, . . . found myself being discussed for the vice presidential nomination." As Bush family *consigliere* James A. Baker III cautioned George W. a quarter-century later, when Rumsfeld's name was bruited for secretary of defense, "You know what he did to your daddy."

Certainly he knew, and one can be forgiven for suspecting that this knowledge might have been a strong part of the attraction, perhaps for both men. When Errol Morris asks Rumsfeld whether his former aide Dick Cheney had brought him into the Bush administration, Rumsfeld replies, "I assume that's the case. I don't think George W. Bush's father recommended it," and then beams with self-congratulatory mischievousness. It is one of several digs at Bush the elder, at whose side he had treaded the perilous path of the highest ambition until, at a critical moment in August 1980, both men found themselves at the Republican National Convention pacing nervously in their Detroit hotel rooms, awaiting a call from Ronald Reagan about who would be his vice-president. In the end it was George H. W. Bush who was called to history.

Errol Morris: It seems to me that if that decision had gone a slightly different way, you would have been vice-president and a future president of the United States.

Rumsfeld: [Pause] That's possible.

Here as at several important moments in his brilliant and maddening film, Morris holds for three beats on that craggy inscrutable face, struggling to penetrate the benign "aw, shucks" good ol' boy persona that Rumsfeld has worn so long he might well have forgotten how to put it aside. A decade ago Morris's camera, focused for those extra beats on the face of Robert Strange McNamara in *The Fog of War*, had seemed to penetrate to some sort of appalling well of pain and pleading, deeply felt or conjured or both, lurking just behind McNamara's rheumy eyes.

Confronted with Rumsfeld's cheerful, hail-fellow-well-met opacity, Morris is mostly forced to plumb the shallows. At a question about his part in the so-called Halloween Massacre, he affects wry surprise. ("I suppose it is" called that, he concedes, with elaborately feigned wonder at the proclivity of reporters and historians to get things so wrong.) His alleged derailing of the elder Bush's ambitions he dismisses as "utter nonsense." ("I suppose it's kind of more fun for somebody to be able to say they were pushed rather than they tripped.") And his legendary ambition? "I never knew what I was going to do next," he tells the filmmaker with chuckling insouciance. "The only thing I've ever volunteered for in my life: one, was to go into the Navy, and the other was to run for Congress."

It is a familiar pose, the modest, even self-effacing man of talent to whom good things just... happen. Such unbidden blessings float down in many guises—for example, in the benevolent and providential interest of a kindly president. In Bradley Graham's account in *By His Own Rules*:

> The conversation in March [1971] was one of a number of private talks, preserved by the White House taping system, in which Rumsfeld sought to advance his career and also draw political advice from Nixon. Rumsfeld showed little inhibition in sounding out the president about various high-level job possibilities....
>
> Nixon told Rumsfeld to consider his counselor post "as temporary, as a very interim period." He said a number of cabinet positions would probably fit Rumsfeld, mentioning Health, Education, and Welfare (HEW), Transportation, Interior, and Commerce....
>
> Rumsfeld tossed out another idea. He suggested "something in the trade area"... indicating this could help his plans "down the road" to run for political office in Illinois....
>
> The president reported that he had tried to find a spot for Rumsfeld at the State Department as undersecretary for development, but Secretary of State William Rogers had objected to Rumsfeld's lack of foreign policy experience.

Undaunted, the thirty-eight-year-old rising star does not hesitate to advise the president how to persuade his secretary of state that, lack of foreign policy experience be damned, Don Rumsfeld is the man for the job:

> Maybe it would be desirable for everyone if... you said to Bill, "Well, we've got a helluva problem in trade and we need a man of his stature,... and I want to do a favor for the Republican Party by giving

our youngest cabinet member some very valuable experience in State...." You wouldn't be saying, uh, "Rogers, you and State need Rumsfeld." You'd be saying, "Bill, I want you to do something that conceivably would be helpful to the party down the road."

Apart from the needling references to Bush Sr., the less worthy rival who *did* manage to become president, this intense will to triumph and dominate shows in the film's protagonist only in his studious denials. Morris's camera struggles with that self-satisfied opacity and so do we, knowing that beneath it, somewhere, lies the bottomless ambition that led Nixon to dub Rumsfeld "a ruthless little bastard." For Nixon there could be no stronger approbation. To his boss's acid observation that though "we've done a hell of a lot for Rumsfeld..., he's ready to jump the ship," H. R. "Bob" Haldeman, Nixon's chief of staff, replies with the cynical assurance born of having made good use of more than one ruthless little bastard in his day:

> No, I don't think he's ready to jump. And I doubt if he ever would, just because it serves his interests more not to. But I sure don't think he's ever going to be a solid member of the ship, except when it's floating high.

That ship was about to founder spectacularly and it was no more than a confirmation of this appraisal that Rumsfeld would gaze on Nixon's final destruction from a safe distance abroad, having engineered his own appointment as ambassador to NATO, and would remain sufficiently untainted by Watergate to return to serve his fellow Midwesterner Gerald Ford as White House chief of staff in his turn, at forty-three years old—his predecessor Haldeman was by then on the way to the federal penitentiary at Lompoc—and finally, as he tells Morris proudly, as "the youngest secretary of defense in history."

Nearly a quarter-century would pass before George W. would bring him back as the oldest, proving by his willingness to hire his father's famous rival that, as Rumsfeld tells Morris, the younger Bush "was his own man, made his own decisions"—and proving it again, not long after, by ordering him during that tearful private chat in the Oval Office to "develop a plan to invade Ir" and to "do it creatively." As for Rumsfeld, the calm, "aw shucks" demeanor was still there, and barely concealed beneath it the driving force of his ambition, which, during a quarter-century mostly spent outside the White House looking in, had only grown.

2.

Nearly two years have passed since the last American soldier crossed the Iraq border into Kuwait, ending in quiet ignominy the American phase of a war that had begun in highly ballyhooed "shock and awe" more than eight years before. In Iraq, the sectarian guerrilla war set off by the invasion goes on, the suicide bombers continue their work, hundreds of Iraqis die in horrific violence every month. That most Americans would prefer to ignore this does not alter the reality that we live in a world the Iraq war has made. Before the war, Iraq had served the United States as a check on the revolutionary ambitions of the Islamic Republic of Iran—a "tilt" to Iraq that Donald Rumsfeld had personally set on course, during talks with Saddam in Baghdad in 1983 as President Reagan's special envoy. It took the American invasion two decades later to make of Iraq an Iranian ally.

Under Saddam, Iraq had been devoid of Islamic jihadists; it took the American occupation to make of Iraq a breeding ground for jihadists and a laboratory for developing and honing their techniques of asymmetric warfare: the car bombs, kidnappings, improvised explosive devices, and other ruthless tactics in a cheap and effective "toolbox" that has been employed with considerable success from Afghanistan to Yemen to Mali. Iraqi jihadists, many of them former soldiers and officers in the Iraqi army that the American occupiers abruptly dissolved in the summer of 2003, have become the proud foot soldiers of the "Islamic State of Iraq and Syria," a proclaimed zone of insurgency and Wild West lawlessness that stretches west from Fallujah through Anbar province and into the heart of Sunni Syria.

While the increasingly repressive Shia government that the Americans helped install in Baghdad collaborates with Tehran in its support of Bashar al-Assad in Damascus, the Sunni insurgents that the Americans unleashed struggle to overthrow Assad in what is becoming the central battle of the three-continent-wide Salafi uprising that al-Qaeda, by its audacious September 11 attacks, had been determined to ignite and foster. Now the Sunnis are increasingly striking back at Hezbollah and its Iranian sponsors in Lebanon.

The Sunni–Shia struggle set in motion by the American invasion of Iraq has become the vortex of a violent political struggle that stretches from South Asia to the Gulf. Meantime, al-Qaeda in the Arabian Peninsula has grown fivefold. Bin Laden is dead, but in Pakistan and Somalia and Yemen the drones go on striking, killing by now several thousand, and more rise to take their place. The jihadists are not winning but they are not disappearing either. There is no end in sight.

Though Bush is long gone, replaced by a president who had seemed to voters to be in many ways his opposite, this geopolitical reality has hardly changed. As Rumsfeld remarks to Morris:

> Barack Obama opposed most of the structures that President George W. Bush put in place: Guantánamo Bay, the concept of indefinite detention, the Patriot Act, military commissions. Here we are, years later, and they're all still here. I think that has to validate, to some extent, the decisions that were made by President George W. Bush.

One needn't accept such "validation" to concede that more than a dozen years later we still live in the world that Bush's "war on terror" made. The "state of exception" that began on September 11, 2001, has not ended, owing not only to the political compromises and misplaced priorities of the Obama administration but to the terribly misbegotten and self-defeating way the "war on terror" was conceived and waged.

It is from this vantage that one must consider the question Donald Rumsfeld posed, in one of his famous "snowflakes"—personal memoranda on white paper that rained down in an unrelenting blizzard on Defense Department officials—with characteristic succinctness and precision:

> Are we capturing, killing or deterring and dissuading more terrorists every day than the madrassas and the radical clerics are recruiting, training and deploying against us?

In its focus on the *political* reality of the war on terror—on the necessity to *deter and dissuade* as well as to kill and capture—the memo is concise, perceptive, astute; it is also, coming in October 2003, very, very late. Americans killing Muslims in Baghdad and Fallujah and other cities of Iraq dominate the television screens. The secretary of defense, after stubbornly resisting the word in a trail of nitpicking snowflakes that Morris's film meticulously follows, can no longer deny that American troops are trying to repress an "insurgency" in Iraq. The images are lurid, indelible: Americans breaking into Muslim homes, pushing Muslim men to the floor with boots to the backs of their heads—and soon, Americans abusing naked Muslims in the garish grotesque prison world of Abu Ghraib.

It is all a great political gift to Osama bin Laden and al-Qaeda, and one that keeps on giving: a worldwide live-action recruiting poster, broadcast 24/7, with the Americans seeming to conform with bullheaded enthusiasm to the caricature the Islamists had made of them. More than two years into the Bush administration's "war on terror," it was too late to be asking, as Rumsfeld does in the next line of his October 2003 memo:

> Does the US need to fashion a broad, integrated plan to stop the next generation of terrorists? The US is putting relatively little effort into a long-range plan, but we are putting a great deal of effort into trying to stop terrorists.

In fact, this "broad, integrated plan" was unfolding before him and every other television viewer on the streets of Baghdad and Fallujah. Rumsfeld had placed it before the president in September 2001, a scant week after their intimate Oval Office meeting, in a memo bearing the portentous title "Strategic Thoughts." In it, the secretary of defense advises that the administration should "avoid as much as possible creating images of Americans killing Muslims." This wise admonition, alas, would conflict rather dramatically with his more grandiose "strategic thoughts." Reading them now, a dozen years into the ongoing "war on terror," the words carry all the poignancy of a vast heroic hubris come to grief:

> A key war aim would be to persuade or compel States to stop supporting terrorism. The regimes of such States should see that it will be fatal to host terrorists who attack the US. . . . *If the war does not significantly change the world's political map, the US will not achieve its aim*. There is value in being clear on the order of magnitude of the necessary change. The [US government] should envision a goal along these lines: *New regimes in Afghanistan *and another key State (or two)* that supports terrorism . . . [My emphasis]

It takes little imagination to glimpse looming out of those memorable words "another key State (or two)" the hirsute visage of Saddam Hussein. Making quick work of "liberating" Iraq would be the first move in the Bush administration's effort to "change the world's political map," without which the "US will not achieve its aim."

This would not be a war in which the president would "send a $2 million missile into a $10 empty tent and hit a camel in the butt" (in Bush's faux-cowboy dismissal of Bill Clinton's response to al-Qaeda). It would be a war to remake the world. George W. Bush, with less foreign policy experience than brash young Don Rumsfeld had had in 1971, was ambitious, impatient, confident; he "was his own man, made his own decisions," and he embraced with enthusiasm his secretary of defense's mission to "significantly change the world's political map." Donald Rumsfeld, experienced, powerful, confident, sharing his president's ambition and thirst for challenges both, was more than happy to show him the way.

3.

DoD has been organized, trained and equipped to fight big armies, navies and air forces. It is not possible to change DoD fast enough to successfully fight the global war on terror. . . .

—DONALD RUMSFELD, October 16, 2003

To explain the rapid shifting of the war on terror from attacking the enemy that had attacked the United States, al-Qaeda, to invading the enemy that hadn't, Iraq, it is not enough to say, quoting Rumsfeld in his notorious response to troops fighting in Iraq in 2004, that "you go to war with the army you have." (By then the soldiers were begging for "up-armored" Humvees to protect them from the IEDs that were maiming and killing them daily on Iraq's roads, and the secretary was trying and failing to explain why they didn't have them.) But if it is true that the post–cold war United States in September 2001 was far and away the world's preeminent military power, it is also true that its splendid arsenal of high-tech tanks and planes and ships had been designed to fight and win a conventional war, not a counter insurgency. The US military had last engaged a guerrilla force in Vietnam, and things had not gone well. Memories of this among senior officers remained vivid, and unpleasant.

No army had attacked the United States on September 11. It had been nineteen men, the vanguard of a worldwide insurgency, and if the attacks on New York and Washington had been bold and shocking and outlandish, the goals behind them had been the classic objects of insurgents for millennia: to encourage recruits to join the insurgent cause, to show the vulnerability of the ruling power, and to provoke that power to overreact—to respond to insurgent attacks in such a way that would reveal to the world the regime's cruelty and repressiveness and so bring the quiescent population (in this case, all Muslims) increasingly over to the insurgents' side.

Bin Laden had counted on the Americans responding to his attacks in New York and Washington by invading and occupying Afghanistan. (Indeed, to prepare for the expected battle he had dispatched, days before September 11, two suicide bombers disguised as television journalists to assassinate Northern Alliance commander Ahmad Shah Massoud.) America's coming occupation was to produce images of suffering Afghans that would outrage Muslims from Indonesia to Morocco; al-Qaeda would lead the Afghans in a guerrilla war against the Americans, producing a quagmire that would engulf the last superpower, as it had—so the legend went—the Soviet Union before it.

In the event, of course, the Americans offered a gift undreamt of in al-Qaeda's philosophy: they invaded and occupied Iraq, a much more important country. The result was catastrophe, not only for Iraq but for the Bush administration's worldwide "war on terror," for the invasion seemed to brand Bush's war, in image after bloody humiliating image of "Americans killing Muslims," as a new Western crusade against the Islamic world, confirming in every newscast the guiding idea of al-Qaeda's politics and propaganda.

These were the very images Rumsfeld had warned against in his

"Strategic Thoughts" memorandum of September 2001; he knew that such images, far from "deterring and dissuading" prospective terrorists, would recruit and nourish them. How was it that he came to preside over a military producing them day after day, month after month? How did the country come to fight, and then badly bungle, precisely the wrong war? Much has been written about the mystery of the Bush administration and its obsession with Iraq. Or rather obsessions, for one could easily construct a typology of these, beginning, first and foremost, with the young evangelical president who already on the evening of the frenzied surreal day after September 11 would confront his counterterrorism adviser Richard Clarke in the hallway outside the Situation Room. "He grabbed a few of us," Clarke writes, "and closed the door."

> "Look," he told us, "I know you have a lot to do and all ... but I want you, as soon as you can, to go back over everything, everything. See if Saddam did this. ..."
>
> I was once again taken aback, incredulous, and it showed. "But, Mr. President, al Qaeda did this."
>
> "I know, I know, but ... see if Saddam was involved. Just look. I want to know any shred ..."
>
> "Absolutely, we will look ... again." I was trying to be more respectful, more responsive. "But, you know, we have looked several times for state sponsorship of al Qaeda and not found any real linkages to Iraq. Iran plays a little, as does Pakistan, and Saudi Arabia, Yemen."
>
> "Look into Iraq, Saddam," the President said testily, and left us.[1]

1. See Richard A. Clarke, *Against All Enemies: Inside America's War on Terror* (Free Press, 2004), p. 32.

Did the president truly believe that Iraq was behind the attacks, or was he looking to find evidence for an invasion he already had in mind? Paul Wolfowitz, Rumsfeld's deputy, almost certainly was a true believer and had—to Clarke's astonishment—insisted on his "Iraq is behind al-Qaeda" theory as early as the previous April, during the administration's single Deputies Meeting on al-Qaeda. Clarke had ardently and doggedly pushed for this meeting—he was convinced another attack was coming—only to see it collapse into a debate about supposed Iraqi state sponsorship. Even after the September 11 attacks, in the first major "war cabinet" meeting at Camp David that Saturday, Wolfowitz insisted that the war on terror should begin not in Afghanistan but in Iraq:

> Rumsfeld turned the table over to Wolfowitz, who began making the case for going after Saddam Hussein. He declared that there was a 10 percent to 50 percent chance that Hussein had been involved in the attacks, although he presented no evidence. Afghanistan would not be a particularly satisfying place to wage a war since it was so primitive that there were few targets; Iraq, on the other hand, had plenty of targets and military action there would be a powerful demonstration that the United States would not sit by idly while a danger like Hussein operated with impunity.[2]

By this account, Bush eventually grows irritated by Wolfowitz's persistence, finally declaring, "We are *not* going after Iraq right

2. See Peter Baker, *Days of Fire: Bush and Cheney in the White House* (Doubleday, 2013), p. 144. We have known about Wolfowitz's role in this discussion since Bob Woodward's *Bush at War* (Simon and Schuster, 2002) but Baker's account brings new details.

this minute. We're going to go after the people we know did this to us."

4.

And so they would, dropping the first bomb on Afghanistan on October 7. The American military had not yet become Rumsfeld's military, with its emphasis on Special Forces; it was CIA officers who led the charge on horseback through Afghanistan, pointing their laser target finders to guide US bombers. Taliban fighters took punishment, then retreated, slipped away; as Wolfowitz had said the targets soon ran out. And when the critical moment came, with Osama bin Laden and much of his al-Qaeda force cornered at Tora Bora, Rumsfeld—so he tells us in his memoir—left the critical decisions to his combatant commander, General Tommy Franks:

> Franks had to determine whether attempting to apprehend one man on the run . . . was worth the risks. . . . Still, the emphasis on bin Laden concerned me. To my mind, the justification for our military operations in Afghanistan was not the capture or killing of one person. Our country's primary purpose was to try to prevent terrorists from attacking us again. There was far more to the threat posed by Islamist extremism than one man.

Still, "I made it clear to Franks that if he believed he needed more troops, he would get them as quickly as possible," and "if someone thought bin Laden was cornered, as later claimed, I found it surprising that [Director of Central Intelligence George] Tenet had never called me to urge Franks to support their operation." We would hear echoes of this in Iraq. As Nixon discovered, the deft shedding of responsibility was a Rumsfeld trademark.

Bin Laden escaped into Pakistan. He would remain defiantly at large, appearing in propaganda videos, for a decade. The Taliban, having fled the wave of heavy bombing that supported the ramshackle advance of the Northern Alliance, would soon begin filtering back into the country. It didn't matter. Amid the celebration of the victory in Afghanistan, the eyes of the Bush administration had already turned to Iraq.

What would Rumsfeld hope to find there? He had argued that the "war on terror" should "significantly change the world's political map." In this belief he was hardly alone. Henry Kissinger, Rumsfeld's old antagonist from the Ford administration, when asked why he supported the Iraq war, had reportedly replied, "because Afghanistan wasn't enough." The radical Islamists had wanted to humiliate us, he went on, "and we need to humiliate them."[3] This was about restoring national credibility, about rebuilding the national power—consisting in no small part of the *image* of power—that had been severely diminished by those world-altering real-time pictures of the collapsing towers. Such images must be vanquished, supplanted by those of American tanks rumbling down the streets of an Arab capital.

Proud realists, neither man put much stock in the "democratic tsunami" that, in the fantasy of neoconservative true believers like Wolfowitz, the Iraq war would send sweeping out of Baghdad to engulf the Middle East. Instead they put their faith in "American

3. See Bob Woodward, *State of Denial* (Simon and Schuster, 2006), p. 408. See also my "Iraq: The War of the Imagination," *The New York Review*, December 21, 2006.

leadership" and the restoration of American power through a decisive demonstration of American strength.

Beneath all the trappings of "Rumsfeld's Rules" and the "Strategic Thoughts" and the cockeyed, self-serving epistemology about unknown knowns and unknown unknowns, one discerns a homespun flag-waving American politician. Morris includes in his film a clip of Rumsfeld at a gathering of former secretaries of defense in 1989, lecturing his predecessors and successors about America's triumph in the cold war:

> The credit belongs to Truman and Adenauer and to steadfastness over a period of forty years.... It went to the concept of peace through strength. And we need to understand how we got to where we are because going forward, we're going to have to make a judgment as to what role our country ought to play, and a passive role would be terribly dangerous. I mean, who do we want to lead—provide leadership—in the world? Somebody else?

The words roll forth, rapid and ardent, an impromptu barn-raiser drawn partly no doubt from his first tour at the Pentagon, and it is evident, as McNamara and Schlesinger and Weinberger and the others look on balefully, that Rumsfeld is first and foremost a patriotic Midwesterner, a politician who nourishes in his soul a primordial and undying belief in the manifest need for, and rightness of, American power. To him this truth is self-evident, imbibed at an Illinois breakfast table. Who do we want to lead in the world? Somebody else? The idea is plainly inconceivable. And it is because of that plain necessity for American leadership that after September 11 American power and credibility must at all costs be restored.

Rumsfeld would offer the "creative" plan for the Iraq invasion that his president had requested that tearful evening in September 2001, one that envisioned a relative handful of troops—150,000, fewer than half the number the elder Bush had assembled a decade before for the much less ambitious Desert Storm—and foresaw an invasion that would begin in shock and awe and an overwhelming rush to Baghdad. As for the occupation—well, if democracy were to come to Iraq it would be the Iraqis themselves who must build it. There would be no occupation, and thus no planning for it. Rumsfeld's troops would be in and out in four months. As he told a then adoring press corps, "I don't do quagmires."

It did not turn out that way. Having watched from the Oval Office in 1975 the last torturous hours of the United States extracting itself from Vietnam—the helicopters fleeing the roof of the US embassy in Saigon—Rumsfeld would be condemned to thrash about in his self-made quagmire for almost four years, sinking ever deeper in the muck as nearly five thousand Americans and hundreds of thousands of Iraqis died. He was smart, brash, ambitious, experienced, skeptical of received wisdom, jealous of civilian control, self-searching, analytical, domineering, and he aimed at nothing less than to transform the American military. The parallels with McNamara are stunning.

And month after month in his arrogance and tenacity he would deny an insurgency had taken root. Month after month, as the shortcomings of the army he had sent into Iraq—too small, too conventional, not configured or equipped or trained to fight an insurgency and thus fated in its impotent bludgeoning to make it ever worse—

became impossible to deny, he would go on denying them, digging in his heels and resisting the change he had to know was necessary. And even as it became undeniable that Rumsfeld's war, far from deterring or dissuading prospective terrorists, increasingly inspired and fostered them—that the image of strength and dominance he sought had become one of bumbling and cruelty and weakness—the power of his personality and of his influence over the president meant that for month after month, year after year, he was able to impose his will—and define the world we still see around us.

Donald Rumsfeld Revealed

January 9, 2014

1.

In my confirmation hearing . . . the best question I was asked was: What do you worry about when you go to bed at night? And my answer was, in effect, intelligence. The danger that we can be surprised because of a failure of imagining what might happen in the world.

—DONALD RUMSFELD TO ERROL MORRIS, *The Unknown Known*

IT IS A STRIKING thought: night after night, the secretary of defense of the world's most powerful country retires to his bed haunted not by some threatening, well-armed foe but by "a failure of imagining what might happen in the world." There is something at once heroic and pleasingly humble about it, with hints of the tragic: the great hero haunted by the boundaries of his own imagination, struggling with all his vast strength to do nothing more than escape the net of his own ignorance.

As Donald H. Rumsfeld speaks those words in Errol Morris's film the familiar burning battleships in Pearl Harbor take shape on the screen before us. "People were chasing the wrong rabbit," he says, in a typically homespun trope that will recur near the film's end, directed at the filmmaker himself. "That one possibility was not something that they had imagined was likely." In the mind's eye the burning ships dissolve into two great New York skyscrapers collapsing against a bright September sky: Rumsfeld's Pearl Harbor. "Was it a failure of the imagination," Morris asks, "or a failure to look at the intelligence that was available?"

It is the film's most telling question, and though it passes quickly, for just an instant the entire elaborate scaffolding of tricked-up epistemological skepticism, promoted in the title of Rumsfeld's memoir and now with lethal irony in that of Morris's film, trembles and wobbles, exposed as the bare rhetoric of self-exculpation. Twice in the film, and with undisguised pride, Rumsfeld offers us this philosophy:

> There are known knowns, the things we know we know. There are known unknowns, the things we know we don't know. There are also that third category of unknown unknowns, the things we don't know we don't know. And you can only know more about those things by imagining what they might be.

To Rumsfeld, it is axiomatic that the attack on Pearl Harbor and those on New York and Washington six decades later have in common that they arose from "gaps in our knowledge, but gaps that we don't know exist." As he tells us bluntly in the author's note that serves as overture to his enormous memoir:

> Nineteen hijackers using commercial airliners as guided missiles to incinerate three thousand men, women, and children was perhaps

the most horrific single unknown unknown America has experienced.

An engaging, even alluring idea and one that Rumsfeld is fond of linking to the analysis of the Harvard economist Thomas Schelling, who attributed, in a famous essay, the success of the Pearl Harbor attacks to a "poverty of expectations" on the part of American officials. "There is a tendency in our planning," Schelling wrote in 1962, "to confuse the unfamiliar with the improbable."[1]

But is this really what happened on September 11, 2001? Throughout that fateful summer, across the reaches of the country's vast intelligence universe, "the system," as Director of Central Intelligence George Tenet put it, "was blinking red," and Tenet himself was said to be running about with his "hair on fire." Meantime, the counterterrorism chief, Richard Clarke, newly demoted from Cabinet level, desperately struggled, as he had since January, to persuade his superiors in the new Bush administration to schedule a "Principals Meeting" on al-Qaeda. Panicked, he finally took to shouting angrily in meetings and e-mailing the national security adviser warning of "hundreds of dead in the streets." He finally got his meeting—on September 4, 2001, a week before the attacks. But that was a month after the president had received this:

1. See Thomas Schelling, "Foreword," in Roberta Wohlstetter, *Pearl Harbor: Warning and Decision* (Stanford University Press, 1962), p. vii.

BIN LADIN DETERMINED TO STRIKE IN US

Clandestine, foreign government, and media reports indicate Bin Ladin since 1997 has wanted to conduct terrorist attacks in the US. Bin Ladin implied in US television interviews in 1997 and 1998 that his followers would follow the example of World Trade Center bomber Ramzi Yousef and "bring the fighting to America."

After US missile strikes on his base in Afghanistan in 1998, Bin Ladin told followers he wanted to retaliate in Washington....

An Egyptian Islamic Jihad (EIJ) operative told an [redacted] service at the same time that Bin Ladin was planning to exploit the operative's access to the US to mount a terrorist strike....

Convicted [millennium] plotter Ahmed Ressam has told the FBI that he conceived the idea to attack Los Angeles International Airport [in 1999] himself, but that ... Ladin lieutenant Abu Zubaydah encouraged him and helped facilitate the operation. Ressam also said that in 1998 Abu Zubaydah was planning his own US attack....

We have not been able to corroborate some of the more sensational threat reporting, such as that from a [redacted] service in 1998 saying that Bin Ladin wanted to hijack a US aircraft....

Nevertheless, FBI information since that time indicates patterns of suspicious activity in this country consistent with preparations for hijackings or other types of attacks, including recent surveillance of federal buildings in New York....[2]

This notorious document is not some random intelligence report that was floating around the bureaucracy and brought out after the

2. See "The Presidential Daily Brief, August 6, 2001," in *The 9/11 Investigations*, edited by Steven Strasser (PublicAffairs, 2004), pp. 293–294.

fact. It is a Presidential Daily Brief, which means it is "finished intelligence" of the highest priority—thought vital enough to be read directly to the president of the United States at his vacation home in Crawford, Texas, on August 6, 2001. It was also distributed to senior national security officials of the US government, including Secretary of Defense Donald H. Rumsfeld.

In the fewer than five hundred words that have been made public—extracted from the understandably reluctant Bush administration with enormous difficulty by the 9/11 Commission—we find several mentions of bin Laden agents within the United States, a confirmation of surveillance of federal buildings, not one but two mentions of their determination to hijack US aircraft, and other quite specific intimations of the attack that was to come less than five weeks later. And it is reportedly only one in a series of Presidential Daily Briefs, dating back to early May, that had carried specific warnings of "imminent" attacks planned for within the United States.[3]

What would have happened had the president upon hearing those words immediately ordered a full National Security Council meeting, discussed the brief with all of his national security officials, ordered increased surveillance at airports, directed the secretary of transportation to issue a threat warning to all civilian pilots, and generally put the various security agencies of the US government on a high alert of the sort that the Clinton administration had ordered before the millennial celebrations?

3. See Kurt Eichenwald, "The Deafness Before the Storm," *The New York Times*, September 10, 2012.

Would, for example, the memorandum sent that July by the FBI special agent in Phoenix who worried over Middle Eastern flight students training at American flight schools have been taken seriously? Would those students—among whom were the September 11 pilots—have been identified and tracked? Would permission have been handed down from the Justice Department in response to desperate appeals from the FBI to search the laptop of Zacarias Moussaoui—the flight student and supposed "twentieth hijacker" who was arrested in Minnesota on August 16—and the September 11 plot itself thereby discovered? Would Moussaoui have been connected to Mohammed al-Qahtani, another supposed "twentieth hijacker" who had been turned away from the Orlando airport in early August? Would the CIA have alerted the FBI earlier to the two September 11 "muscle" hijackers who had been living openly in San Diego for more than a year, and the plot been foiled?

We will never know the answers to these questions. We do know that the senior officials brought in by President Bush, unlike their predecessors in the Clinton administration, did not consider al-Qaeda or the threat it posed one of their highest security concerns. Despite the increasingly panicked and exasperated warnings of Clarke and Tenet, among others, the "principals" preferred to focus their attention on the threat of Saddam Hussein and the challenge of a rising China. Indeed, some senior officials, including a number in Rumsfeld's Pentagon, suspected that "bin Laden was merely pretending to be planning an attack to distract the administration from Saddam Hussein" and they exhorted the White House not to be "fooled."[4]

4. See Eichenwald, "The Deafness Before the Storm." See also Eichenwald's *500 Days: Secrets and Lies in the Terror Wars* (Touchstone, 2012).

In the midst of this flurry of warning, the secretary of defense, as was his wont, wrote himself a memorandum, "Subject: Pearl Harbor Post-Mortem."

> In some future hearing I am going to say that I do not want to be sitting before this panel in a modern day version of a Pearl Harbor post-mortem. Who didn't do what, when, where, and why? None of us would want to have to be back here going through that agony.

The date was July 23, 2001. There had been several Presidential Daily Briefs warning of imminent attacks; "Bin Ladin Determined To Strike in US" would come two weeks later. "It would be wrong," Rumsfeld tells Morris of his memo, with scrupulous humility, "to think that someone who wrote it—namely me—was prescient. I wasn't. I simply had read enough history that I worried."

And these worries led him . . . to write a memo. So far as we know, they did not lead him, even in the face of very specific warnings, to *do* anything, or push for any action. Nor did President George W. Bush himself, after sitting impatiently through his briefing on August 6, 2001, call an immediate National Security Council meeting or indeed move to take any other decisive action. Instead he gazed evenly at the briefer, paused, and uttered the imperishable words, "All right. You've covered your ass, now."[5]

Did the September 11 attacks truly arise from "gaps in our knowledge, but gaps that we don't know exist"? To use Rumsfeld's parlance, we knew what we knew: that terrorist attacks "in the US" were likely being planned, that they might well involve hijackings and

5. See Ron Suskind, *The One Percent Doctrine* (Simon and Schuster, 2006), p. 2.

target federal buildings. And we knew what we *didn't* know: precisely when the attacks might be carried out, what the targets would be, how they would be attacked—though in truth even here there were clues, among them al-Qaeda's obsession with the World Trade Center (the 1993 attack is mentioned in the Presidential Daily Brief) and an Islamic terrorist group's earlier hijacking of a commercial airliner and its failed attempt to fly it into the Eiffel Tower.

What exactly were those "gaps that we didn't know existed" that made the September 11 attacks, in Rumsfeld's words, "the most horrific single unknown unknown America has experienced"? Was the failure to stop the attacks truly a failure of the imagination or was it a failure, as Morris says, to look at the intelligence that was available? And if it was the latter—a failure by senior leaders to look at and take seriously enough and act upon what was actually known—then the success of the attacks stemmed not from some universal human "failure of the imagination" or "poverty of expectations" but from the arrogance and willfulness of certain people to whom the country had entrusted the highest responsibility.

2.

When you say, "How can you know?" the answer is, you can't. Wouldn't it be wonderful if we could see around corners—have our imaginations anticipate every conceivable thing that could happen, and then, from that full array and spectrum, pick out the ones that will happen?

—DONALD RUMSFELD TO ERROL MORRIS, *The Unknown Known*

How could Donald Rumsfeld, as he stood at his Pentagon desk on the morning of December 2, 2002, and scrawled his name on one of the hundreds of Action Memoranda he saw, "anticipate every conceivable thing that could happen"? Plainly, he could not—not even the fact that the memorandum, which asked him to approve certain "Counter-Resistance Techniques" to be used on detainees at Guantánamo Bay, Cuba, was destined to be the most controversial document he would sign.

By now, of course the "war on terror" had been at full boil for more than a year; failure of the imagination had become an unbounded terror of what might happen next. Morris has the striking idea of having his subject read out the list of eighteen "enhanced interrogation techniques" he approved that December morning, and so we hear Rumsfeld's disembodied voice intoning the odd phrases, one dissolving into another, offering the viewer a strange and haunting litany in which one bureaucratic euphemism falls softly over the next:

> Yelling at the detainee; techniques of deception; multiple interrogator techniques; interviewer may identify himself as a citizen of a foreign [country] with a reputation for harsh treatment....
>
> Stress positions, like standing, for a maximum of four hours; falsified documents or reports; the use of isolation facility for up to thirty days; deprivation of light and auditory stimulus; a hood placed over his head during transportation and questioning; twenty-hour interrogations; removal of all comfort items, including religious items; removal of clothing; forced grooming (shaving of facial hair); using detainees' individual phobias, such as fear of dogs, to induce stress....

At the end of the list Rumsfeld looks up, gazes at Morris with feigned or real surprise, and exclaims: "Good grief, that's a *pile* of stuff." Indeed, it is. Which makes one wonder what led the secretary of defense to scrawl in his own hand, after signing his name on the "Approved" line:

> However, I stand for 8–10 hours A day. Why is standing limited to 4 hours? D.R.

Though he tells Morris that during his six years as secretary of defense he dictated 20,000 memos—the famous "snowflakes"—it would be possible to argue that these fifteen words are the most celebrated he wrote during his tenure. In my experience people react to them with instinctive shock or repugnance—and Rumsfeld is plainly sensitive to this, volunteering to Morris:

> I remember one of the things required that he stand for three or four or five, six hours. When I approved it, I wrote down that, you know, "I stand for eight or ten hours a day." I forget what I said, but something like that. Needless to say, I did not intend that my memo would then be sent back down the chain of command.

In his memoir Rumsfeld is a bit more specific:

> My offhand comment was a statement of fact. I used a stand-up desk and spent much of the day on my feet. The note received enormous attention when detainee abuse became a major public issue. It was a mistake to make that personal observation to my general counsel.

It certainly was not a signal to the Department that it would be okay to stretch the rules, as some have suggested.

But what exactly was Rumsfeld's "personal observation" meant to signal? What could the secretary of defense have meant in comparing his daily work at a stand-up desk in his vast office—signing memoranda, reading reports, drinking coffee, taking phone calls, meeting with subordinates, running off to lunch—to the experience of a hooded, shackled man standing naked, bolted to the floor in a freezing room, deprived of sleep for day after day, bathed in light or cloaked in darkness, forced to listen to an endless loop of ear-splitting music, or white noise, or screaming, at an offshore prison in Guantánamo Bay, Cuba?

We know a lot now about what went on in those rooms. We have, among many other documents, the minute-by-minute interrogation logs for Mohammed al-Qahtani, the supposed "twentieth hijacker" who was turned back at Orlando airport in August and later captured in Pakistan. It was Qahtani for whom Rumsfeld's eighteen "counter-resistance techniques" were specially devised, and during his fifty-four days of interrogation he was subjected to nearly all of them: prolonged sleep deprivation—he endured forty-eight twenty-hour interrogations—forced nudity; prolonged stress positions; unremitting, almost unbearable noise; and humiliations of various kinds, sexual and otherwise. He was forced to wear women's underwear, and to appear nude in front of female interrogators. He was made to wear a leash and bark and perform "dog tricks," and forced to endure enemas and intravenous drips. The log, scrupulously compiled by the military interrogators, charts Qahtani's reactions in mind-numbing and often revolting detail.[6] Here are some of Qahtani's responses:

> Detainee began to cry... Visibly anxious... Very emotional... Detainee cried... Disturbed... Detainee began to cry... Butted SGT R in the eye... Bit the IV tube completely in two... Started moaning... Uncomfortable... Moaning... Began crying hard spontaneously... Crying and praying... Began to cry... Claimed to have been pressured into making a confession... Falling asleep... Very uncomfortable... On the verge of breaking... Angry... Detainee struggled... Detainee asked for prayer... Very agitated... Yelled... Tired... Agitated... Yelled for Allah... Started making odd faces... Near crying... Irritated... Annoyed... Detainee attempted to injure two guards... Became very violent and irate... Attempted to liberate himself... Struggled... Made several attempts to stand up... Screamed.[7]

If Rumsfeld was not suggesting by his note—"However, I stand for 8–10 hours A day. Why is standing limited to 4 hours?"—that some of the techniques he had approved did not go far enough, then what exactly was he suggesting?

Rumsfeld tells Morris that "some of the things that were done to [Qahtani] were not approved, and the interrogation plan involving the duration and the combination of the techniques was not proper."

6. See "Interrogation Log Detainee 063," *Time*, March 2, 2006.

7. See Philippe Sands, *Torture Team: Rumsfeld's Memo and the Betrayal of American Values* (Palgrave Macmillan, 2008), pp. 170–171.

He remarks in his memoir that "any technique that is legal and humane on its own could conceivably be applied in ways that are not legal and not humane if, for example, it is done repeatedly, over long periods of time or used in an inappropriate combination with other techniques."

There is an implication that he wasn't informed of the "interrogation plan"—that things had gotten out of hand down there in Cuba and when he found out about it he put a stop to it. And yet Pentagon investigators of detainee abuse at Guantánamo later concluded that Rumsfeld was in fact "personally involved" in Qahtani's interrogation plan, that he spoke at least weekly to the general officer in command of it.

Indeed, when he had met in his Pentagon office with this commander's predecessor at Guantánamo he had told him, "General, I want you to call me every morning." After the meeting he remarked to an aide, according to Bradley Graham's *By His Own Rules*, "I've found that when you take on something so sensitive it could come back and bite you, it's best to keep it firmly in hand yourself until you gain confidence and can delegate it to somebody else."

All the available evidence, including a series of insistent memos quoted in Morris's film, suggests that Rumsfeld kept high-level interrogations at Guantánamo "firmly in hand." But before signing off on these techniques he had required only a legal review—in the event, a shockingly cursory one—and ordered no policy review at all. Like other Bush officials when it came to "enhanced interrogation," he'd asked only what *could* be done, not what *should* be done.[8]

8. The phrase is Philip Zelikow's, who has made this argument persuasively and eloquently. See, for example, "Codes of Conduct for a Twilight War," *Houston Law Review*, Symposium 2012. See also my commentary, "The Twilight of Responsibility: Torture and the Higher Deniability," in the same issue.

It was a failure of the moral imagination. Much later, according to an army investigator, Lieutenant General Randall M. Schmidt, who interviewed Rumsfeld twice during the investigation, he "expressed puzzlement" that his approval could have led to the abuse. "My God," Rumsfeld told Schmidt, "did I authorize putting a bra and underwear on this guy's head?"[9]

Did he? What might it mean to "use detainees' individual phobias . . . to induce stress"? What might follow, if you authorize removal of clothing, "forced grooming," "deprivation of light and auditory stimulus," hooding during questioning, which could last twenty straight hours a day, day after day? What effect might this have on—in the words of one experienced interrogator—"the gravitational laws that govern human behavior when one group of people is given complete control over another in a prison," where "every impulse tugs downward"?[10]

3.

When the [Abu Ghraib] pictures came, it had an impact that was well beyond anything that I had experienced. . . . What it showed was people engaging in acts of abuse that were disgusting and revolting. . . . They were engaging in sadistic things and there was nudity involved.

9. See Michael Scherer and Mark Benjamin, "What Rumsfeld Knew," *Salon*, April 14, 2006.

10. See Chris Mackey and Greg Miller, *The Interrogators: Task Force 500 and America's Secret War Against Al Qaeda* (Little, Brown, 2004), p. 471. Chris Mackey is the pseudonym of an army reservist who worked in Kandahar, Afghanistan, in 2001 and 2002, where he interrogated many detainees who were sent to Guantánamo.

I knew that it would create an advantage for the terrorists, for al-Qaeda, and for the people in the insurgency who were out recruiting.... It worked against everything we were trying to do.

—DONALD RUMSFELD TO ERROL MORRIS, *The Unknown Known*

Here, as with Robert McNamara in *The Fog of War* a decade ago, Morris is interested in history and how it is made, how it *feels* to make it. "When you're in a position like secretary of defense," he asks Rumsfeld, "do you feel that you actually are in control of history, or that history is controlling you?" The politician/philosopher is blithe, dismissive; affects modesty: "Oh neither," he says. "Obviously, you don't control history. And you are failing if history controls you." The lessons of the defeat in Vietnam? "Some things work out. Some things don't. That didn't." And yet the Vietnam War had coincided with his rise as a politician and as a leader; he had witnessed the helicopters fleeing the roof of the US embassy in Saigon from the Oval Office, at the side of President Gerald Ford. Had he nothing more to say about it than this?

Though he had a startling political rise, attaining the highest positions—White House chief of staff, secretary of defense—when he was in his early forties, history will likely remember Rumsfeld as the man who presided over a disastrous lost war in Iraq. In this he resembles Robert McNamara, another man of great early achievement, vast ambition, and impatient, restless, domineering take-no-prisoners intelligence, undone by a war he could not win. And as McNamara's war will likely be forever symbolized by the images of those helicopters fleeing the US embassy roof, Rumsfeld's will be known by the grotesque images of twisted naked bodies at Abu

Ghraib. Both men were intelligent enough to know this and willful enough to reject it. Before Morris's camera, in their different ways, they fight and struggle, Laocoöns in the coils of the sea serpent, at the unfairness of a life of such high-gloss achievement reduced to a single, monumental failure.

Morris mostly lets them enact this struggle on the screen. As much as McNamara is tortured, tearful, pleading, Rumsfeld is—as he tells us—"cool ... and measured." His arguments course beneath the surface in the form of a self-serving philosophy of what can be known and what cannot. Too often this near mysticism about history and its causes seems meant to obscure lines of responsibility that aren't in the end obscure at all. Mostly the technique is indirect, a shadow play; but we see it in full light in the film's most striking sequence, which begins with Morris pointing out that "there's a claim that the interrogation rules used in Guantánamo migrated to Iraq, where they led to incredible abuse." The verb here, "migrate," is carefully chosen, as Morris, who created a film about Abu Ghraib, *Standard Operating Procedure*, plainly knows. With some heat Rumsfeld leaps at the bait:

> The evidence is to the contrary. There were twelve investigations that looked at these issues—some by civilians, distinguished people like Dr. Harold Brown and Dr. James Schlesinger, former secretaries of defense, others by military officials. To suggest that the procedures from Guantánamo migrated over to Iraq is to suggest that the procedures in Guantánamo would have encouraged the kind of unbelievably bad, illegal, improper behavior that took place at Abu

Ghraib. And there was nothing that would have permitted anything like that. Anyone who reads the investigative reports knows that's not the case.

But Morris *has* read the investigative reports and he is waiting for him. He has to hand the relevant quotation from the Schlesinger Report and reads it out to Rumsfeld:

> Changes in DoD interrogation policies between December 2, 2002 and April 16, 2003 were an element contributing to uncertainties in the field as to which techniques were authorized. Although specifically limited by the Secretary of Defense to Guantánamo..., the augmented techniques for Guantánamo migrated to Afghanistan and Iraq where they were neither limited nor safeguarded....

It is a classic so-called gotcha moment, atypical in Morris's films, and it is immensely revealing, for Rumsfeld is not only shown to be diametrically wrong but proved to be so with a direct quotation drawn from the very document he cited. Techniques *did* "migrate" from Guantánamo to Abu Ghraib. Decisions he made, behind his stand-up desk, *were* embodied in those grotesque images of naked, tortured detainees at Abu Ghraib. Confronted with the actual words from Schlesinger, he does not grow angry or embarrassed, does not demand with outrage to see the text. Instead he says imperturbably, even helpfully, "Yeah, I think that's a fair assessment."

It is a startling moment. Rumsfeld had commissioned the Schlesinger Report, and would have been familiar with its most important findings. He would have been aware that the report he was citing proved precisely the opposite of what he said it did. It is not the first time he has tried to win an argument in this way, but perhaps the first time he'd been called out on it. After all, who reads those reports anyway? Caught by Morris, he is not embarrassed or nonplussed. Nor does he acknowledge that he'd been wrong, or indeed engage Morris's question—the question about his own responsibility—at all. We get only a blank stare, and the same mild serious attentiveness. The dogged indomitable wrestler will not admit that he has been prevaricating. The filmmaker, determined to pierce the opacity, persists:

Morris: Are you saying stuff just happens?

Rumsfeld: Well, we know that in every war there are things that evolve that hadn't been planned for or fully anticipated, and that things occur which shouldn't occur.

Morris: Wouldn't it have been better not to go there at all?

Rumsfeld: Well, I guess time will tell.

We have reverted here to the bureaucratic passive tense that attained its true fame in the mouth of Rumsfeld's mentor, Richard M. Nixon: "Mistakes were made. . . ." He will not go deeper. Responsibility is shrugged off, abandoned to the fates, bespeaking a strain in him of deeply political self-protectiveness that must have its roots very far back indeed. If his scrawl at the bottom of that memo or the images that followed haunt him, there is no sign of it—only, at bottom, tenacious ambition, here embodied in the unrelenting determination to make his case, to win and to conquer. Perhaps this is Donald Rumsfeld's true "failure of imagining what might happen in the world."

He Remade Our World

April 3, 2014

1.

Why didn't I know about this?

—George W. Bush

Almost exactly a decade ago, Vice President Dick Cheney greeted President George W. Bush one morning in the Oval Office with the news that his administration was about to implode. Or not quite: Cheney let the president know that something was deeply wrong, though it would take Bush two more days of increasingly surprising revelations, and the near mass resignation of his senior Justice Department and law enforcement officials, to figure out exactly what it was. "On the morning of March 10, 2004," as the former president recounts the story in his memoirs,

> Dick Cheney and Andy Card greeted me with a startling announcement: The Terrorist Surveillance Program would expire at the end of the day.

"How can it possibly end?" I asked. "It's vital to protecting the country."

The Terrorist Surveillance Program, then known to the handful who were aware of it only as "the Program" or by its code name, "Stellar Wind," was a highly secret National Security Agency effort—eventually revealed by *The New York Times* in December 2005 and then in much greater detail by former NSA contractor Edward Snowden last June. Among other things, Stellar Wind empowered the agency to assemble a vast collection of "metadata," including on the telephone calls and e-mails of millions of Americans, that its analysts could search and "mine" for information.

Though the program would appear on its face to violate the Fourth Amendment and the Foreign Intelligence Surveillance Act of 1978, President Bush had approved it three weeks after the September 11 attacks, securing the signature of Attorney General John Ashcroft after the fact. To remain in force the program had to be recertified by the president and the attorney general every forty-five days.

And now, two and a half years later, Cheney and White House chief of staff Andrew Card told Bush, Justice Department lawyers "had raised a legal objection to one component of the program." Unless that "component"—apparently, the sweeping up of Internet metadata—was eliminated or modified, they told the president, the lawyers would refuse to certify that the program was legal.

"Why didn't I know about this?" I asked. Andy shared my disbelief. He told me he had just learned about the objection the previous night.

What did the third member of the triumvirate, Vice President Cheney—who had known about the conflict for weeks—say at this moment? Did he profess to share the disbelief of the president and his chief of staff? Or did he, as so often, say nothing at all? President Bush does not say but as we read his account—a remarkable two-and-a-half-page aria on what the president knew, what he didn't, and, even as the crisis that threatened his administration was breaking all around him, what he still doesn't—the president's painfully protracted series of discoveries makes sense only if we assume Dick Cheney's persistent and stubborn silence.

Bush knows he has a crisis on his hands—confronting him with a "decision point," as the title of his memoirs has it. By his account, before flying off to deliver a speech in Cleveland, the president orders Card and his White House counsel Alberto Gonzales "to work with" the attorney general "to solve the problem." On his return, however, he finds that "little progress had been made."

> "Where the hell is Ashcroft?" I asked.
>
> "He's in the hospital," Andy replied.
>
> That was news to me.

The second revelation: John Ashcroft has been in intensive care for nearly a week. Though Ashcroft is the chief law enforcement officer of the United States—and though it is the attorney general's signature that is required to recertify Stellar Wind—no one seems to have thought it relevant to tell the commander in chief. No matter; Bush telephones intensive care, insists on speaking to the heavily sedated Ashcroft, and tells him he is sending over his chief of staff and White House counsel "to talk to him about an urgent matter." What follows is the famous Hospital Room Showdown, the great melodramatic set piece of the Bush administration, which features, as Barton Gellman describes it in the superb *Angler: The Cheney Vice Presidency*, "men in their forties and fifties, stamping on the brakes, abandoning double-parked vehicles, and running up a hospital stairwell as fast as their legs could pump."

The White House men were clutching the paper they were determined to persuade the attorney general to sign, and the Justice Department lawyers, led by James Comey, Ashcroft's deputy, were determined to prevent him from signing it. They converged in a hospital room around the IV-festooned body of the ailing attorney general, who "looked half dead." Nonetheless, Gellman tells us, in the midst of this coven of lawyers, like some unvanquishable horror movie character, Ashcroft "raised himself up stiffly" off the bed.

> He glared at his visitors and said they had no business coming. He gave a lucid account of the reasons that Justice had decided to withhold support. And then he went beyond that. Ashcroft said he never should have certified the program.
>
> . . . If it were up to him now, he would refuse to approve. But it was not up to him. Gesturing at his deputy, Ashcroft said, "*There* is the attorney general." Spent and pale, Ashcroft sank back down.

In the face of this defiance, the White House chief of staff and counsel ignore Comey and stride from the room and then race back to the White House where, Bush informs us rather laconically, "they told me Ashcroft hadn't signed." Why not? Apparently they didn't say and the president doesn't ask. Instead, he decides to overrule the objections of the Department of Justice and sign "an order keeping the TSP alive based on my authority as head of the executive branch."

It is, as will soon become clear, a momentous decision, though there is no sign he realizes quite how momentous. Still, the president isn't happy. "I went to bed irritated," Bush tells us, "and had a feeling I didn't know the full story."

The following morning, when Bush arrives at the Oval Office, his chief of staff confirms these suspicions. "Mr. President," Card tells him, "we've got a major problem."

> "Jim Comey is the acting attorney general, and he's going to resign.... So are a bunch of other Justice Department officials."
>
> I was stunned. Nobody had told me that Comey, John Ashcroft's deputy, had taken over Ashcroft's responsibilities when he went in for surgery.

Revelation Three: it is Comey who is now in charge at Justice. After that morning's FBI briefing, where Comey is sitting in for Ashcroft, the president takes the deputy attorney general aside:

> I started by explaining that I had an obligation to do what was necessary to protect the country.... He explained his concerns about the problematic aspect of the program. "I just don't understand why you are raising this at the last minute," I said.
>
> He looked shocked. "Mr. President," he said, "your staff has known about this for weeks."

Revelation Four: what Bush had believed, had been led to believe, was a last-minute disagreement was in fact a policy conflict that had been raging for weeks between the White House and the Department of Justice. And that is not all:

> Then [Comey] dropped another bomb. He wasn't the only one planning to resign. So was FBI Director Bob Mueller. I was about to witness the largest mass resignation in modern presidential history, and we were in the middle of a war.

"Witness" is, alas, the appropriate word. Bush has finally reached the innermost Russian doll: a score or more of top lawyers in the Justice Department, including the deputy attorney general and possibly the attorney general himself, and the director of the FBI, and perhaps other attorneys at the CIA and elsewhere in the national security bureaucracy, are about to resign en masse over a secret, highly intrusive, warrantless surveillance program less than eight months before Bush will have to face the voters. And it is all going to happen today—and Bush has up until this moment known nothing about it. It will be an enormous scandal with George W. Bush playing hapless witness to his own destruction.

2.

I basically would have let them resign....

—DICK CHENEY

Bush, the self-described "decider," author of *Decision Points*, knows, he tells us, he has "to make a big decision, and fast." He can agree to modify Stellar Wind as Comey and Ashcroft demand and thus avert their resignations, and allow it to continue; but this would mean reversing his decision of the day before, something Bush simply does not do. Or, as "some in the White House believed," he could "stand on my powers under Article II of the Constitution and suffer the walkout."

Who are these "some in the White House" who go so conspicuously unnamed in Bush's account? "I had little patience with what I saw happening," Dick Cheney tells us his memoirs, *In My Time*. "The program had been in place more than two years and the attorney general had approved it some twenty times." Speaking to R. J. Cutler for his film *The World According to Dick Cheney*, the former vice-president is rather more explicit:

> I basically would have let them resign because I thought the program was perfectly legitimate, it was totally necessary, and it had been totally approved and signed up to twenty separate occasions by the Attorney General of the United States. . . .

On its face this argument seems sophistical: Ashcroft, as he suggested from his hospital bed, had been able to do little if any legal research or consultation before he first certified the program, and in any event the requirement that it be recertified every forty-five days was meant to allow for reevaluation of it and the emergency conditions that supposedly required it. Cheney's refusal to accept the lawyers' refusal was in effect an admission that he believed the president hadn't needed the lawyers to begin with; their approval of the program was so much decoration draped over the bedrock of the president's "Article II powers."

Cheney believed in a "unitary executive," believed quite literally that "the executive Power shall be vested in a President of the United States of America." He believed that the various post-Watergate hearings of the mid-1970s, the Church and Pike committees and others—he had watched their progress as the thirty-four-year-old chief of staff in President Gerald Ford's White House—and the laws that had followed their exposé—had "neutered" the intelligence agencies, had "put the gloves on," and that a vital part of the Bush administration's post–September 11 mission, his mission, was to take those gloves off.

One of those "gloves" was the Foreign Intelligence Surveillance Act of 1978—the law Comey and now Ashcroft believed that Stellar Wind's sweeping warrantless metadata collections violated. The president had approved Stellar Wind on October 4, 2001, a few weeks after the September 11 attack, and given the temper in Washington and in the country at that time he likely could simply and easily have amended the law. "We could have gone to Congress, hat in hand, the judicial branch and the executive together," Royce Lamberth, then the chief FISA court judge, tells Gellman, "and gotten any statutory change we wanted.... But they wanted to demonstrate that the president's power was supreme, and the judiciary was just a tagalong when necessary, but not appreciated." They didn't want to change the law, that is; they wanted to circumvent it, and so demonstrate that, in the face of the president's wartime powers, the law didn't matter.

Cheney and his allies—most prominently the vice-president's formidable counsel, David Addington—seem to have had a similar attitude toward the Department of Justice. The lawyers worked for the president; if they forgot that, let them go ahead and resign. Yet in the end the Stellar Wind confrontation—with whose consequences, in the form of the Snowden revelations, among other things, we are still living—serves as a kind of reductio ad absurdum of this particular position. Bush himself summarizes it rather eloquently: "I was willing to defend the powers of the presidency under Article II," he writes in *Decision Points*, "but not at any cost."

> I thought about the Saturday Night Massacre in October 1973, when President Richard Nixon's firing of Watergate prosecutor Archibald Cox led his attorney general and deputy attorney general to resign. That was not a historical crisis I was eager to replicate. It wouldn't give me much satisfaction to know I was right on the legal principles while my administration imploded and our key programs in the war on terror were exposed in the media firestorm that would inevitably follow.

This is the mundane, pragmatic truth. Such a mass resignation would certainly have led immediately to high-profile hearings on Capitol Hill, though the intense press coverage probably would have exposed Stellar Wind before they could be convened—exposed it and likely severely curtailed or ended it, given the circumstances: senior Justice Department lawyers, who resigned rather than violate the law, criticizing advocates of a secret program that snooped on Americans' telephone calls and e-mails without a warrant.

Cheney, no less able a politician than Bush, could certainly see this. And yet, at the end of the day, standing on principle—making the "tough decision" and taking the political hit for it—was more important to him than the survival of the program itself. Principle trumped pragmatism, even when "these programs and keeping them secret," as he tells us in his memoirs, "are critical for the defense of the nation." Gellman claims that this makes Cheney "the nearest thing there was to an antipolitician in elected office."

The statement is provocative, the word alluring; but if he means by "antipolitician" that Cheney was "above politics," as he seems to ("A vice president . . . could afford to be. Bush could not"), then the term seems hardly adequate. In this vital instance Cheney would choose purity and toughness even though such a course would have led to the exposure and destruction of the program itself. Perhaps the word "ideologue"—"an adherent of an ideology, especially one who is uncompromising or dogmatic"—better captures the cold sterility of such a choice, where dead "principle" is deemed more important than a living, supposedly vital program. But if Cheney is better described as an ideologue, what precisely was his ideology?

3.

It is a truism and a quite inadequate one to say that Richard Bruce Cheney was the most powerful vice-president in American history. It was Cheney's singular genius to take an oddly archaic constitutional office that had at best been regarded as a useful if perilous stepping stone to a presidential run and at worst as "not worth a bucket of warm piss" (in the imperishable words of John Nance Garner), and to reshape it, by force of will, quiet audacity, and a peculiar institutional brilliance, into the most powerful position in the American government. In doing this he doubly benefited from that vital attribute of the successful politician: luck.

Cheney was lucky to be vice-president during the attacks of September 11, a national security crisis that drew on precisely the encyclopedic knowledge and bureaucratic skills he had cultivated in a quarter-century spent at the heights of power in Washington, from White House chief of staff in the 1970s to leading member of the House Intelligence Committee in the 1980s to wartime secretary of defense in the 1990s. And he was particularly lucky in serving an untested president who, while intelligent and strong-willed, found himself at the apex of a government suddenly under attack, a government that he knew he lacked the experience and knowledge and confidence to effectively lead.

While the caricature of George W. Bush as his vice-president's puppet is plainly false—"The alpha male in the White House was the president," as former Joint Chiefs Chairman General Richard Myers put it—after September 11 Bush clearly needed Cheney, and he knew it. He needed Cheney's knowledge of foreign and security policy, particularly his familiarity with "the dark side" where Cheney proclaimed, less than a week after the attacks, a major part of the war on terror would be fought, and even more he needed Cheney's deep knowledge of the government and his unique ability to push forward effectively what was a truly radical transformation. These changes could not have been imposed without experience, dedication, and ruthlessness. For as Gellman remarks, while the death and destruction of September 11 were horrible, "decisions made in the White House, in response, had incomparably greater impact on American interests and society."

It is an astute point, all the more so for seeming obvious: the unique policies put into effect by Bush and Cheney were not consequences of the September 11 attacks but calculated responses to them. There was nothing fated about Stellar Wind, or "black sites" and the "enhanced interrogation techniques" that were practiced in them, or Guantánamo and military commissions; these and the other distinctive post–September 11 policies that still cast their shadows over us were born of choices made by government officials and, in the event, by a vanishingly small number of them. Cheney, Gellman writes, "freed Bush to fight the 'war on terror' as he saw fit, driven by a shared belief that the government had to shake off old habits of self-restraint." As noted, some of these "habits" Cheney, as President Ford's chief of staff, had seen inscribed in law during the post-Vietnam revolution of the 1970s, when government misdeeds, not only those by the White House but by the FBI, CIA, and NSA, were exposed, and Congress acted to restrain those institutions, and the president's power to make use of them, with new legislation. September 11 offered the opportunity for a counterrevolution, which Gellman neatly summarizes:

> With Bush's consent, Cheney unleashed foreign intelligence agencies to spy at home. He gave them legal cover to conduct what he called "robust interrogation" of captured enemies, using calculated cruelty to break their will. At Cheney's initiative, the United States stripped terror suspects of long-established rights under domestic and international law, building a new legal edifice under exclusive White House ownership. Everything from capture and confinement to questioning, trial, and punishment would proceed by rules invented on the fly.

The depth of this transformation is truly breathtaking and its surface signs are still visible all around us, if we take the trouble to look: in the detainees still languishing at Guantánamo, in the unpiloted drones tracking and killing thousands of people, and indeed in the sweeping up of our telephone and Internet metadata by the four programs that have been the successors of Stellar Wind. These revolutionary changes in our government's policies toward holding prisoners, toward waging war, and toward surveilling its citizens could never have been effected without the imagination, experience, and audacity of Dick Cheney.

The "interagency process" embodied in the National Security Council system, whereby policies are carefully developed and evaluated across the bureaucracy, rising stepwise through the assistant secretary, deputy secretary, and finally principal levels, is inherently conservative, making substantive systemic changes slow and cumbersome. As Gellman shows in detail, Cheney made use of secrecy and a cadre of dedicated and ruthless allies that he, as chief of Bush's transition—unprecedented for a vice-president-elect—had seeded at strategic points throughout the government. This enabled Bush to circumvent that process and instead make policy in tiny, highly secret groups. And it was Cheney who urged Bush to impose those policies unilaterally, relying on his own asserted authority as commander in chief—even policies like Stellar Wind that appeared to violate express provisions of the law.

4.

In the end, perhaps inevitably, Bush would disappoint Cheney, bowing, in the steely unforgiving view of the older man, to the shoddy demands of politics and the fear of "negative press stories." As Cheney describes the end of the Stellar Wind confrontation in his memoirs, one can almost hear the condescending disappointment in the former vice-president's voice:

> Faced with threats of resignation, the president decided to alter the NSA program, even though he and his advisors were confident of his constitutional authority to continue the program unchanged.

Talking to Cutler for his film, Cheney is more explicit and in his typically precise phrases lets peep through more than a hint of a sneer:

> If you're a man of principle, compromise is a bit of a dirty word. The President made the decision that he wanted to avoid major controversy. It was his call so that's what we did.

It is clear who is the man of principle and who is not. There is a hint here of the complicated emotional strains of mutual dependency inherent in this relationship. Cheney needed Bush, of course, for without him his high title would have been what it had been for so many of his predecessors: empty words. Bush alone had the power to give Cheney power—and because Cheney's power came from him personally the president could expect loyalty and discretion in return. But in Cheney's recollections of Bush one also senses resentment and a kind of moral trumping that is none too subtle. "If you're a man of principle, compromise is a bit of a dirty word."

We see a more obvious sign of the instability built into this mutual dependency in Bush's own account of the Stellar Wind crisis, where Cheney, strikingly, is hardly mentioned. Behind the scenes the vice-president is very much the lead actor in the drama—the conflict is inconceivable without the central part he played in pushing forward Stellar Wind, in maintaining that it could be recertified without Department of Justice approval, and in insisting that the resulting high-profile resignations could be survived. But the reader is left to puzzle out who exactly Bush is referring to when he writes that "some in the White House" wanted him to let Comey, Mueller, and their colleagues, and perhaps Ashcroft himself, resign. Even writing his memoirs years after leaving office Bush is loath to identify Cheney as the antagonist who almost scuttled his presidency—though had he done so, his account, which portrays an incurious president very much out of touch, might have been less embarrassing to him personally.

"I made clear to my advisers that I never wanted to be blindsided like that again," he writes in *Decision Points*. In the film Gellman tells Cutler that with that confrontation the high-water mark of Cheney's power had passed, that Bush understood that the incident had been "a mortal threat to his presidency. He understood . . . that Cheney had walked him right to the edge of a cliff and it changed their relationship forever." Perhaps; but is it resentment, embarrassment, or even lingering gratitude, or a mixture of the three, that leaves Bush unable to mention Cheney by name?

The final irony is that Stellar Wind survived because Bush, when faced with a political crisis that would have exposed it, was willing to compromise, while Cheney, "the antipolitician," preferred to hold to principles that would have meant watching Stellar Wind collapse into controversy. If there had been a mass resignation, there can be no doubt that the principled objections of the high Justice Department officials would have been widely heard. It is quite possible that had Bush followed the chosen course of "the man of principle"—and had the Justice Department officials resigned while their objections were leaked to the public—the metadata collection would have ended in the spring of 2004, and eight months later, very possibly, the presidency of George W. Bush.

Instead, Stellar Wind lived on, first without the Internet metadata collection that Ashcroft, Comey, and other Justice Department lawyers had refused to approve, and then, three months later, in its original form but according to a different legal theory under the authority of the FISA court. Meanwhile a lawyer farther down the hierarchy in the Justice Department who found himself deeply troubled by the program, and who was warned, after raising his concerns with a superior, "not to go there," put in a call to Eric Lichtblau and James Risen of *The New York Times*. After the *Times*, under heavy administration pressure, held their story for a year, the paper finally revealed Stellar Wind to Americans in December 2005.

The story brought shock and controversy but in the event there were no high Justice Department officials who had resigned their posts rather than approve warrantless surveillance; there was just the *Times* and its unnamed sources. The controversy cooled, the collection of metadata went on under Stellar Wind's successor programs, only to be revealed again, thanks to Edward Snowden, by Glenn Greenwald of *The Guardian* and Gellman himself in *The Washington Post* in June 2013.

It goes on still. This is the way of the post–September 11 world, where whistleblowers and news organizations reveal what would have once been considered illegal and then, years later, find themselves "revealing" it yet again, and then again. So it has been with torture and extrajudicial killing and warrantless wiretapping. We might call these frozen scandals, which begin in revelation and white-hot controversy and end with our learning to live with secret wrongdoing that is in fact no secret at all. This is our new normal—and a vital attribute of the world Dick Cheney bequeathed us.

Cheney: "The More Ruthless the Better"

May 8, 2014

If you want to be loved, you know, go be a movie star.

—Dick Cheney, in *The World According to Dick Cheney*

1.

I came upon the half-destroyed truck atop a highway overpass outside Fallujah, the cab all shot to hell, the trailer bloodstained and askew, propped at a crazy angle on its blown tires. On the highway below a great black burn scarred the concrete and over it a rust-red slash, the soot and blood marking the spot where, earlier that day in October 2003, the insurgents had used a cheap remote control to ignite barrels of concealed explosives just as the US armored patrol rumbled by, killing one paratrooper, wounding several. Insurgents, hidden in houses nearby, followed with bursts from their AK-47s.

The Americans promptly dismounted and with their M-16s and M-14s began "hosing" everything they could see, starting with the truck passing on the highway above—eviscerating the unfortunate driver—and then poured fire into the houses.

How many Iraqis had they killed and wounded? The more the better, as far as insurgent leaders were concerned. "The point," the commanding general of the 82nd Airborne told me the next day, "is to get the Americans to fire back and hopefully they'll get some Iraqi casualties out of that and they can publicize that." By week's end family and close friends of those killed and wounded would join the insurgents, for honor demanded they kill Americans to wipe away family shame.

American firepower plus Iraqi deaths equals more insurgents: an axiom in the strategy of provocation. Provoke your enemy to kill civilians and thereby call to battle the sleeping population. You have no army? Use the occupier's to help raise one of your own. In Iraq insurgents used that strategy to grow and prosper, recognizing the characteristic American quickness to react with overwhelming firepower as their best friend. Across continents, al-Qaeda used it as well. Blow up towers in New York, creating an indelible recruiting poster for the worldwide cause while provoking self-defeating responses. Lure the Americans into Afghanistan, where they'll sink into the quagmire that trapped their superpower rival twenty years before.

Such was Osama bin Laden's strategy. Who dreamed that the Americans would prove so cooperative by also invading Iraq? Like a celestial slot machine daily pouring forth its golden bounty, the September 11 attacks had produced a wonderfully telegenic invasion of a major Muslim country. To an attack by a small group that called for a worldwide uprising of Muslims to throw off American oppression, the United States had responded by sending 150,000 armed Americans to oppress a Muslim country. The tiny fringe movement could point to the television screens as American tanks rumbled down the streets of an Arab capital, as American soldiers rousted Muslims from their beds, threw them to the ground, placed unclean boots on their backs—as they stripped them and tortured them at Abu Ghraib, as they had hooded them and forced them to their knees at Guantánamo.

If the Iraq insurgency sat atop the worldwide jihadist insurgency like the second layer of a cake, it was the Americans who made that possible. Guantánamo did for al-Qaeda what Abu Ghraib had for the Iraqi insurgents, affirming in powerful images their political arguments about who Americans were, what they did to Muslims, and why they must be defeated.

2.

"But it's not Guantánamo that does the harm," Dick Cheney writes in his memoirs. "It is the critics of the facility who peddle falsehoods about it."

> Even if, for the sake of debate, one were to accept the image argument, I don't have much sympathy for the view that we should find an alternative to Guantánamo... simply because we are worried about how we are perceived abroad.

If it was true, as Barack Obama said, that Guantánamo was "probably the number one recruitment tool" of al-Qaeda, Cheney wrote,

> one would expect to see al Qaeda mention Guantánamo frequently, but a review of thirty-four messages and interviews by top al Qaeda

> leaders issued in 2009 and 2010 shows the word *Guantánamo* appearing in only three.

Instead, this "recruitment tool theory," Cheney told an audience at the American Enterprise Institute in the spring of 2009,

> after a familiar fashion, . . . excuses the violent and blames America for the evil that others do. It's another version of that same old refrain from the Left, "We brought it on ourselves."[1]

Dick Cheney is a highly experienced public official, but what strikes one about these comments is how shallow, provincial, and uninformed they seem, and also how tendentious, mistaking a discussion about facts—for the dynamics of insurgency and counterinsurgency are facts—for a dispute about politics. That images of repression and torture were enormously important as a means to stoke Muslim anger and recruit insurgents was a commonplace for any soldier who fought in Iraq—or indeed anyone who noticed the graffiti and improvised murals on the walls. "Top al Qaeda leaders" had no need to talk about Guantánamo and Abu Ghraib in interviews; the images were everywhere.

In Baghdad in the fall of 2003, six months before the photographs of them were broadcast, the tortures at Abu Ghraib already formed part of a generalized rage among Iraqis over their treatment at the hands of Americans. Indeed, a grim joke I heard often in Baghdad

1. "Remarks by Richard B. Cheney," the American Enterprise Institute, May 21, 2009.

at the time melded the anger over the Americans' failure to restore power with rumors of what they were doing to helpless prisoners in Saddam's former torture chambers:

> I knew the Americans would finally get the electricity back on but I didn't know that when they did they'd be shooting it up my ass....

Like any insurgency, the "war on terror" was in its essence a political struggle in which occupier and insurgent fought over the allegiance of the population. In 2004, long after the Iraq war had descended into fiasco, this larger dynamic was captured by Cheney's one-time mentor, Secretary of Defense Donald Rumsfeld, in a single question: "Are we capturing, killing or deterring and dissuading more terrorists every day than the madrassas and the radical clerics are recruiting, training and deploying against us?"

This was about the time that Cheney was boasting that the insurgency was "in its last throes." His comments on the dynamics of the war were blinkered, ignorant, ideological: that American repression and atrocity help fuel insurgency he believes an echo of "that same old refrain from the Left" about crime. The comparison is striking and peculiar and it serves as a window into a worldview that, generally concealed beneath a crisp technocratic mastery born of deep experience in government, is dogmatic and deeply reactionary. In answer to the vice-president's complaint, in the bunker beneath the White House on September 11, that "the comms in this place are terrible," counterterrorism adviser Richard Clarke, as he tells us in his memoir,

Against All Enemies, bemoaned the fact that the funds he'd requested to renovate the bunker's communications had never been approved:

> "It'll happen," Cheney promised. "Are you getting everything you need, everybody doing what you want?" Cheney asked, placing his hand on my shoulder. I had known Dick Cheney for a dozen years and for that long had been fascinated at how complex a person he was. On the surface, he was quiet and soft-spoken. Below the surface calm ran strong, almost extreme beliefs.

Only rarely did these beliefs become visible—for example, during the 1980s, when, as Clarke notes, Cheney "had been one of the five most radical conservatives in the Congress." But mostly, as a powerful official within the executive branch—as White House chief of staff when he was in his thirties, secretary of defense when he was in his forties, and now, in his sixties, as a vice-president whose power and influence were unmatched in the history of the country—Cheney kept his own counsel. "The quiet," as Clarke delicately observes, "often hid views that would seem out of place if aired more broadly."[2] Views, he might have added, that would surely have attracted opposition. Mostly Cheney chose to air those opinions in private, to the one man who could give them life: George W. Bush. In those weekly lunches and daily private conferences, the words could be passionate, even taunting: "Are you going to take care of this guy, or not?" Cheney demanded of Bush about Saddam Hussein.[3]

2. See Richard A. Clarke, *Against All Enemies: Inside America's War on Terror* (Free Press, 2004), p. 19.

3. See George W. Bush, *Decision Points* (Broadway, 2010), p. 251.

Self-directed, restrained, disciplined, Cheney was concerned not with words but with power and what it brought. In the aftermath of September 11, the silent vice-president, serving a fledgling president who had won half a million fewer votes than his Democratic opponent, who knew little of the workings of government and less of the world, and who had just failed to prevent the most damaging attack on the homeland in the history of the United States, had an unprecedented opportunity to embody, in matters of interrogation, detention, counterterror, and war, his "extreme beliefs" in the policies of the country. That those beliefs originated in a mind that seems not to have grasped, or credited, the basic dynamics of the war itself was a particular misfortune that still weighs on American foreign policy.

3.

Late in the afternoon of September 11, Dick and Lynne Cheney and a few aides, as he tells filmmaker R. J. Cutler, emerged from the bunker, "went out and got on a helicopter on the South Lawn on the White House and flew off to a secure undisclosed location." The flight path took them across the Potomac:

> Everything I'd seen up till that point had been, you know, over television and so forth. But when you fly over the Pentagon and there's a big hole in the side of it and all the signs of the attack and it's still smoking from the damage that was done that morning was a dramatic sort of reinforcement of what we knew was happening. I started thinking about how we should respond, how can we bring to bear the power and influence of the United States to take down whoever had launched this attack against us.

It is indeed a problem: How does one "bring to bear the power and influence of the United States"—the greatest military power in the history of the world and now, more than a decade after the fall of the Soviet Union, the great unrivaled champion of "the unipolar moment" in international affairs[4]—on a tiny group of a few hundred conspirators hiding in the mountains of Afghanistan and scattered across various other hard-to-find places in South Asia, Africa, and the Middle East? The United States, the muscle-bound giant, with technology generations more advanced than any in the world—what nation could produce fighter planes that could survive a dogfight with those of the United States, or aircraft carriers that could remain afloat in the seas?—had been presented with its gravest military challenge by... a small, lightly armed network of insurgents.

Thus the problem of "asymmetrical warfare": How could the giant, groping about in the caves and crevices, even find that group, let alone join it in a worldwide struggle commensurate with its own "power and influence"? Thus the consternation over the fact that Afghanistan, "since it was so primitive that there were few targets," as Paul Wolfowitz put it at the first war cabinet meeting after the attacks, "would not be a particularly satisfying place to wage a war."

One answer was to make the enemy larger. The insurgents of al-Qaeda, the president told the nation on September 20, were "heirs of all the murderous ideologies of the twentieth century. By sacrificing human life to serve their radical visions... they follow in the path of fascism, Nazism, and totalitarianism." Al-Qaeda, with no state under its control, no army, no nuclear missiles, nonetheless

4. See, for example, Charles Krauthammer, "The Unipolar Moment," *Foreign Affairs*, Vol. 70, No. 1 (1990/1991).

would assume, in the administration's eschatology, the mantle of the Nazis and the Soviets; the war against it would be a new cold war—or rather a continuation of the old one, which, it turns out, had only been suspended. The Communist threat became the terrorist one. Though the weapons of choice on September 11 had been mundane—box cutters and airliners—terrorists henceforth would be considered armed with "weapons of mass destruction." In fact, though it was well known that the organization had kept up a steady rhythm of attacks against American targets that required careful planning and one and two years of delay in between—

November 1995—Riyadh, Saudi Arabia
August 1998—US embassies, Nairobi and Dar-es-Salaam
October 2000—USS *Cole*, Aden, Yemen

—now the country was panicked with the false certainty of near-immediate "second-wave" attacks, perhaps even "dirty bombs," that might destroy shopping centers or high-rises or cities at any time. Against this imminent, apocalyptic threat, anything—*anything*—was justified, even if that anything was quite demonstrably counterproductive. Thus the heart of Cheney's "one percent doctrine," which he set out during a CIA briefing in November 2001:

> If there's a one percent chance that Pakistani scientists are helping al Qaeda build or develop a nuclear weapon, we have to treat it as a certainty in terms of our response. It's not about our analysis.... It's about our response.[5]

5. See Ron Suskind, *The One Percent Doctrine: Deep Inside America's Pursuit of Its Enemies Since 9/11* (Simon and Schuster, 2007).

The response, by definition, meant acting: though the chance might be one in a hundred, the danger of that tiny possibility, if realized, was so great that one must act as if that one percent were in fact a hundred percent certainty. *One must always act.* The Cheney Doctrine was put into effect in Iraq—which, as Wolfowitz said, "had plenty of targets"—and it was in those Iraqi streets that the doctrine showed itself to be a crackpot faux profundity of the most damaging kind. For to act has its own risks. To act can place one in a weaker, more vulnerable position than before—for example, by attacking a Muslim country that has no al-Qaeda presence and, by so acting, encouraging in that country a rebellion full of such insurgents (who fight on in Iraq to this day).

The philosophy of leadership embodied in terse, tough action, the tougher and more ruthless the better—"it was more important to be successful than it was to be loved," Cheney tells Cutler—was already well displayed in that bunker beneath the White House on September 11. At 10:39 AM that day, Vice President Cheney spoke to Secretary of Defense Rumsfeld, his old mentor who had first brought him to the White House:

> *VP*: There's been at least three instances where we've had reports of aircraft approaching Washington—a couple were confirmed hijacked. And, pursuant to the president's instructions, I gave authorization for them to be taken out. Hello?...
>
> *SecDef*: Okay, let me ask the question here. Has that directive been transmitted to the aircraft?
>
> *VP*: Yes, it has.

SecDef: So, we've got a couple of aircraft up there that have those instructions at this present time?

VP: That is correct. And it's my understanding they've already taken a couple aircraft out.

SecDef: We can't confirm that....

Secretary Rumsfeld couldn't confirm that because it wasn't true. In fact, very little of what Cheney said in this exchange, which he quotes in full in his memoir, turned out to be true. Two aircraft approaching Washington had not been confirmed hijacked. His directive to "take them out" had not been transmitted to the aircraft. And though it was his "understanding" that the US pilots had "already taken a couple aircraft out," they in fact hadn't.

The military ignored the vice-president's terse, tough orders—and in any case, Cheney had not "conveyed" the order to "take out" the Washington-bound airliner until eight minutes or so after it crashed in Pennsylvania. President Bush finally gave the authority to shoot down planes fifteen minutes after the plane had crashed. Indeed, despite a lot of misleading testimony to the contrary, the simple fact is that if the passengers on that plane hadn't desperately tried to seize control of it, causing it to crash into a field, the plane likely would have destroyed the Capitol or the White House itself. What saved the country from damage and loss of life of a much greater magnitude on September 11 was not tough and ruthless orders by the vice-president, which were literally falling on deaf ears, but the random fact that that flight had been forty-two minutes late taking off from Newark—which allowed the passengers time to learn while in the air that the earlier planes had been made into suicide flights.

That the government's real-time response to the attacks was a maelstrom of panic and confusion is not news.[6] What strikes one is Cheney's insistence on reprinting this error-riddled and embarrassing transcript in his memoirs a decade after the fiasco. What is he trying to tell us? Not that he "took out" civilian airliners but that however impotent the actual result, he had not hesitated to try to do so, and that he displayed that willingness with some pride in reporting to his former mentor. He writes that "the enormity of the order I had just conveyed"—and conveyed, he tells us, "without hesitation"—"struck all of us in the [bunker], and a silence fell over the room."

It is doubtful, as Barton Gellman shows in a painstaking reconstruction in his study *Angler*, that Cheney was "conveying" an order at all, for though he claims that the president had "approved my recommendation" that fighter pilots be authorized to fire on hijacked airliners "in one of our earlier calls," in fact, as the 9/11 Commission noted, "there is no documentary evidence for this call," and as Gellman writes, the relevant two-minute conversation with Bush "began shortly *after* the vice president cleared"—or thought he had—"Air Force fighters to open fire."

Cheney, though both he and Bush have steadfastly denied it, seems to have given the order to "take out" the plane at least ten minutes before Bush had actually approved it. Both directives came long after United 93 crashed. Even if the airliner hadn't crashed, the two fighter pilots, who—like their flight controllers—had no idea where it was and who did not receive clearance to fire until long after the airliner would have reached Washington, almost certainly

6. For the most thorough account of what actually happened between the military and civilian air controllers that morning, see Michael Bronner, "9/11 Live: The NORAD Tapes," *Vanity Fair*, September 2006.

could not prevented its striking the Capitol or the White House, its intended targets.[7]

For al-Qaeda, phase one of the attack—causing mammoth destruction and loss of life—would be an unprecedented success. Phase two, luring the superpower into taking actions that would foster the movement by producing more insurgents, had already been set in motion, confirmed with the determination of Dick Cheney to "bring to bear the power and influence of the United States to take down whoever had launched this attack against us."

4.

Five days later Cheney would speak from his "secure undisclosed location"—the phrase was his, though in fact he was at the presidential retreat in Camp David—to tell the country on *Meet the Press* that in responding to the attacks the government would "have to work through, sort of the dark side, if you will."

7. The 9/11 Commission calculated that had it not crashed in Pennsylvania at 10:03, "United 93 could not have reached Washington any earlier than 10:13, and probably would have arrived before 10:23." At the time there were only two fighter planes in the air near Washington, and at 10:10 the pilots of these planes had been told emphatically that they had "negative clearance to shoot." In the event, and despite the vice-president's conviction that his orders had been transmitted, "shootdown authority was first communicated to [the flight controllers] at 10:31"—almost certainly long after United 93, had it survived, would have struck its target in Washington. The commission members conclude that they "are sure the nation owes a debt to the passengers of United 93. Their actions saved the lives of countless others, and may have saved either the Capitol or the White House from destruction." See "'We Have Some Planes,'" *The 9/11 Commission Report* (Norton, 2004), pp. 44–45.

> We've got to spend time in the shadows in the intelligence world. A lot of what needs to be done here will have to be done quietly, without any discussion, using sources and methods that are available to our intelligence agencies, if we're going to be successful. That's the world these folks operate in....

At the time, one might have found much to commend in these remarks: the proper response to the attacks should have been targeted and discreet, directed solely and effectively at the small group responsible—and careful to avoid any broader actions that could politically bolster that group's cause. But such measured action was not quite what the vice-president had in mind: "So it's going to be vital for us to use"—as he put it—"any means at our disposal, basically, to achieve our objective."

These "means" would include establishing an archipelago of secret prisons—so-called "black sites"—whose existence, with each highly publicized capture of the latest terrorist, soon became all too public—and one, at Guantánamo, that was public from the start, where Muslims were imprisoned indefinitely under harsh conditions and subjected to "enhanced interrogation techniques" improvised by bumbling amateur "experts" hired by the CIA and the military.

It was in creating and pushing through these programs on detention, interrogation, and surveillance that the vice-president showed his true brilliance. With his discipline, determination, and experience he was able to show the president how to circumvent the "interagency process" and develop and impose policies on detention and interrogation that would otherwise never have been approved. His genius for working the bureaucracy, and making use of the close associates he had seeded, as head of the Bush transition, at strategic posts within it, allowed him to implement, with the help of only a handful of like-minded people, policies that constituted a revolution when it came to American practices of human rights.

There is little evidence that this tiny group ever did much to think through these policies—for example, when it came to interrogation, to delve into the history of what the country had done in previous wars or to consult allies with rich experience of what worked and what did not. The key words were "any means at our disposal." To insist on such means was not a mark of knowledge or analysis; it was a necessary sign of will, of toughness, of the unspoken terse readiness to do what Cheney thought needed to be done, even if evidence would have suggested—had evidence been sought—that these were distinctly poor decisions representing not knowledge or experience but a predilection for toughness at any cost. "If you want to be loved," as Cheney tells Cutler, "go be a movie star."

In this way, the blinkered narrow ignorance of a few was imposed with great effectiveness on the actions of the entire government. And if the war on terror was still a giant floundering about in search of a small insurgent group, soon Iraq would offer the chance to display American "shock and awe" and—just what al-Qaeda had wanted—American tanks rumbling down the streets of an Arab capital. The tough, terse philosophy of power of Dick Cheney was al-Qaeda's dream.

Did anyone trouble to point out that such images might be a boon to the small jidhadist group who had attacked the country? In January 2003, with the invasion of Iraq a few months off, President Bush met with his CIA director, George Tenet, and other officials for "an in-depth review of the administration's counterterrorism efforts." The mood was dark:

> One of the biggest challenges they faced, Tenet said, was al-Qaeda's continued success in attracting new foot soldiers. Rice and Wolfowitz agreed, fretting that American efforts had failed to stem the influx of jihadist recruits.
>
> Bush waved a hand dismissively. "Victory will take care of that problem."

At the bravado of this remark, Kurt Eichenwald writes in *500 Days*, "some of the people in the room were flabbergasted." The victory the president meant, of course, was the quick overwhelming one he was certain would come in Iraq:

> In a single sentence, . . . Bush had revealed volumes about his strategic thinking. . . . Somehow, Bush had come to believe that ousting Saddam would—what? frighten? impress?—extremists so much that they would abandon jihad.
>
> It was, one aide believed, an extraordinarily dangerous assumption.

How might the president have come by this "extraordinarily dangerous assumption"—which, it seemed, would come to motivate the entire government on a war of choice launched halfway around the world against an enemy that had not attacked the country? We are not told. Nor whether one of "the people in the room" was the vice-president—that terse, unsentimental Westerner, the firm believer in the universal effectiveness of power and force, who would offer this wisdom about torturing detainees:

> With many thousands of innocent lives potentially in the balance, we didn't think it made sense to let the terrorists answer questions in their own good time....

Asked about waterboarding by filmmaker R. J. Cutler, his retort is equally quick and brutal:

> Are you gonna trade the lives of a number of people because you want to preserve your, your honor, or are you going to do your job, do what's required first and foremost: your responsibility to safeguard the United States of America and the lives of its citizens. Now given a choice between doing what we did or backing off and saying, "We know you know their next attack against the United States but we're not gonna force you to tell us what it is because it might create a bad image for us." That's not a close call for me.

Cheney's is a simple philosophy of toughness, its crystal clarity unblemished by any question of whether torture might actually work or what its use might cost the country. Anyone who hesitates to torture can only be a weakling worrying pitifully about creating "a bad image for us" or struggling to preserve, even more pathetically, "your honor." Could it be from this terse tough man of action that the president had gotten the idea that, when it came to worries over "al-Qaeda's continued success in attracting new foot soldiers," he ought not to worry at all, because "victory will take care of that"?

In truth, we don't know if Cheney was in the room. If he was, it is pretty certain he would have had nothing to say.

Obama and Sweet Potato Pie

October 23, 2008

1.

You would think first of all of a village fair: the entire community of Germantown, Northwest Philly, taking itself up on the brightest of bright sunny fall days and moving en masse, clumps of people—groups of young men in the obligatory hoodies and low-riding jeans, moms pushing strollers, dads lugging car seats, and everywhere children, from toddlers on up, being pulled along ("You'll remember this all your life!")—almost all of them African-American and all melding together, as they crowded toward the entrance to Vernon Park, into a full running, laughing stream. Hawkers hawked "Obamaniana"—the man's face glowing on posters, some huge, floating above the crowd; his name carved in wood or stone; the Obama keychains and wallets and everywhere the volunteers with their blue buttons and their clipboards, making sure it all works smoothly.

Once in the park, enfolded in those several thousand happy people, there was the dancing. Over the loudspeakers, inevitably, "The Power of One!" and of course "Power to the People," and beneath where I stood on the riser, among the generally bored press corps, two blond girls danced and laughed and bumped hips. I chat with a local volunteer, a middle-aged lady with a café au lait face, and when I ask her how it's going she fixes me first of all with a slightly scolding look—how can you *ask* that?—and then says it simply and without doubt, "Oh, we're gonna do it this time. This time it's ours!"

Knowing politicians and his schedule of four appearances on this one bright day in Philly I'd been prepared to wait but it was only twenty minutes after the appointed time when after a series of very quick introductions from the young black mayor, Michael Nutter, and Senator Robert Casey, and the gravel-voiced bearish Governor Ed Rendell—hardly more than a minute each, a never-before-glimpsed discipline from politicians—he rose from a stairway at the back of the stage into an explosion of sound, grinning with pleasure in an open-collared white dress shirt and black dress slacks.

He seems slender and slight and young, astonishingly young, and you notice first of all, for it is impossible not to, the physical grace; he moves like an athlete much more than a politician, taking pleasure in his body: bursting up onto the stage, the lanky highly stylized movement, shoulders bent slightly concave, gathering everything into those constantly clapping hands, using the hands in their clapping to acknowledge the crowd, his head nodding all the while, as if he is drawing his energy only from them and showing that energy with his clapping and nodding, with the bursting energy of his body that is an embodiment of theirs, an embodied picture of what they're giving him. He prances with evident pleasure around the little stage, moving his head in big theatrical nods, embracing each politician in turn, big full-bodied embraces, and again one thinks of an athlete on the sidelines or in the dugout: all of it is done with the unhindered pleasure of the body, all of it says confidence and pleasure, as if this, being bathed in the huge cheers, taking sustenance and energy from the wave of sounds and the shouts of his name, is the place where he breathes his true oxygen, where he really lives. He seems made to be precisely here—in the midst of these thousands of sun-drenched cheering people. On this perfect mid-October day, there is only him and them and what is between them.

"*How's it goin', Northwest?*" That salutation, and the enormous opening roar in response, tells you that he knows these people and they know him. "What a beautiful day the Lord has made!" It's a black crowd and his speech immediately acquires, not broadly but noticeably, a tinge of blackness: the Southern tones, the slight mid-Carolina or mid-South softening, the falling final *g*'s. He knows these people, each one of them, that's what the grin says—wherever he comes from he will be this day the local boy made good: *theirs*. They can take pleasure in that and he can, too, and he is telling them he knows it.

He goes quickly through the thanks to the local politicians and then moves into the stump speech, a stripped-down version for this heavily packed day, and I was impressed again by the absolute clarity and simplicity of the language. The transformational "post-partisanship" of the primaries is nowhere to be seen, burned away in the fires and fears of the financial crisis. Frank, rousing Democratic populism now: jobs and the hurt people are feeling. "Now's not the time for fear," he declares. "Now's the time for leadership. The disastrous policies of the last four years cannot continue. We have seen the final verdict of Bush economics. We don't need four more years of *that*."

The ease and simplicity of the message: Things are bad now, real bad. Do you want that to continue or do you want things to get better? In this construction McCain is Bush. The two are identical and that identification, which handcuffs the Republican to the disaster wrought by the incumbent in the White House, and which is taken for granted here, is all you need to know.

In the midst of this he lets drop today's "bite." "I want to acknowledge," he says, "that Senator McCain tried to tone down the rhetoric at his town hall meeting yesterday." It is the line the traveling press, who know his stump speech by heart, have been waiting for. Looking across from my riser toward the reporters gathered at the long card tables arrayed on the grass, I see heads suddenly bend over laptops, fingers flying. The day before, in a town meeting in Lakeville, Minnesota, McCain had taken the microphone from an elderly woman who was saying she didn't "trust Obama" because she had "read about him and he's"—a big pause here—"an Arab." McCain, who had been shaking his head, took the mic and said, "No ma'am, no ma'am, he's a decent, family man, citizen, that I just happen to have disagreements with on fundamental issues, and that's what this campaign is all about." Earlier he had told another angry supporter, a man who had shouted that he would be "scared" to bring up his child in a country with a President Obama, that Obama was "a decent person, and a person that you do not have to be scared of as president of the United States."

Now Obama, in the midst of this increasingly raucous conversation with the crowd, has issued his answer and by the time I would return to my hotel room a few hours later there it would be leading that day's news on all the cable networks. For the purposes of the "national campaign," what the bloviators bloviate about, what the commentators comment about, what most Americans manage to glimpse of the campaign, this is what "really" happened that day: the campaigns continued to "dial back the rhetoric," which in previous days "had grown increasingly poisonous."

Indeed, the other bit of political news, which reinforced this now superseded "poisonous" plotline, had congressman and civil rights hero John Lewis issuing a statement that seemed to compare the McCain campaign, in the increasing vehemence of its language, to George Wallace, whose overheated rhetoric had also led to an "atmosphere of hate," and "because of this . . . , four little girls were killed on Sunday morning when a church was bombed in Birmingham, Alabama"—itself an overheated comparison Obama could now declare "inappropriate."

Watching the day's events, and their televised packaging, one is struck once again by the profound bifurcated strangeness of American politics. Impossible to know what is the "real" campaign. Was it that rousing event I was attending, full of uplifting words and calls to arms and inspiration, which so many children and young people will never forget? Or is it this battle of sound bites, carefully crafted each morning by the campaign "strategists" and tossed with casual precision by each candidate into the maw of the hungry press corps? Seen from Vernon Park the national campaign is a strange disembodied electronic cloud, floating out there in the ether, with an almost laughably tangential relation to what actually occurs before the people themselves. What would those who had attended the rally feel when they looked at their television sets that evening? Bewilderment? Disgust? Bemusement? Pity?

For the national campaign, on the other hand, for the commentators and bloviators and battalions of Democratic and Republican "strategists" ushered in and out of the television studios, the battle of the bites was the campaign, and that campaign had reached the point where "things were getting increasingly ugly." There was no trace of this whatever at the event in Vernon Park, beyond that wisp of a sentence from the candidate acknowledging that his opponent had tried to "tone down the rhetoric . . . yesterday." But he knew and every member of the campaign and press present knew—all the "professionals" knew—that this was all that had been said that day that would be part of the national campaign. And to all the commentators and strategists, and all the millions who that day would see and hear, on the cable stations and on talk radio and on the networks and the blogs only what they had produced, this was the real campaign, for which the rallies only existed as a kind of artificially constructed pageant. It was comprised of the cheering ranks of those who had already committed, out of which one could daily extract those tiny preformed packets of "news," intended to persuade, via the electronic ether, those who had not.

Everything else they would never see. It existed only for the several thousand cheering people in Vernon Park on that bright morning in Germantown. They would never see, for instance, Obama's riff on sweet potato pie. It came as he told a story about his campaigning "the other day in a little town in Ohio, with the governor there," about how he and the governor suddenly felt hungry and "decided we'd stop right there and get some pie." Now here began a little gem of a story, which had at its center the diner employees who wanted to take a picture with Obama, not least because, as they told him, their boss was a die-hard Republican and "they wanted to tweak him a little with that picture." All this was heading toward a carefully choreographed finale, where the owner appeared personally with the pie for candidate and governor and Obama looked at the pie and looked at the pie-carrying die-hard Republican owner and "then I said to him"—perfectly elongated pause—"How's business?"

This brought on great gales of laughter from the crowd. For the joke turned on a point already precisely made: How can even the most die-hard of die-hard Republicans, if he is thinking of his self-interest, how *can* he vote Republican this year? "If you beat your head against the wall," Obama demanded of that faraway Republican with his pie, to a blizzard of "oh yeahs!" and "you got *that* right!" from the crowd, "and it hurts and hurts, how can you keep doing it?" But it was those two words, "How's business?"—that casual greeting thrown at the Republican diner owner that showed that there simply could *be* no other choice this year—that showed the case proved, wrapped up, unassailable.

And yet what struck me in this little model of political art was a tiny riff the candidate effortlessly worked into it from his banter with the crowd. When Obama launched into his story with "Because I *love* pie," a woman out in that sea of cheering, laughing people shouted back, "*I'll* make you pie, baby!" and to the general hooting laughter the candidate returned, "Oh yeah, you gonna *make* me pie?" Then, after a beat, amid even more raucous laughter, and several other female voices shouting out invitations, "You gonna make me *sweet potato pie*?" More shouts and laughter. "*All* you gonna make me pie?"

"Well, you know I love sweet potato pie. And I think what we're going to have to *do* here"—and the laughter and the shouting rose and as it did his voice rose above it—"what we're going to have to do here is have a sweet potato pie *contest*.... That's right. And in this contest, I'm gonna be the *judge*." The laughter rose and you could hear not only the women but the deep laughter of the men taking delight in the double entendre that was not only about the women and their laughing, teasing offers and about their pie that that lanky confident smiling young man knew how to eat and enjoy and judge, but even more now, amazingly, as people came one by one to recognize, about something else. To those people gathered in Vernon Park that bright sun-drenched morning, it was an even more titillating and more pleasurable double entendre, for it was most clearly about something they'd never had but hoped and dreamed of having and now had begun to believe they were within the shortest of short distances of finally tasting. "Because you all know," their candidate told them, "that I *know* sweet potato pie."

2.

Two days later I made my way past the long lines of people moving slowly in the glare of the seaside sun, through the half-dozen brightly colored tables of McCain-Palin tchotchkes ("You're going to a rally. You need a *rally towel*!"), toward the glinting glass-skinned magnificence of the Virginia Beach Convention Center. The people moving in such good-natured and patient order were easy and handsome and prosperous, and if those in the urban precincts of Germantown had come to Senator Obama on foot in a vast pilgrimage of baby carriages and bicycles and skateboards, these enthusiasts for Senator John McCain and his superstar consort from Alaska, Governor Sarah Palin, came mostly in a glinting-bright armada of SUVs and pickup trucks and late-model sedans rolling in from the suburbs.

The crowd was white, blond, and well fed, with many sport shirts, much silver hair, and a good deal of makeup in evidence. Women were well coiffed, men well tanned, and everyone I spoke to unfailingly polite. But if the crowds in the two rallies were almost comically distinct and complementary, seeming to form a parody of the respective bases of the two political parties, both were plainly rooted in the middle class, with Obama's urban followers shading downward, toward working class, and hoping to rise, and McCain's suburbanites shading upward, toward the well-to-do, and fearing to fall. Like Obama, these confident and prosperous-looking men and women already had their sweet potato pie and did not want to lose it.

After the warm-up speeches delivered by the local politicians and after the entertainment, brought to you live by the inimitable brand-name voice and bearded, sun-glassed, cowboy-hatted figure of Hank ("Are You Ready for Some *Football*?!") Williams Jr., who offered a memorable anthem to the stubborn survival of "true American values" in "Country Boy Can Survive"—

> We say grace and we say ma'am
> If they ain't into that, we don't give a damn.
> And a country boy can survive....

—a pungent song of besieged resentment, determination, and transcendence lustily cheered by the several thousand SUV-driving country boys and girls in the hall, and later converted into more explicitly and topically political terms:

> The left-wing liberal media has always been
> A real close-knit family.
> But most of the American people

Don't believe 'em anyway, you see.
John and Sarah tell you just what they think
They're not gonna blink,
And they don't have radical friends
To whom their careers are linked....

After all this the McCains and the Palins mounted the stage, into an ocean of cheers and waving signs and chants. ("*No Bama! No Bama!*") I was struck by the magnetic smiling beauty and charisma of Governor Palin—whose mix of proper white blouse, black skirt, and black glasses just failed to suppress and thus enhanced a pert, naughty-librarian sexiness of the sort evoked in a thousand *Playboy* photo spreads of the early Sixties—and by the crabbed, wounded, unavoidable physicality of John McCain. For this oft-proclaimed "most important election of our lifetimes," some playful deity seems to have determined that the candidates shall serve as one another's perfect mirror images: the first black major-party candidate versus the whitest of white men ("We need first of all to get McCain some sun," one of his supporters joked mirthlessly to me afterward); the forty-seven-year-old versus the seventy-two-year-old (the widest difference in age—more than a generation—between presidential candidates in history); the cool lawyer-professor versus the daring naval aviator—and, above all, the young lithe basketball-playing athlete versus the crippled hero, the wounded Fisher King of the American post-Vietnam wasteland.

The prolonged suffering that determined McCain's career is marked indelibly on his body. He is a politician who can't make the gesture of embracing a crowd, who can't even raise his arms. The burden of that acknowledgment is borne, inevitably, by his face, by his slightly uncomfortable smile and his endlessly blinking eyes. He does not seem at ease as the waves of applause flow over him. Obama's frank pleasure, his gleeful imbibing of the crowd's energy, is reflected here in the dark mirror of McCain's inability to do what should be natural to any leader. Everyone in the hall knows the tale of how he was brutally deprived of it, McCain's own Passion Story, chapter and verse.

Indeed, as the cheers rose, and even more after Palin's call—"*Those of you who have served your country raise your hands!*"—and the impenetrable forest of hands rose up in answer (leaving the press corps on its risers looking very isolated), it was clear not only that everyone here knew the story but that for them it *meant something*. Late the night before, driving from Philadelphia to Virginia Beach, I had listened again to a recording of McCain recounting it, intoning the horrors in a singsong, nearly affectless voice:

> One guard would hold me while the others pounded away. Most blows were directed at my shoulders, chest and stomach. Occasionally, when I had fallen to the floor, they kicked me in the head. They cracked several of my ribs and broke a couple of teeth. My bad right leg [which had been broken, along with both arms, when he had ejected over Hanoi, and had never been set] was swollen and hurt the most of any of my injuries. Weakened by beatings and dysentery, and with my right leg again nearly useless, I found it almost impossible to stand.
>
> On the third night, I lay in my own blood and waste, so tired and hurt that I could not move. The Prick came in with two other guards, lifted me to my feet, and gave me the worst beating I had yet experienced. At one point he slammed his fist into my face and knocked me across the room toward the waste bucket. I fell on the bucket,

> hitting it with my left arm, and breaking it again. They left me lying on the floor, moaning from the stabbing pain in my refractured arm.[1]

Oceana Air Station, a few miles up the road, had been McCain's first duty station. The men and women here knew these beatings came in part because he had refused, unlike some others, to accept early release from the POW camp, and had refused, thus far, to sign a confession. To them McCain's "story" and the campaign's propensity to advert to it in order to deflect all criticism was not a running joke, as it had become for much of the press, but an unassailable monument to character and trustworthiness—notions that, they firmly believed, the "larger culture," morally bankrupt as it now was, could acknowledge with nothing more than snickers. And when Rick Davis, McCain's campaign manager, had said that "this election is not about issues. This election is about a composite view of what people take away from these candidates," they had regarded this not as the scandalous self-revelation of a harshly negative Republican campaign which, devoid of ideas, had resorted to unremitting personal attacks, but as a simple, self-evident truth.

So his body, crabbed, restricted, frozen as if in a body cast, seemed a kind of talisman to this crowd, and they cheered him as he hobbled about the little stage. When later he uttered the "takeaway lines" of that particular day, the lines that were destined to be extracted and vacuumed up into the electronic ether by the several score cameras and recorders bristling around me and arrayed that evening before the hundreds of millions of fellow citizens—

1. See John McCain, with Mark Salter, *Faith of My Fathers: A Family Memoir* (Random House, 1999), pp. 242–243.

> We have 22 days to go. We're six points down. The national media has written us off. Senator Obama is measuring the drapes, and planning with Speaker Pelosi and Senator Reid to raise taxes, increase spending, take away your right to vote by secret ballot in labor elections, and concede defeat in Iraq. But they forgot to let you decide. My friends, *we've got them just where we want them*!

—when he uttered those last words, bringing on a great explosion of laughter and applause, they meant something very specific to this well-heeled, largely ex-military crowd. They meant that you don't give up the struggle, even though most of the weak "popular culture" crowd would. That you fight for what you have. That, as McCain shouted out to them with increasing vehemence as the cheering rose, "we have to change direction now and we have to fight and you know and I know how to do that. I've been fighting for this country since I was 17 and I have the scars to prove it...."

They cheered lustily at this, for if anything they wanted him to fight still harder. TAKE THE GLOVES OFF OR YOU WILL LOSE! read one hand-lettered sign, its young female bearer pumping it up and down urgently in front of the candidate's face, and I heard this sentiment expressed repeatedly, that McCain must fight harder, using "everything he had." If one pointed out that as the financial crisis had spread its fear and Obama's lead in the polls had begun steadily to grow, McCain's campaign had in fact turned increasingly harsh, that the vast majority of his advertisements, and now his "robocalls," were attacks on Obama, most focusing on his "association" with, as McCain put it, the "washed-up old terrorist," Weatherman founder and now education professor William Ayers—if one pointed all this out the answer came back from his frustrated and fearful supporters that this was simply not enough, not in an election where "everything was at stake."

Where, they asked, were the ads featuring the Reverend Jeremiah Wright Jr. exhorting his First Trinity congregation, at the time Barack Obama's congregation, with the call that "God damn America!" and with all those other horrible words? Had I not seen the videos of these awful sermons? If it was true, they said, that McCain's honor now led him to forbid his campaign the use of this particular image (which Hillary Clinton, after all, had exploited in the Pennsylvania primary with great success), if it was true that his campaign advisers were even now pushing him to use Wright and that the candidate still "wouldn't budge," then what good had this vaunted honor really done him?[2] After all, shouldered with a historic financial crisis and an incumbent president as unpopular as any in history, he had already "gone negative" some time ago, and his reputation had long since been tarnished among a press corps and a public increasingly disgusted by the persistent references to Ayers, among others. Why Ayers and not Wright?

This was, needless to say, a rather utilitarian definition of honor, something far from the code McCain, with whatever contradictions, seemed to embrace. To McCain the distinction was clear: on the

2. See, for example, Tucker Carlson: "This spring, McCain said he wouldn't use Wright as a campaign issue, and so far he's stuck to that pledge.... The campaign hasn't run a single ad featuring Wright, and neither have the RNC or pro-McCain 527s. Late last week, senior McCain advisers broached the topic with their candidate, but McCain wouldn't budge." "Bring Back Rev. Wright," *The Daily Beast*, October 13, 2008.

one hand a "domestic terrorist" who had tried to undermine and destroy his beloved country at the very moment he was suffering for it; on the other, a black preacher shouting out his righteous anger to a black congregation, whom he, McCain, could not and would not attack in order to destroy the country's first major-party black candidate—even if it meant losing the election. The first "association" was by his lights ignoble and unpatriotic and Obama should be held to account. The second—well, he had said he would not run a "racist" campaign and he would not.

That this distinction was lost not only on his opponents but on some of his more aggressive supporters, who in their bewilderment and fear saw *le déluge* approaching, was perhaps not surprising. Listening to these bitter words from this man in his red MCCAIN-PALIN COUNTRY FIRST T-shirt, gazing over his shoulder at the white-haired candidate turning and lumbering about the stage with his arms stiffly extended at the waist, a haunting line of Kafka's floated into my mind: "The condemned man has to have the law he has transgressed inscribed on his body."[3] Was that contradictory and confounding and self-aggrandizing sense of honor, marked as it was on his broken rigid body, the "honor" that led him to forswear the black preacher while flaunting the "broken-down terrorist," to be McCain's pride, his burden, and his tragedy all at once?

Later, out in the bright glare of the seaside light, as the crowds flowed back toward the endless parking lots, I spotted bouncing along the sidewalk one of the more innovative homemade signs—THE OBAMANATION ENDS HERE! it declared in an admirable

3. See Franz Kafka, "In the Penal Colony," in *Metamorphosis and Other Stories*, translated by Michael Hofmann (Penguin Classics, 2007).

rainbow of hand-painted colors—and I asked its smiling creator, a forty-four-year-old Air Force veteran named Brad Crum, what exactly he feared in "The Obamanation."

"I think there'll be a lot of moves toward socialism," he told me, growing serious. "I've been all around the world, Spain, Germany"—he had served twenty-five years, as an electronics technician, and was about to start work for the FAA:

> I've seen it. I know it doesn't work. You hear what he's been saying? Health care for everyone? Sounds good but taxes would have to be so high it wouldn't be worth it.
>
> I grew up in East Kentucky. I knew a lot of people there whose ambition was really in the end just to game the system. You know, to get a job and then get on the draw. . . .

The people with him, including a woman carrying a GUN TOTIN' LIPSTICK WEARIN' WOMEN 4 MCCAIN/PALIN sign, nodded, a bit sheepishly. Just as their understanding of McCain was a deeply personal one—they knew him, understood what he represented and what he would protect them from—their sense of what Obama stood for was murky and dark, fearful. They were bewildered by him, mistrusted him: Where had he come from, after all? What had he ever done? What accomplishments did he have that could compare to what McCain had achieved, what he had suffered? McCain had served right here. His father and grandfather had been admirals. In Meridian, Mississippi, there was an air station, McCain Field, named for his grandfather. And who was . . . Barack Obama?

I thought for a moment of telling them about the Kansas grandparents and the years in Chicago. Then I remembered the recording of Obama's rich voice filling the dark car as I sped down the interstate highway from Philadelphia the night before, reciting the litany from *Dreams from My Father*, when his Kenyan "Granny," whom as a young man he seeks out in the upcountry town of Kisumu, tells him the story of his origins:

> First there was Miwiru. It's not known who came before. Miwiru sired Sigoma, Sigoma sired Owiny, Owiny sired Kisodhi, Kisodhi sired Ogelo, Ogelo sired Otondi, Otondi sired Obongo, Obongo sired Okoth, and Okoth sired Opiyo. The women who bore them, their names are forgotten, for that was the way of our people. . . .[4]

We are a long way here from Virginia Beach—or rather, in any event, from white Virginia Beach—and even farther from the known and cherished formalities of the old military culture of McCain's father in prewar Pearl Harbor:

> Newly arrived officers, dressed in white uniforms, took their wives, who were attired in white gloves and hats, to call on the families of fellow officers every Wednesday and Saturday between four and six o'clock. The husband laid two calling cards on the receiving tray, one for the officer in residence and the other for the lady of the house. His wife offered a single card for her hostess, for it was inappropriate for an officer's wife to call on another officer.[5]

4. See Barack Obama, *Dreams from My Father: A Story of Race and Inheritance* (Three Rivers, 1995), p. 394.

5. See McCain, *Faith of My Fathers*, p. 65

One might have said, I suppose, that the evident differences here, as clear and glaring as black and white, masked many striking parallels—that here were two accomplished men obsessed with origins, with their fathers, men overshadowed by the myths of those who had sired them and with the worlds that they had made. Men who couldn't help struggling with the past. One might even have pointed to more fortuitous crossing points—McCain's sepia-colored Pearl Harbor, for example, a later version of which is also lodged firmly in the memories of Obama, who writes of the "appeal that the military bases back in Hawaii had always held for me as a young boy, with their tidy streets and well-oiled machinery, the crisp uniforms and crisper salutes." It may not be white gloves and visiting cards, and the view of the young black outsider is not that of the young white admiral's son; but given the litany of Granny in Kisumu, it is much closer than one might think possible.

Standing in the glaring sun, beads of sweat trickling down my face, with my friend holding his THE OBAMANATION ENDS HERE! sign, I thought of offering these reflections and seeing what response they would bring. I held my tongue. They would think, I knew, that I had not been listening. They offered a simple and rough-hewn story. They had worked hard to get from East Kentucky to here. They had worked hard for what they had. Why should they let Obama, with his prettied-up socialism, open the door for others—others who had never worked as hard—to take a much easier route? Especially when that much easier route would be paved with their taxes, with the sacrifices that they and their families had already made? "Like my idea of community organizing," Obama writes of the late Mayor Harold Washington of Chicago, "he held on to a promise of collective redemption."

These people in the parking lot holding their homemade signs bleached by the sun did not believe in "collective redemption." They believed in patriotism. And to them—unlike, perhaps, to those I had seen in Northwest Philly—"collective redemption" and "patriotism" meant very different things. Obama could talk and talk, spinning those long and beautiful sentences, reasoning so unassailably with that golden tongue ("He certainly has the *symbolism* down pat," as one McCain supporter told me grimly); but whether he said so or not, what he really wanted to do was to *take things away*. They, too, *knew their pie*—and they feared they could see whose fingers were reaching for it now.

After September 11
Our State of Exception

October 13, 2011

We are in a fight for our principles, and our first responsibility is to live by them.

—GEORGE W. BUSH, September 20, 2001

1.

WE ARE LIVING in the State of Exception. We don't know when it will end, as we don't know when the War on Terror will end. But we all know when it began. We can no longer quite "remember" that moment, for the images have long since been refitted into a present-day fable of innocence and apocalypse: the perfect blue of that late summer sky stained by acrid black smoke. The jetliner appearing, tilting, then disappearing into the skin of the second tower, to emerge on the other side as a great eruption of red and yellow flame. The showers of debris, the falling bodies, and then that great blossoming flower of white dust, roiling and churning upward, enveloping and consuming the mighty skyscraper as it collapses into the whirlwind.

To Americans, those terrible moments stand as a brightly lit portal through which we were all compelled to step, together, into a different world. Since that day ten years ago we have lived in a subtly different country, and though we have grown accustomed to these changes and think little of them now, certain words still appear often enough in the news—Guantánamo, indefinite detention, torture—to remind us that ours remains a strange America. The contours of this strangeness are not unknown in our history—the country has lived through broadly similar periods, at least half a dozen or so, depending on how you count; but we have no proper name for them. State of siege? Martial law? State of emergency? None of these expressions, familiar as they may be to other peoples, falls naturally from American lips.

What are we to call this subtly altered America? Clinton Rossiter, the great American scholar of "crisis government," writing in the shadow of World War II, called such times "constitutional dictatorship."[1] Others, more recently, have spoken of a "9/11 Constitution" or an "Emergency Constitution." Vivid terms all; and yet perhaps too narrowly drawn, placing as they do the definitional weight entirely on law when this state of ours seems to have as much, or more, to do with politics—with how we live now and who we are as a polity. This is in part why I prefer "the state of exception," an umbrella term that gathers beneath it those emergency categories while emphasizing that this state has as its defining characteristic that it transcends the borders of the strictly legal—that it occupies, in the words of the philosopher Giorgio Agamben, "a position at the limit between politics and law... an ambiguous, uncertain, borderline fringe, at the intersection of the legal and the political."[2]

1. See Clinton Rossiter, *Constitutional Dictatorship: Crisis Government in the Modern Democracies* (Princeton University Press, 1948; Transaction, 2002).

2. See Giorgio Agamben, *State of Exception* (University of Chicago Press, 2005), p. 1. The second phrase Agamben quotes from François Saint-Bonnet, *L'État d'exception* (Presses Universitaires de France, 2001).

Call it, then, the state of exception: these years during which, in the name of security, some of our accustomed rights and freedoms are circumscribed or set aside, the years during which we live *in a different time.* This different time of ours has now extended ten years—the longest by far in American history—with little sense of an ending. Indeed, the very endlessness of this state of exception—a quality emphasized even as it was imposed—and the broad acceptance of that endlessness, the state of exception's increasing normalization, are among its distinguishing marks.

For the overwhelming majority of Americans the changes have come to seem subtle, certainly when set beside how daily life was altered during World War II or World War I, not to mention during the Civil War. Officially sanctioned torture, or enhanced interrogation, however dramatic a departure it may be from our history, happens not to Americans but to others, as do extraordinary rendition and indefinite detention; the particular burdens of our exception seem mostly to be borne by someone else—by someone other. It is possible for most to live their lives without taking note of these practices at all except as phrases in the news—until, every once in a while, like a blind man who lives, all unknowingly, in a very large cage, one or another of us stumbles into the bars.

Whoever takes the time to peer closely at the space enclosed within those bars can see that our country has been altered in fundamental ways. When President Barack Obama in his elegant address accepting the Nobel Peace Prize declares to the world that he has "prohibited torture," we should pause in our pride to notice that torture violates international and domestic law and that the notion that our new president has the power to prohibit it follows insidiously from the pretense that his predecessor had the power to order it—that during the state of exception, not only because of what President George W. Bush decided to do but also because of what President Obama is every day deciding not to do (not to "look back" but "look forward"), torture in America has metamorphosed. Before the War on Terror, official torture was illegal and anathema; today it is a policy choice.

2.

> I woke up, naked, strapped to a bed, in a very white room. The room measured approximately 4m x 4m. The room had three solid walls, with the fourth wall consisting of metal bars separating it from a larger room. I am not sure how long I remained in the bed. After some time, I think it was several days, but can't remember exactly, I was transferred to a chair where I was kept, shackled by [the] hands and feet for what I think was the next 2 to 3 weeks. During this time I developed blisters on the underside of my legs due to the constant sitting....
>
> I was given no solid food during the first two or three weeks, while sitting on the chair. I was only given Ensure and water to drink. At first the Ensure made me vomit, but this became less with time.
>
> The cell and room were air-conditioned and were very cold. Very loud, shouting type music was constantly playing. It kept repeating about every fifteen minutes twenty-four hours a day. Sometimes the music stopped and was replaced by a loud hissing or crackling noise....
>
> During this first two to three week period I was questioned for about one to two hours each day. American interrogators would

> come to the room and speak to me through the bars of the cell. During the questioning the music was switched off, but was then put back on again afterwards. I could not sleep at all for the first two to three weeks. If I started to fall asleep one of the guards would come and spray water in my face.[3]

By now, sometime in the summer of 2002, as he sits woozy and drooling, chained naked to the chair, and though he doesn't know it, Zayn al-Abidin Muhammad Husayn is a famous man, his knowledge and status debated in the world's press and argued over in the White House. When he was captured on March 28, 2002, in a spectacular raid in Faisalabad, Pakistan, during which he leapt from a building's rooftop and was shot three times, the man we now know as Abu Zubaydah, of Saudi birth and Palestinian nationality, had just turned thirty-one. His capture was an event of great moment, a trophy in the War on Terror. "The other day, we hauled in a guy named Abu Zubaydah," President Bush proclaimed at a Republican fund-raiser in Greenwich.

> He's one of the top operatives plotting and planning death and destruction on the United States. He's not plotting and planning anymore. He's where he belongs.

Abu Zubaydah, as Secretary of Defense Donald Rumsfeld told the world from his Pentagon lectern two days after his capture, was

3. *ICRC Report on the Treatment of Fourteen "High Value Detainees" in CIA Custody*, February 2007, pp. 28–29.

"a close associate of [Osama bin Laden], and if not the number two, very close to the number two person in the organization. I think that's well established."[4]

It is an intriguing phrase, "well established": What does it take to make a fact a fact? What we actually know about Abu Zubaydah—and, even more, what we know he knows—would become a matter of intense debate. At this point we know he has bullet wounds in the stomach, thigh, groin, loses huge amounts of blood, falls into a coma. On the other side of the world, in Baltimore, a trauma surgeon is awakened by an urgent call from the CIA director, rushed to a private jet, and flown to Pakistan, where he manages, just barely, to save the prisoner's life. Abu Zubaydah, bleeding, still unconscious, will be carried off to a famously "undisclosed location" and his whereabouts will remain a closely guarded secret, not least to him, even as he sits, several months later, chained immobile in his white room.

Once again, we know a bit more than he does: the white room is likely on a military base in Thailand, but in any event at one of the so-called black sites that the CIA improvised hurriedly in the days after September 11, secret prisons in Pakistan, Afghanistan, Romania, Morocco, Poland, Lithuania, and perhaps elsewhere to hold and interrogate prisoners, pursuant to President Bush's secret order, issued six days after the attacks, which gave this task to the CIA, an agency that had had nothing whatever to do with detention or interrogation for two decades or more.

4. See "DoD News Briefing—With Secretary Rumsfeld and General Myers," April 1, 2002. Remarks by the President, Connecticut Republican Committee Lunches, April 9, 2002.

*

So the critically wounded Abu Zubaydah is "disappeared" into secrecy; but in fact all that is secret is his location. Abu Zubaydah's capture and his "disappearance" quickly became highly public victories in the War on Terror. That he was now in American hands, and "where he belongs"—being interrogated at an "undisclosed location": this was known, discussed, debated, gloated over. This peculiar fiction of "public secrecy" allows the government to withhold not mainly knowledge from the public—though narrow and vital bits of information are withheld—but responsibility and liability from itself. Not officially acknowledging the situation of the man—and, eventually, of scores more such prisoners—the United States will reject all claims that it has any obligation to account for them or to answer for their treatment, as other countries have done in the case of their own "disappeared." Without legal status or even government confirmation that they are alive and in custody, such prisoners become the objects, as Agamben writes, of "a detention that is indefinite not only in the temporal sense but in its very nature. . . ."[5] That is, we have reached, when it comes to detainees, the opposite end of the spectrum from the presiding liberal idea of a government inherently limited in its powers.

A few days later Abu Zubaydah wakes from his coma to find at his bedside in this unfamiliar location in an unknown country a man he doesn't know, who asks him his name. Abu Zubaydah shakes his head: he has heard the American accent. "And I asked him again in Arabic," remembers John Kiriakou of the CIA.

5. See *State of Exception*, pp. 3–4.

And then he answered me in English. And he said that he would not speak to me in God's language. And then I said, "That's okay. We know who you are."

They did not quite know, as it happened. The facts that Secretary Rumsfeld had crowed about at the Pentagon as "well established" were not facts at all. Abu Zubaydah was not "a close associate" of Osama bin Laden, nor was he "number two," nor even "very close to the number two person in the organization"—nor, as the Department of Justice admitted in court documents in 2009, did he have any role in or advance knowledge of the September 11 attacks, nor was he a member of the organization or "formally" identified with it at all.[6] To US officials desperate for information on al-Qaeda six months after the attacks on New York and Washington, he seemed, however, a very rich prize indeed—as Abu Zubaydah seemed to

6. In documents filed in US District Court in Washington in September 2009, the Justice Department conceded that the government was no longer contending that Zubaydah "was a 'member' of al-Qaeda in the sense of having sworn bayat (allegiance) or having otherwise satisfied any formal criteria that either [Zubaydah] or al-Qaeda may have considered necessary for inclusion in al-Qaeda.... Rather, [the government's] detention of [Zubaydah] is based on conduct and actions that establish [Zubaydah] was 'part of' hostile forces and 'substantially supported' those forces."

Earlier, at his Combatant Status Review Tribunal at Guantánamo, Zubaydah noted that his interrogators had "told me sorry we discover that you are not number three [in al-Qaeda], not a partner, even not a fighter." See, for example, Jason Leopold, "Government Recants Major Terror Claims on 'High Value' Detainee Abu Zubaydah," *TruthOut*, March 30, 2010, and Andy Worthington, "Abu Zubaydah: Tortured for Nothing," *Commentaries: The Future of Freedom Foundation*, April 5, 2010. See also Barton Gellman, "The Shadow War, in a Surprising New Light, *The Washington Post*, June 20, 2006.

recognize, according to Kiriakou's recounting of the initial bedside interview at that undisclosed location:

> And then he asked me to smother him with a pillow. And I said, "No, no. . . . We have plans for you."[7]

The plans even then were being fought over. The interrogation would be led at this initial stage by two experienced interrogators from the FBI, using "traditional methods": helping to nurse the wounded man back to health, changing his bandages, washing his wounds, building a relationship, respect, rapport, etc. One of these men, the Lebanese-born Ali Soufan, would startle the prisoner by addressing him as Hani, the nickname his mother had used with him.

Soufan has argued strenuously, first as an unnamed source for journalists and now in newspaper articles and congressional testimony and a book in his own name, that all the valuable information that was gained from Abu Zubaydah—including the identity of so-called dirty bomber Jose Padilla and the code name of Khalid Sheikh Mohammed—was gained in those initial discussions.[8] Traditional interrogation, he and his colleagues contend, was working. Torture was not needed.

7. See "CIA—Abu Zubaydah. Interview with John Kiriakou," pp. 8–9," an unedited, rough, and undated transcript of a video interview conducted by Brian Ross of ABC News, apparently in December 2007, and available at https://humanrights.ucdavis.edu/projects/the-guantanamo-testimonials-project/testimonies/testimonies-of-the-cia/brianross_kiriakou_1.pdf

8. See Ali Soufan, "My Tortured Decision," *The New York Times*, April 22, 2009. See also Ali Soufan and Daniel Freedman, *The Black Banners: The Inside Story of 9/11 and the War Against al-Qaeda* (Norton, 2011).

Others in the government, particularly in the CIA, did not believe it; they were convinced, as a Justice Department report has it, that "he was not telling all he knew." How did they come to this conclusion? It is a fascinating question. Unlike the fantasy parable of the Ticking Bomb, in which officials know everything—that the nuclear bomb has been planted, that it will be detonated soon, that the man in custody who denies knowing its location actually knows it, that only torture will make him speak—in the real world it is the vast unknowns we fear, the deserts of ignorance, unbounded by any certain facts.

Donald Rumsfeld famously distinguished between the "known unknowns"—what we know we don't know, which can be frightening—and the "unknown unknowns"—what we don't even know we don't know, which can be terrifying. After September 11, that terror was expressed in a simple calculus of action, well described by the CIA inspector general in 2004:

> Lack of knowledge led analysts to speculate about what a detainee "should know," [versus] information the analyst could objectively demonstrate the detainee did know.... When a detainee did not respond to a question posed to him, the assumption at Headquarters was that the detainee was holding back and knew more; consequently, Headquarters recommended resumption of [enhanced interrogation techniques].[9]

9. Inspector General, Central Intelligence Agency, *Special Review: Counterterrorism and Detention Activities* (September 2001–October 2003), May 7, 2004, p. 83.

In an atmosphere of fear and anxiety, it seems the prudent course to assume what the detainee "should know" and proceed accordingly. And make no mistake, the critical decisions laying the basis for the state of exception were made in a state of anxiety and fear. How could they not have been? After September 11, as Richard Clarke put it simply, "we panicked." Terrorism, downgraded as a threat by the incoming Bush administration, now became the single all-consuming obsession of a government suddenly on a "war footing."

Every day the President and other senior officials received the "threat matrix," a document that could be dozens of pages long listing "every threat directed at the United States"[10] that had been sucked up during the last twenty-four hours by the vast electronic and human vacuum cleaner of information that was US intelligence: warnings of catastrophic weapons, conventional attacks, planned attacks on allies, plots of every description and level of seriousness. "You simply could not sit where I did," George Tenet later wrote of the threat matrix, "and be anything other than scared to death about what it portended."[11]

One official compared reading the matrix every day—in an example of the ironic "mirroring" one finds everywhere in this story—to "being stuck in a room listening to loud Led Zeppelin music," which leads to "sensory overload" and makes one "paranoid." He compared the task of defending the country to playing goalie in a game in which the goalie must stop every shot and in which all

10. Jack Goldsmith, *The Terror Presidency: Law and Judgment Inside the Bush Administration* (Norton, 2007), p. 71.

11. Quoted in Goldsmith, *The Terror Presidency*, p. 72.

the opposing players, and the boundary lines, and the field, are invisible.[12]

All this bespeaks not only an all-encompassing anxiety about information—about the lack of map rooms displaying the movements of armies, the maddening absence of visible, identifiable threats, the unremitting angst of making what could be life-and-death judgments based on the reading and interpreting of inscrutable signs—but also, I think, guilt over what had been allowed to happen, together with the deep-seated need to banish that guilt, to start again, cleansed and immaculate. Thus "the War on Terror"—a new policy for a new era, during which the guardians of the nation's security could boast a perfect record: no attacks on American soil. The attacks of September 11 would be banished to a "before time" when the "legalistic" Clinton rules applied, before "the gloves came off." The successful attack could thus be blamed on the mistaken beliefs of another time, another administration. The apocalyptic portal of September 11 made everything new, wiping out all guilt and blame.

The argument escalated, between the FBI and CIA interrogators at the "black site," between various factions back in Washington. CIA officers, led by two "contractors" who had been Air Force instructors in the so-called SERE program in the military—a program designed to prepare downed pilots for hostile questioning—prepared an interrogation plan for the detainee, and it was passed to CIA headquarters and discussed in the White House. By mid-May the national security adviser let it be known that the plan could

12. Goldsmith, *The Terror Presidency*, pp. 72–73.

go forward, subject to Justice Department approval. The FBI interrogators, the most experienced on the scene, were withdrawn. In their wake CIA officers began to apply—as President Bush preferred to call them—an "alternative set of procedures."

We should remember that the contractors hired by the CIA improvised these from a cold war–era program the Air Force had "designed to simulate conditions to which [pilots] might be subject if taken prisoner by enemies"—that is, the Soviets and the Chinese—"that did not abide by the Geneva Conventions." Which is to say, SERE training, as one former instructor told the Senate Armed Services Committee, from whose report I am quoting, was "based on *illegal* exploitation . . . of prisoners over the last fifty years [emphasis added]."[13]

We see here perhaps the prime example of the improvisation inherent in the state of exception. First, the critical security bureaucracies in the US government—the CIA and the military—derived their "enhanced interrogation techniques" from a cold war–era pilot-training program that had been intentionally designed to reproduce illegal techniques. They then placed before government attorneys the through-the-looking-glass task of proving that those interrogation techniques are perfectly permissible under the tenets of international and domestic law that they were expressly designed to violate.

This history means that a central line of reasoning running through the so-called torture memos is the peculiar notion that

13. See "Executive Summary and Conclusions," *Inquiry into the Treatment of Detainees in US Custody*, Senate Armed Services Committee, December 2008, p. xiii; quoted in my *Stripping Bare the Body: Politics Violence War* (Nation Books, 2009), p. 526.

because the pilot trainees, who were volunteers and who could, of course, halt the procedures at any time, did not suffer, for example, long-term psychological harm, then detainees subjected to these techniques, as it were, for real, would not suffer any either. An interrogation program deemed absolutely essential to protect the country during a national emergency was thus "reverse-engineered" from a training program for pilots by contract instructors who had never carried out an actual interrogation. However much this might seem to be a fantasy, in fact it is true.

The leaders of the new War on Terror would not be "reading terrorists their Miranda rights." They would launch their new War on Terror with an unblemished record and with a willingness, a commitment, to do whatever it took. That meant gaining the most vital fuel: information. When it came to the interrogation of Abu Zubaydah, the victor in the struggle between the FBI and its traditional "law enforcement methods" and the CIA and its improvised "alternative set of procedures" was preordained. The judgment would seem to be built on evidence, on the thinness of what the detainee was providing, but in fact was based on conviction. Abu Zubaydah was known to be a high official in al-Qaeda—a "lieutenant of Osama bin Laden," as Vice President Cheney is still describing him in his recent memoir, *In My Time* (2011). If he gives up only relatively modest information, mustn't that very fact mean he is concealing things that are important? The conviction of secret knowledge, set beside the paucity of what is revealed, proves the conclusion of deception. (It is a familiar, if distinctive, chain of reasoning. Mustn't, after all, the failure of the UN inspectors to find weapons of mass destruction in Iraq be confirmation that Saddam is hiding them?)

Back at the Department of Justice Deputy Assistant Attorney General John Yoo and a young colleague were working furiously on a memorandum that judged whether twelve proposed techniques—including slamming the captive's head against a wall and suffocating him with water—violated the statutes of the US criminal code and the US government's international undertakings forbidding torture. Their memos went through several drafts. "Bring the Bad Things Memo," Yoo e-mailed his young colleague before a White House meeting during that heady spring. "I like your new name for it," she replied brightly. There is in these exchanges all the breathless excitement of young professionals breaking new legal ground.

Experimentation and improvisation are inherent in the very genes of our state of exception—as Abu Zubaydah seems to realize in recounting the second, or "correction," phase of his interrogation, which followed his weeks sitting chained to the chair in the cold white room:

> Two black wooden boxes were brought into the room outside my cell. One was tall, slightly higher than me and narrow. . . . I was taken out of my cell and one of the interrogators wrapped a towel around my neck, they then used it to swing me around and smash me repeatedly against the hard walls of the room. . . .
>
> I was then put into the tall black box for what I think was about one and a half to two hours. The box was totally black on the inside as well as the outside. . . . They put a cloth or cover over the outside of the box to cut out the light and restrict my air supply. It was

> difficult to breathe. When I was let out of the box I saw that one of the walls of the room had been covered with plywood sheeting. From now on it was against this wall that I was then smashed with the towel around my neck.

Abu Zubaydah suggests that "the plywood was put there" because the "interrogators realized that smashing me against the hard wall would probably quickly result in physical injury." No doubt he is right: the plywood is the answer to the perennial problem of the torturer: how to inflict sufficient pain without causing injury of the sort that will make further "exploitation" of the detainee difficult or even impossible. But where precisely, between the first time Abu Zubaydah was smashed into the wall and then placed inside the standing black coffin-like box for "close confinement" and then emerged to be "walled" again, did that plywood come from?

I suspect it was the idea of someone back at CIA headquarters, in Langley, Virginia. As CIA officer John Kiriakou reminds us,

> Each one of these steps ... had to have the approval of the Deputy Director for Operations. So before you laid a hand on him, you had to send in the cable saying, "He's uncooperative. Request permission to do X." And that permission would come.... The cable traffic back and forth was extremely specific....

Beyond the hour-by-hour approval of particular techniques issuing out of headquarters came an assiduous effort to brief "NSC policy staff and senior Administration officials," for, as the CIA inspector general put it, "the Agency specifically wanted to ensure that these officials and the [Congressional Oversight] Committees continued to be aware of and approve CIA's actions."[14] One detects here a further echo of the 1970s and the scandals after the revelations of agency assassinations, coups, and other misdeeds before the Church and Pike committees: CIA leaders and officers were determined that this time, however much national attitudes on these matters might change—after the emergency had passed—they could never be accused of "rogue" behavior. This time, high officials couldn't claim they didn't know; instead of "nothing on paper," this time CIA officers would insist on briefings, meetings, records, memos, documents—explicit approval. In so doing they ensured that responsibility was spread very high and very wide indeed.

Again, Abu Zubaydah:

> After the beating I was then placed in the small box. They placed a cloth or cover over the box to cut out all light and restrict my air supply.... The wound on my leg began to open and started to bleed....
>
> I was then dragged from the small box, unable to walk properly and put on what looked like a hospital bed, and strapped down very tightly with belts. A black cloth was then placed over my face and the interrogators used a mineral water bottle to pour water on the cloth so that I could not breathe. After a few minutes the cloth was removed and the bed was rotated into an upright position. The pressure of the straps on my wounds was very painful. I vomited.

14. *Special Review: Counterterrorism and Detention Activities* (September 2001–October 2003), p. 23.

> The bed was then again lowered to horizontal position and the same torture carried out again with the black cloth over my face and water poured on from a bottle. On this occasion my head was in a more backward, downwards position and the water was poured on for a longer time. I struggled against the straps, trying to breathe, but it was hopeless. I thought I was going to die. I lost control of my urine. Since then I still lose control of my urine when under stress.

This is the famous waterboarding, a time-honored technique deployed by the priestly interrogators of the Spanish Inquisition, by French paratroopers during the Algerian War, by the Argentines during their "dirty war," by the Khmer Rouge and the Salvadorans during their civil wars. Techniques vary but the principle remains the same: drown the prisoner, provoking suffocation and panic, then interrupt the drowning in time to save his life. That American interrogators were waterboarding prisoners first appeared in the press, to my knowledge, in May 2004, in a report in *The New York Times*. This of course is another side of "public secrecy": the two narratives—what was done and what we know—crossed very early on.

Of the eleven "enhanced interrogation techniques" deemed legal by the Department of Justice, ten, according to John Yoo, "did not even come close to the [legal] standard [of torture]," but "waterboarding did." In a rather striking admission to Department of Justice investigators that has received too little attention, Yoo confessed that "I had actually thought that we prohibited waterboarding. I didn't recollect that we had actually said that you could do it." He went on:

> The waterboarding as it's described in that memo is very different than the waterboarding that was described in the press. And so when

I read the description in the press of what waterboarding is, I was like, oh, well, obviously that would be prohibited by the statute.[15]

It should be said, of course, that the International Committee of the Red Cross, legally charged with investigating and judging the treatment of prisoners, had no problem whatever declaring that this treatment "amounted to torture and/or cruel, inhuman, or degrading treatment." But Yoo's observation underlines again that the differences between what is prescribed in the legal and policy documents—in which Yoo memorably describes waterboarding as a "controlled acute episode" short of torture—and what actually happens at the black sites is often dramatic. In waterboarding Abu Zubaydah, the interrogators used more water and performed the procedure much more frequently—eighty-three times, in this case—than prescribed in the documents, part of a general "drifting downward" into greater cruelty that we see throughout the various plotlines of this story.

It seems a general rule of what we might call the early state of exception that those officials—at the White House, the CIA, the Pentagon, and the Justice Department—who could point to the desert of knowledge, who could dwell on and profit from the fear of that dark unknown, were victorious, and indeed nothing more dramatically embodies the style of the exception: Assume the worst. Act

15. Office of Professional Responsibility, Department of Justice, *Investigation into the Office of Legal Counsel's Memoranda Concerning Issues Relating to the Central Intelligence Agency's Use of "Enhanced Interrogation Techniques" on Suspected Terrorists*, July 29, 2009, pp. 53–54.

preemptively, aggressively. Don't hesitate. When in doubt, act. If there is a risk, the possible consequences are so grave that you must not let worries over evidence slow you down.

This kind of thinking reached a kind of apotheosis in Vice President Cheney's so-called one percent doctrine, which Ron Suskind summarized as follows: "If there was even a one percent chance of terrorists getting a weapon of mass destruction . . . the United States must now act as if it was a certainty."[16] This remarkable attitude toward risk—that only lack of action, and not mistaken action, posed dangers to the country—had peculiar and contradictory effects when embodied in the vast worldwide detention regime spawned by the state of exception: the five thousand arrested and detained by the Immigration and Naturalization Service in the United States; the tens of thousands detained in Abu Ghraib and Bagram and other prisons in Iraq and Afghanistan; the hundreds detained in Guantánamo Bay, Cuba; the scores detained in the "black sites." This vast system, which stretched around the world and at one time held nearly one hundred thousand prisoners, was intended to extract the vital intelligence that would supply the "front line" in the War on Terror.

But the sweeping arrests and indefinite detention—the failure to make discriminations of risk (which would have meant a willingness to get it wrong) in favor of wholesale, blanket judgments based on pervasive fear—had the perverse effect of crippling the intelligence-gathering system itself. That system was flooded with detainees who knew nothing "actionable," or even relevant—and

16. See Ron Suskind, *The One Percent Doctrine: Deep Inside America's Pursuit of Its Enemies Since 9/11* (Simon and Schuster, 2006), p. 62.

who could not be released, either, because, as in Abu Ghraib, the officers who were responsible for detaining them objected or because, as Colonel Lawrence Wilkerson says of the Guantánamo detainees, "it was politically impossible to release them." Wilkerson, who served as chief of staff to Secretary of State Colin Powell, notes that if those detainees who should never have been imprisoned were released, "the detention efforts at Guantánamo would be revealed as the incredibly confused operation that they were."[17]

The injustice of the system, of course, was pervasive, and this was increasingly recognized around the world and had its own grave political effects in what was, after all, a political war—a war in which al-Qaeda's primary goal was to recruit young Muslims to its cause. But it is important to recognize that it was failing on its own terms. A system meant to be gathering the most vital and precious resource to fight the existential dangers of the War on Terror in fact was debilitating itself.

Though his moment of secret fame is long past, Abu Zubaydah is still with us. After three and a half years in the black sites, he was moved in 2006 to Guantánamo, where he is now in his ninth year of imprisonment. Thinking of him there, it is difficult to embrace fully the presiding philosophy of the Obama administration on these matters: that when it comes to torture we must "look forward," not back. Impossible, thinking of Abu Zubaydah and the questions he embodies, not to think as well of his American partners in these

17. See the Declaration of Colonel Lawrence B. Wilkerson in *Adel Hassan Hamad* v. *George W. Bush, Donald Rumsfeld, Jay Hood, and Brice Gyurisko*, US District Court for the District of Columbia, CV 05-1009 JDB, March 24, 2010.

scenes a half-dozen years ago. Many of course have moved on, to private law firms, to corporate security jobs, to university faculties. But the story is not over. The documents are full of the drama of the interrogators and the officials of the CIA demanding that they be granted, if not advance immunity for what they were about to do—a so-called letter of declination—then at least a "golden shield" that would protect them from any future attempt at prosecution. They received one, indeed a series of them, in the so-called torture memos produced by the Justice Department and, later, in the Military Commissions Act passed by Congress in 2006.

As we look back today at these ghostly figures, at the policymakers sitting in their offices who ordered these techniques, and the lawyers who deemed them legal, and the interrogators who practiced them on men chained naked in cold sunless rooms, we can have the sense, haunting as it is, that they are all looking forward at us, as we stand here today judging what they did. If we know anything, it is that they knew this moment would come. They were determined to prepare for it, and in a sense they succeeded brilliantly. The legal memos, however grotesque in their reasoning and however widely denounced, have in effect held sway, and imposed a painful unremitting moral limbo on all of us.

Waterboarding, prosecuted within the United States as recently as 1983—and reaffirmed, explicitly, to be illegal by the present attorney general in his confirmation hearings—now amounts, in these exhaustively documented cases, to no more than the "controlled acute episode" of John Yoo's description. The former vice-president can speak proudly in his memoirs of his approval of these techniques, asserting, in direct contradiction to findings of the International Committee of the Red Cross, that "they complied with the law, including international treaty obligations such as the United Nations Convention Against Torture." The current president is on record asserting that waterboarding is illegal—even as his predecessor proudly recounts in his own memoirs that when asked for approval to waterboard Khalid Sheikh Mohammed he replied without hesitation, "Damn right!"

Americans, believing themselves to stand proudly for the rule of law and human rights, have become for the rest of the world a symbol of something quite opposite: a society in which lawbreaking, approved by its highest elected officials, goes unpunished. Thus President Obama's exhortation that the country look forward and not back takes on a different coloring: the country has entered a twilight world when it comes to the law and is unlikely soon to emerge from it.

At the same time, in the Middle East itself, where torture had underpinned the power of every national security state, the most notorious images of the state of exception—the obscenely twisted naked figures at Abu Ghraib, the kneeling hooded prisoners in their orange jumpsuits at Guantánamo—provoked a debate about torture and human rights that had heretofore been impossible. Egyptians, forbidden to talk about Egyptian torture, could freely discuss, analyze, and condemn American torture, and thereby initiate a discussion of human rights and dignity that was a motivating element in the early upheavals of the Arab Spring. As Shadi Mokhtari writes:

> Because the torture and abuse depicted was so widely seen as directed towards the Arab or Muslim man, many felt a profound sense of personal violation. As they grappled to formulate a response, they often found themselves invoking human rights.... Instead of viewing

> human rights as a Western imposition, increasingly it became a language that Arab populations embraced.... It did not take long however for the focus to turn inward to the Arab world's own "Guantánamos," "Abu Ghraibs," and widespread practice of torture. Activists began exploiting limited openings to draw compelling analogies to the repression pervading their own societies.[18]

This raises a question for Americans: Are we still waiting to have that debate in the United States—or is it already over? The story of torture is widely known, voluminously documented. It is part of our present, not our past. When Umar Farouk Abdulmutallab, the so-called Christmas Day Bomber, was apprehended after failing to detonate his "underwear bomb" over Detroit, a number of prominent politicians, both Republican and Democratic, demanded he be sent to Guantánamo and subjected to "enhanced interrogation techniques." That Obama officials handed him over to the FBI provoked outrage and warnings about the grave danger such a decision represented for the country. "Eleven months after the president had shut down the enhanced interrogation program and revealed the techniques in the program publicly," former Vice President Cheney writes in his memoir, "the replacement [for the interrogation program] did not exist. Abdulmutallab was read a Miranda warning."

The accuracy of this—in fact, Abdulmutallab seems to have cooperated with the FBI interrogators—is less important than what it says about the centrality of "enhanced interrogation techniques" as a political touchstone in the era of the state of exception. Torture

18. See Shadi Mokhtari, "George Bush and the Turn to Human Rights in the Arab World," OpenDemocracy.net, February 25, 2011.

shows that officials are willing to do anything to protect the country. Reluctance to use torture shows weakness, an ambivalence in the determination to protect the country no matter what the cost. Reluctance to use torture shows a reversion to the "law enforcement model," which, as we know, is now held to be responsible for the success of the September 11 attacks in the first place.

As long as there is no successful attack on American soil an unstable equilibrium persists—a gray world different but recognizable. In the wake of the next attack, however, the subtle changes all around us, the ways the state of exception endures, will leap into vivid color. And for all the talk of the "strategic defeat" of al-Qaeda, that next attack is almost certain to come—indeed, the very weakening of al-Qaeda makes such a success more likely. The organization is no longer strong enough to insist that America, the showcase for its most dramatic efforts, is suited only for a "spectacular," a grand mass-casualty event on the scale of September 11. Now any attack, even a "lone wolf" car bombing, will serve, and we see this in the pattern of recent attempts:

> In the post-9/11 world, we had an average of about four plots targeting US soil, or emanating on US soil, a year. In 2008–2009, that jumps to nine and then ten. In 2011, we are already on a pace to pass that.

Thus John Miller, a high official of the Office of the Director of National Intelligence and a former television reporter who interviewed both Osama bin Laden and Ayman al-Zawahiri. Miller goes on:

> Something has happened, a better maturation of ideology, a better way to get the message out, that has caused those plots to be coming at us literally at a rate or a pace of almost one a month. And when you deal in that kind of volume, you have a special challenge. Number one, we are operating at nearly 100 percent in interdicting all of them and shutting them down. But the odds of being able to maintain that batting average, as the numbers go up, those [odds] go down.[19]

What is this "better way of getting the message out"? One of the most damaging failures of the early War on Terror was the willingness of the Bush administration to act in a way that seemed to embody the caricature that bin Laden and al-Qaeda had made of the United States: a muscle-bound, arrogant, crusading, hegemonic superpower intent on repressing and abusing and humiliating Muslims. The naked obscenities from Abu Ghraib, the images of shackled, hooded Muslims in their orange jumpsuits at Guantánamo, were immense victories for al-Qaeda in a war whose foremost strategic goal was the recruitment of young Muslims to the cause of extremist, anti-American Islamic fundamentalism. It is this "battle of the story" that Dick Cheney, for example, still fails utterly to grasp. "I don't have much sympathy for the view that we should find an alternative to Guantánamo . . . ," he tells us in his memoir, "simply because we are worried about how we are perceived abroad."

The president who followed him has shown—most notably in his Cairo speech to the Muslim world—that he has a deeper understanding of the politics of this conflict; but his failure to close Guantánamo, after vowing on his second day in office to do so

19. See *Piers Morgan Tonight*, CNN, September 6, 2011.

within the year, shows how deeply the state of exception has embedded itself in our politics. No one, Republican or Democrat, wants to be accused of "coddling terrorists." To this President Obama, in a typically eager capitulation to reality, has acceded. It is a compromise with the state of exception for which, in the political whirlwind certain to follow hard on another successful attack, he is unlikely to be granted much credit. Meanwhile the one element that, since the early Roman dictatorships, all states of exception have shared—that they are temporary, that they *end*—seems lacking in ours. Ten years later, what was the exceptional has become the normal. The improvisations of panic are the reality of our daily lives.

The Politics of Fear

October 24, 2012

AMID THE CLAMOROUS CONTROVERSIES of this election campaign, what strikes one here on the west bank of the Jordan is the silences. Though the issue of Palestine promises to have a much more vital part in the volatile, populist politics of the Middle East's new democracies—whose vulnerable governments actually must take some account of what moves ordinary people—here in Ramallah we have heard virtually nothing substantive about it, apart, that is, from Mitt Romney's repeated charge that President Obama, presumably in extracting from Israel a hard-fought ten-month freeze on settlement building early on in his administration, had "thrown Israel under the bus."

In fact, the West Bank is perhaps the place on the globe that has seen the least of President Obama's promised "change you can believe in." Nearly fifty years after Israel conquered the territories, its young soldiers are still on patrol, herding millions of Palestinians through and around an increasingly elaborate labyrinth of checkpoints, walls, and access roads, while Israeli settlers, now numbering in all more than half a million, flow over the hills, swelling their gated and fortified towns, creating one "fact on the ground" after another. Even as the land of the long-promised Palestinian state vanishes behind these barricades, the phrase "two-state solution" lives on, hovering like a ghost over the settlements, a remnant mirage of a permanently moribund "peace process" that has produced no agreement of consequence in twenty years, since the Oslo Accords vowed a Palestinian state would be declared no later than 1999.

Governor Romney's own view of how to achieve Middle East peace is decidedly more modest—indeed, almost Buddhist in its fatalism. As he told guests at the now-infamous Boca Raton "47 percent" fund-raiser:

> You hope for some degree of stability, but you recognize that it's going to remain an unsolved problem. . . . And we kick the ball down the field and hope that ultimately, somehow, something will happen and resolve it.

Whatever that "something" that will "somehow . . . happen" might be, it will presumably not come at the initiative of a Romney administration, since, as the governor went on, "the idea of pushing on the Israelis to give something up, to get the Palestinians to act, is the worst idea in the world."[1]

Since this attitude mirrors that of Israeli prime minister Benjamin Netanyahu, the governor's former colleague at Bain Capital, it would seem to accord perfectly with Romney's vow that "the world must never see any daylight between" the US and Israel. Five months after he made these statements, after his return as "ol' moderate

1. See "Full Transcript of the Mitt Romney Secret Video," *Mother Jones*, September 19, 2012.

Mitt" in the first debate, Governor Romney declared that he would "recommit America to the goal of a democratic, prosperous Palestinian state living side by side in peace and security with the Jewish state of Israel"[2]—a "goal" Prime Minister Netanyahu has also publicly embraced, no doubt with like sincerity.

The blanket of near silence cast over the Middle East "peace process" extends south and east, to the United States' most active current "shooting war"—the undeclared and seemingly permanent covert war being fought mostly with unmanned drones in South Asia and, increasingly, the Horn of Africa. Every day, twenty-four hours a day, American airmen serving their shifts at bases in Nevada, upstate New York, and elsewhere in the United States are "piloting" these lethal flying robots, gazing at computer screens through which they track from above the movements of men on the other side of the world.

Sometimes the men they shadow in Pakistan and Yemen and Somalia are known militant suspects (targets of so-called personality strikes), sometimes they are military-aged men behaving in ways deemed to fit with known terrorist "profiles" (so-called signature strikes). In either case the land-borne pilots, whether working for the Central Intelligence Agency or the United States military, spend their hours and days observing them—and often pulling the trigger that launches the missile that streaks down and kills them. These pilots working quietly on US bases have so far killed several thousand people—credible estimates range as high as 3,500—and perhaps as

2. "Romney Speech Transcript on Foreign Policy and His Plans for the White House," Virginia Military Institute, October 8, 2012. The words "ol' moderate Mitt" are of course former President Bill Clinton's, in the wake of the first debate.

many as one in four have been noncombatants.[3] At least four executed in this manner have been American citizens.

This quiet war, President Obama's "focused" version of George W. Bush's Global War on Terror, shows no sign of coming to an end. No doubt some of those killed pose an imminent threat to American citizens—though the definition of what exactly that means, what criteria must be satisfied for our government to order someone's death, remain classified and unmentioned. But there is much evidence to suggest that many, at least by any reasonable definition of "threat," do not—indeed, that in as many as 94 percent of the cases the targets are "mere foot soldiers" about whom, according to terrorism expert Peter Bergen, "it's hard to make the case that [they] threaten the United States in some way."[4] What is not in dispute is that these killings of thousands of Muslims, conducted by remote control by a distant superpower, have caused enormous resentment and hatred of the United States in Pakistan and throughout the Islamic world, a consequence that helps revivify and perpetuate the political sentiments at the root of the War on Terror.

More than a decade after the attacks of September 11, one might have thought a great democracy in choosing its leader could have found time at least to consider this ongoing and seemingly endless war: to debate, for example, whether the drone strikes, deeply unpopular as they are among Muslims, might be creating as many terrorists as they are killing; or to ask whether Americans truly believe that their president should have "the unreviewable power to kill anyone,

3. See "Covert Drone War—The Data," The Bureau of Investigative Journalism.

4. See Greg Miller, "Increased U.S. Drone Strikes in Pakistan Killing Few High-Value Militants," *The Washington Post*, February 21, 2011.

anywhere, at any time"—including their fellow citizens—"based on secret criteria and secret information discussed in a secret process" with no judicial oversight whatever;[5] or even to inquire of their leaders, actual or prospective, how many thousands will need to be killed in this manner before the War on Terror could finally be declared at an end—if in fact it ever can be. Behind the targeted killings, does the Obama administration have a strategy that will bring this war to some conclusion? Does Governor Romney?

As I write, amid the inescapable racket over what may or may not have happened one afternoon in Benghazi, these basic questions about the drone war, like the question of Palestine, remain unanswered and indeed largely unasked, beneath the ocean of silence. When the moderator of the last debate finally uttered the word "drones," Governor Romney was quick to say, "I support that entirely, and feel the president was right up to the usage of that technology," and, having noted earlier that "we can't kill our way out of this mess," went on to call for "a far more effective and comprehensive strategy"—focused on education and economic development—"to help move the world away from terror and Islamic extremism."

If the word "drone" has hardly been uttered—and if, when it finally was, the Republican challenger found himself vigorously supporting their use while spouting faintly progressive-sounding calls for regional development—it is not least because on this question, President Obama has taken a position so strongly in favor of unremitting military violence that he has left his Republican rival,

5. See Rosa Brooks, "Take Two Drones and Call Me in the Morning," *Foreign Policy*, September 12, 2012.

struggle though he may to shoulder his way past him, no place to stand. On the lingering war in Afghanistan and the possible one in Iran, Romney and Congressman Paul Ryan have harshly criticized Obama's policies even as they have largely embraced them. Caught in a vise of Obama's devising, the Republicans find themselves pressed on one side by the president's surge of troops into, and now withdrawal from, Afghanistan, and by his strong sanctions on Iran; and on the other side—should they be tempted to advocate perpetuating the Afghan war or starting a new one against Iran—by the country's lingering fatigue with the wars begun by George W. Bush.

Obama's dramatic escalation and prosecution of the drone campaign, his "surge" of troops into Afghanistan, his embrace of many of George Bush's national security policies (including warrantless wiretapping and military commissions and indefinite detention) that he bitterly criticized during his election campaign, even his failure to investigate and perhaps punish the use of torture, or to pay the political price to fulfill the promise, embodied in his executive order, to close Guantánamo: all these policies, even as they have disappointed and appalled supporters of human rights, have served to fortify the president's right flank, making him the first Democrat president since Harry S. Truman to enter a reelection campaign with few if any vulnerabilities on national security.

Truman is not a bad place to start if we want to make some sense of what has become the "Libya Scandal" or, simply, "Benghazi." How could one begin to explain to a visitor from another world that during the campaign to elect the leader of the most powerful nation on the planet the single clamorous foreign policy "debate" concerns the circumstances of the death of a single US ambassador and three US employees in a small backwater city on the Mediterranean littoral? Perhaps one might begin by pointing out that American electoral politics have less to do with policies than with the manipulation of symbols and with the search to find and artfully present that particular complex of symbols that together most powerfully evoke the emotions desired—in this case, a sense of vulnerability, of loss of control, of looming threat, and of panic and fear—that can begin to make plausible the Republicans' claim that what we were witnessing that afternoon in Benghazi, in the words of Paul Ryan, was "the absolute unraveling of the Obama administration's foreign policy."

President Truman would have well understood this, for it was he who in 1949 "lost China"—in the phrase his Republican adversaries coined to describe the Chinese Revolution—and thereby helped to begin a half-century of mostly Republican Party ascendancy when it came to national security and its governing cold war political question: In a world of unremitting danger, who can best keep us safe? In both cases, of course, the threats were real—though al-Qaeda's terrorism, unlike, say, the Soviet nuclear arsenal, never posed an existential threat to the country. But what matters is extracting from that threat the political gold—fear, the most lucrative political emotion—and artfully inflating, maintaining, and exploiting it.

But of these cold war origins—the world of "fellow travelers" and "security risks," of "red-baiting" politicians for their being "soft on communism"—came the lineaments of the politics of fear that we saw reemerge in the War on Terror. Indeed, within ten days of the attacks President Bush was arguing quite explicitly that the two "wars" were continuous, insisting that the terrorists who had attacked New York and Washington were "heirs of all the murderous ideologies of the 20th century."

> By sacrificing human life to serve their radical visions, by abandoning every value except the will to power, they follow in the path of fascism, Nazism and totalitarianism.[6]

This powerful rhetoric firmly anchored the War on Terror in the familiar political constellation of a four-decade-long cold war that, when it finally ended a decade before, had deprived Republicans of their most potent foreign policy issue. The September 11 attacks restored it, as President Bush's political Svengali, Karl Rove, pointed out a few months after they took place. "We can go to the American people on this issue of winning the war [against terror]," Rove told the Republican National Committee, "because they trust the Republican Party to do a better job of protecting and strengthening America's military might and thereby protecting America."[7] And indeed a few months later, President Bush, following the most murderous attacks on America in the country's history, accomplished what very few first-term presidents had before: he led his party to a decisive victory in a midterm election, winning back control of the Senate (with the help of a notable "terrorist-baiting" campaign against Senator Max Cleland of Georgia, in which a notorious advertisement superimposed the face of the severely wounded Vietnam war hero with that of... Osama bin Laden).

We still know little about the features of Ahmed Abu Khattalah or the other leaders of Ansar al-Sharia, the "local militant group determined to protect Libya from Western influence"—in David D.

6. See "Transcript of President Bush's address to a joint session of Congress on Thursday night, September 20, 2001," CNN.com.

7. Scott McClellan, *What Happened: Inside the Bush White House and Washington's Culture of Deception* (PublicAffairs, 2008), pp. 112–113.

Kirkpatrick's description in *The New York Times*—that attacked the US consulate in Benghazi on the evening of September 11, 2012, and after "an intense, four-hour firefight," burned it to the ground, leaving US Ambassador J. Christopher Stevens and three other Americans dead. I daresay if one of Ansar's leaders proves as photogenic as bin Laden, the airwaves and political advertisements will be flooded with his image soon.[8] Whether we'll ever know more of the facts of what actually happened that night is another matter. As I write they remain murky and disputed, notably regarding who exactly planned the attack and when, whether al-Qaeda really had any hand in it, and precisely how the evolving information about what happened made its way through the American government. Of course, the difficulty of answering definitively these central questions, and the drip drip drip of information emerging day by day, hour by hour, mainly from leaks within various parts of the government with their own interests at stake, are essential to keeping the scandal alive and thriving.

Early reports tell us that members of the group had been angered by the circulation on YouTube of a by-then-notorious "anti-Islam video," and attacked the consulate in Benghazi. According to *The New York Times*, there was "some level of advance planning," but according to Bloomberg News, the raid on the embassy was "a hasty and poorly organized act by men with basic military training and access to weapons widely available in Libya."[9] They assaulted the compound with mortars, rocket-propelled grenades, and, perhaps,

8. See David D. Kirkpatrick, "Suspect in Libya Attack, in Plain Sight, Scoffs at US," *The New York Times*, October 18, 2012.

9. John Walcott and Christopher Stephen, "Evidence Points to Hasty Strike on US Compound in Libya," Bloomberg News, October 16, 2012.

an antiaircraft weapon. Unable to breach the consulate's "safe room," the militiamen set the building on fire using canisters filled with diesel fuel, trapping the ambassador inside. Looters later found him unconscious, overcome by smoke inhalation, and carried him to the hospital, where attempts to revive him failed.

For all the ambiguities, according to the *Times*, "Libyans who witnessed the assault and know the attackers" have "little doubt what occurred":

> A well-known group of local Islamist militants struck the United States Mission without any warning or protest, and they did it in retaliation for the video. That is what the fighters said at the time, speaking emotionally of their anger at the video without mentioning Al Qaeda, Osama bin Laden or the terrorist strikes of 11 years earlier.

Which is to say, though there appear to have been demonstrations against the YouTube video in Benghazi that evening, the attack on the consulate did not emerge from those demonstrations, as officials of the Obama administration initially maintained (and as did, it should be said, the *Times* and other reporters)—and as at least some officials were still maintaining five days after the fact. At the same time, while Republicans asserted with increasing vehemence that the attack was a pre-planned terrorist operation directed by al-Qaeda, they have produced no evidence to support that or to contradict the officials of the National Counterterrorism Center, who told Bloomberg News that "the al-Qaeda groups learned of the assault only after one of the attackers called to boast of it."

Seizing hold of this rather unpromising germ of sordid violence, the well-tuned scandal machinery of the right—the oversight committees in the Republican-controlled Congress working hand in glove with ardent publicists on Fox News and other outlets—probed and exploited its ambiguities and, with the considerable help of the administration's own initial mistakes, inflated it into, in Governor Romney's words, an "attack by terrorists . . . [that] calls into question the president's whole policy in the Middle East." In this task they were helped immeasurably not only by the ongoing inability of intelligence officials and reporters to answer definitively some critical questions—such as the group's true relationship to al-Qaeda—but by an initial shading of the story by some Obama officials that may have been politically motivated, for the wedge needed to broaden the disputed events of Benghazi into this broad indictment was the implication, and later the assertion, that the administration lied. Though President Obama did refer vaguely to "acts of terror" in his Rose Garden statement the morning after the attack, the insistence by other officials that the attack was "spontaneous, not premeditated" led Republicans to charge what has become necessary for the construction of any respectable American political scandal: a cover-up.

What was being covered up? Since the White House was "trying to sell a narrative, quite frankly, about the Mideast that the wars are receding and that al-Qaeda's been dismantled," as Senator Lindsey Graham, Republican of South Carolina, put it, acknowledging that "an al-Qaeda-affiliated militia" had attacked the US consulate in "the first successful terrorist attack on our country since September 11, 2001"—the words are Ari Fleischer's, George W. Bush's former spokesman—would not only have undermined that story but revealed instead "the absolute unraveling of the Obama foreign policy." The Republican vice-presidential candidate went on to shape that argument in familiar terms:

> What we are witnessing is the projection of weakness. And that projection of weakness emboldens our adversaries and scares our allies. You see, if we look weak, our adversaries are more willing and more brazen [*sic*] to test us, and our allies are less willing to trust us. It's a dangerous world. We are at war with terrorists. Let's not forget that.

The words recall not only President Bush's 2004 reelection campaign—when Vice President Cheney warned voters that "if we make the wrong choice then the danger is that we'll get hit again and we'll be hit in a way that will be devastating"—but echo cold war warnings not to "show weakness" before the monolithic power of the Soviet Union. Governor Romney expanded the analogy in his foreign policy address on October 8:

> The attack on our Consulate in Benghazi on September 11th, 2012, was likely the work of forces affiliated with those that attacked our homeland on September 11th, 2001.... These attacks were the deliberate work of terrorists who use violence to impose their dark ideology on others...; who are fighting to control much of the Middle East today; and who seek to wage perpetual war on the West....
>
> This is the struggle that is now shaking the entire Middle East to its foundation... a struggle between liberty and tyranny, justice and oppression, hope and despair.
>
> We have seen this struggle before. It would be familiar to George

Marshall. In his time, in the ashes of world war, another critical part of the world was torn between democracy and despotism.

In the face of this challenge, as the governor put it during the second debate on October 16, "the president's policies throughout the Middle East began with an apology tour and—and—and pursue a strategy of leading from behind, and this strategy is unraveling before our very eyes."

The logic here is shaky indeed: that Obama officials shaped their early accounts for political motives has by no means been proved; indeed, according to a report in *The Wall Street Journal* published on the morning of the third and final debate, the president himself "was told in his daily briefing for more than a week after the consulate siege . . . that the assault grew out of a spontaneous protest."[10] One might expect this information would dim the ardor of Republicans convinced that the administration was trying to cover up the facts. Still, whatever new leaks may or may not tell us in coming days about what the government knew, what happened in Benghazi seems a very far cry from the unraveling of the country's Middle East policy.

But the terms here preexisted the event; the constellation of words and symbols meant to elicit apprehension and vulnerability and fear have been established by long practice and only await the "content" that will set them in motion. Still, this content, at least what we know of it so far, seems unequal to the task. It is as if a large, mechanical monster, complete with frightful grimace and bared

10. See Adam Entous and Siobhan Gorman, "Intelligence Stressed Libya Protest Scenario," *The Wall Street Journal*, October 22, 2012.

teeth, has been dragged, clanking and clattering, back out on stage, but though the great old beast still engenders apprehension, the figure its masters are hoping to fit inside to reanimate it is simply too small and too puny to put it convincingly through its paces.

The second problem is that in place of Obama's "unraveling" foreign policy Governor Romney offers little more than ... Obama's foreign policy, after adding a sprinkling of platitudes and a strong dose of nostalgia. A Romney administration would supply not a new initiative in the Middle East—an effort to address the Palestinian issue, for example—but ... "leadership," along with "confidence in our cause, clarity in our purpose and resolve in our might." In practical terms, this would seem to mean maintaining Obama's sanctions on Iran, and perhaps tightening them; pursuing Obama's "real and successful transition to Afghan security forces by the end of 2014" while "evaluat[ing] conditions on the ground"; supplying arms through third parties to some factions of the Syrian rebels, as the Obama administration is reportedly already doing; "reaffirm[ing]" the country's "historic ties" to Israel; and "deepen[ing] our critical cooperation with our partners in the Gulf." President Romney would add fifteen new ships a year to the US Navy, doubling the current building program, and would "roll back President Obama's deep and arbitrary cuts to our national defense"—though these do not in fact exist, having been agreed to with Republicans in a wholly notional budget deal (called "sequestration"). Finally, bringing together all these minute "initiatives," we have the capstone in Romney's foreign policy address:

> There is a longing for American leadership in the Middle East.... It is broadly felt by America's friends and allies in other parts of the

world as well—in Europe, where Putin's Russia casts a long shadow over young democracies.... I believe that if America does not lead, others will—others who do not share our interests and our values—and the world will grow darker....

The music is familiar here, the tunes a half-century old, but in the lyrics we find no new ideas, no creative policies—to deal with Egypt, for example, and the other challenges presented by the young, struggling democracies of the Middle East and North Africa. Here a new initiative on the Palestinian issue, vigorously pursued, might actually reduce the influence of extremist forces, and the anti-American sentiments on which they thrive, and help to stabilize struggling moderate governments of countries, like Egypt, that have long been allied to the US. But what we get is only a vague reference to negotiations and the hope, privately expressed and no doubt more sincere, that when it comes to this conflict a President Romney would "kick the ball down the field and hope that ultimately, somehow, something will happen and resolve it."

Though Obama's policies in the Middle East, after the grand rhetorical gestures at the start of his term, have been largely improvisational and opportunistic—and though those policies are now dangerously "unraveling"—to replace them Romney can offer only a longing for an imagined past in which aircraft carriers and the "leadership" they convey could keep the old familiar order, autocratic, sclerotic, predictable, firmly in place. Whatever else one can say about today's Middle East, that order is largely gone. In response to the roiling political struggles that have overtaken it, we hear only a pale conjuring of fear, and behind that only silence.

Against this inarticulate longing stands President Obama and his ferocious prosecution of the War on Terror. If the politics of fear has lost its magic for the Republican right it is not least because its methods have been co-opted by the Democrat in the White House, who has been relentless in hunting down terrorists, and those who may look like terrorists, and killing them by the thousands. No one can criticize him for investigating the CIA for torture, for he has conducted no such investigation. No one can attack him for abandoning President Bush's indefinite detention policy because he has, in the case of the prisoners who "can neither be tried nor released," regularized and legalized it. And no one can denounce him for closing Guantánamo because Guantánamo has not been closed.[11]

Indeed, Republicans, who reportedly plan to reinstate "enhanced interrogation techniques against high-value detainees" in a Romney administration, make the plausible claim that the president, after officially halting torture on his second day in office, has in practice avoided the knotty questions of interrogation, "enhanced" or otherwise, by managing during his War on Terror to avoid taking prisoners.[12] Drones have largely replaced the interrogation room. And our leaders and those seeking to replace them will not debate drone warfare because on this as on other pressing matters raised by our

11. Today 166 detainees remain in Guantánamo, down from a peak of 779 under George W. Bush and 242 under Obama. See "Guantanamo by the Numbers," Human Rights First. [As of July 2026, fifteen detainees remain in Guantánamo.]

12. See " Interrogation Techniques," a campaign policy paper written by former Bush and Reagan officials, which notes that "Governor Romney has recommended for years that a sounder policy outcome is the revival of the enhanced interrogation program" and urges him to "expressly endorse such an outcome during the campaign," or risk "signaling to the bureaucracy that this is not a deeply-felt priority." Also Charlie Savage, "Election to Decide Future Interrogation Methods in Terrorism Cases," *The New York Times*, September 27, 2012.

permanent War on Terror there is no longer an opposition. Both parties have embroiled themselves full-force in the struggle to be tough, and tougher. If President Obama has made himself largely invulnerable to the politics of fear it is because he has to a great extent taken it over in advance by his cool and ruthless methods, and left little political space for discussion.

This then is the final silence of our election campaign, particularly resonant here in the hills of Palestine. Across eleven years of the War on Terror, and two presidents, the politics of fear have not been forestalled, or banished, or defeated. The politics of fear have been embodied in the country's permanent policies, without comment or objection by its citizenry. The politics of fear have won.

How, and What, Obama Won

December 20, 2012

1.

Columbus, Ohio

CLAMOROUS AND OVERPOWERING, campaign images are vivid as dreams and vanish as quickly. Was it real, that huge white aircraft hangar in Columbus, Ohio, the night before the election? I'd raced there from downtown Columbus's Nationwide Arena, where President Obama, introduced by Bruce Springsteen and Jay-Z, his voice hoarse and his face worn, had addressed fifteen thousand or so enthusiastic, mostly young supporters. From the moment Springsteen had begun singing ("*No retreat, baby, no surrender…*"), they had risen to their feet, cheered, shouted and stomped, and, on hearing Romney's name, lustily booed. ("Don't boo—*vote*!" Obama had answered. "Folks can't hear you boo, but they can hear you *vote*!")

But the sound at Nationwide Arena, though the crowd was larger, had been nothing compared to the volcano of noise erupting in that aircraft hangar. Its white metal walls seemed to reverberate back the shouts and cheers ("One More Day! One More Day!") of thousands of sweating partisans, packed cheek by jowl, hip to hip, the press of bodies becoming almost unbearable beneath the country music whining over the tinny sound system—until finally, blessedly, a bit of breeze seeped in and the realization swept visibly through the throng that the great hangar doors were slowly clattering open to reveal an enormous blue and white airliner—*his* plane!—rumbling directly into the crowd. Or trying to rumble in, for as the cheers rose to an almost unendurable pitch, the pilot managed to miss the door, backed up, revved his engines, and on a second try barely nosed his way in. And then the stairway is wheeled up and the door opens and, waving and beaming to the whining, deafening strains of "Born Free," out comes . . . *the next president of the United States!*

Mitt Romney is a handsome man and, in a slightly exaggerated, Senator Forehead kind of way, truly does look like he was born to be president. What strikes one, though, at this impossibly sound-drenched moment in a Columbus aircraft hangar on the evening before the election, is that along with this crowd of deliriously certain supporters, the candidate himself, in his benevolent, confident gaze over the crowd, appears completely convinced that he will indeed be elected president the next day.

On this election eve I receive incredulous, faintly hostile stares when I ask supporters whether they think Romney will be elected tomorrow. "What do you mean?" a young blond woman in her thirties asks me in turn, stopping in her tracks, her pretty face crunching into perplexity. "How do you . . . just what are you asking?" She'd been friendly as we'd chatted but in the chill half-light outside the hangar I see her face darken, as she realizes I really am one of *them*—one of the heathen, unbelieving press, who have been penned inside a little holding area in the midst of the crush, crouching over laptops or perching behind cameras under uniformly unforgiving stares.

It is a peculiarity of this election that the Republicans embraced up until and indeed after the moment of voting a conviction that the entire public information and polling apparatus of the country, with a few exceptions, was lying. "All of it, the reporters, the commentators, all the damn so-called 'news'—and the polls, especially the polls, you can't trust any of it," a retired businessman told me in early October at a Romney rally in Port St. Lucie, Florida. "I mean, who the hell are they talking to? Not any of us, certainly," he said, sweeping his arm in an arc around him. And, turning away, "They're all in the bag for Obama. Can't believe a word of it."

This was in the wake of the first debate, when Obama, faltering and shuffling about behind his podium with downturned eyes, had shown himself to be what they had always known he was: a myth and a fraud, a dark nightmare version of the tiny wizard quailing behind the immense Oz-like image built of him in 2008 and still sustained by the press and the commentariat and the grasping members of the 47 percent. "You saw what he really was, once you take away his teleprompter"—I heard this again and again from Romney supporters. Obama was a fake, a fabrication of the liberal media and of those who drew sustenance from the programs of dependency he distributed like so much candy. When Romney first uttered the president's name at Port St. Lucie, a beefy T-shirted young man behind me, a football player by the well-fed looks of him, cupped his hands about his mouth and roared out, "He's an *idiot*!"—convulsing the entire all-white crowd in laughter.

The notion of a pervasive constructed world of falsehood and illusion built on the fabrications of the press and the liberal establishment has long been central to the American far right.[1] And since Ronald Reagan and Barry Goldwater before him, the knowledge that its supporters have their own truth, that they are forced to battle continually against an intensively propagandized false reality, has been a vital energizing trump of "movement" Republicans. It means that Republicans, whether in power or not, are always in opposition. Even when they hold the White House and Congress, still the great bulk of the news media in New York and Washington with its vaunted "objectivity"; the culture industry in New York and California with its Hollywood vulgarity and easy virtues; the permanent bureaucracy of unionized government employees and teachers with their sinecures and perks—all remain immovably liberal. Republicans, "in power" or not, are forced to struggle always to conquer false truth, and that constant struggle has been a source of great motivating mobilizing power, as we last saw during the town meetings against the health care bill in the summer of 2009 and the Tea Party electoral triumph that followed.

Of course occasionally into these great self-sustaining master narratives comes a rude interruption from something . . . real. Holding my hands over my ears as I gazed at Romney's plane struggling to make its resplendent way into the Columbus hangar I suddenly thought of George W. Bush's flight-suited swagger against the deck of the USS *Abraham Lincoln* on May 1, 2003: the *Lincoln*, within sight of the California coast, had been carefully turned so that live

1. See Richard Hofstadter, *The Paranoid Style in American Politics and Other Essays* (Harvard University Press, 1996).

shots of the triumphant "war president" would not reveal the cityscape of San Diego—but on the other side of the globe Baghdad was being looted and all the Leni Riefenstahl "Mission Accomplished" moments in the world would not prevent Americans from eventually realizing that the Iraq war was an unholy mess: a war of choice badly planned, catastrophically executed, and impossible to escape. It took a year or more and a couple thousand American lives, and in the meantime President Bush, after a negative, base-dependent campaign not all that different from Obama's this year, scraped to reelection.

Reality's reemergence in the 2012 election followed a more precise timeline. Before the polls closed, Romney's campaign was pointing to clear victory:

> On a midafternoon conference call with political insiders, Romney campaign brass ticked off a list of data points about turnout—in mega-swing states such as Colorado, Ohio and Florida—that they called signs that victory was at hand. They warned that people shouldn't take the media consortium exit polling too seriously, since it would most likely be wrong.[2]

Unfortunately, the campaign's own highly touted get-out-the-vote operation, presided over by an elaborate "state-of-the-art" data manager dubbed Project ORCA, had already shown itself to be "dysfunctional." "At the end of the day," a Romney worker told *Politico*, "they told us that every single swing state was looking either

2. See Maggie Haberman and Alexander Burns, "Mitt Romney's ORCA Program Couldn't Stay Afloat," *Politico*, November 9, 2012.

pink or red and the worst one was Virginia, where they were a little concerned."

Romney and reality were still traveling along parallel tracks, not touching. "The polling we had. The numbers we were looking at looked like we stood a pretty good chance of winning," Paul Ryan said later. "So, when the numbers came in, going the other direction. When we saw the turnout that was occurring in urban areas which were really fairly unprecedented, it did come as a bit of a shock."[3]

In truth, this "turnout . . . in urban areas" was not far from a repeat of 2008. And for the Republicans, that was the problem: 2008 was the mythical year, the illegitimate year, the year of illusions when a young unknown African-American community organizer and senator-for-a-minute with virtually no experience managed to hoodwink the American electorate and, with the help of two unpopular wars and an economic catastrophe, seize the White House. All the confident and specific predictions of a Romney landslide by prominent conservatives like Michael Barone, George Will, Karl Rove, and Dick Morris were built on the conviction that 2008 could not be repeated.[4] As Morris said later:

> All of my analysis of the polling that suggested to me . . . that in fact Obama would lose by a significant margin were all based . . . on the assumption that they were *wrong*, the media was *wrong*, in saying that there would be the same high level of black, Latino, and young

3. See Tom Kludt, "Ryan: It 'Looked Like We Stood a Pretty Good Chance of Winning' on Election Day," *TPM LiveWire*, November 13, 2012.

4. See, for example, Michael Barone, "Prediction: Romney Beats Obama, Handily," *National Journal*, November 5, 2012. See also "Eight Conservatives Predicting a Romney Victory Tomorrow," Fairfaxunderground.com.

voter turnout in 2012 that there was in '08.... I figured that '08 was just an excrescence....[5]

This "excrescence" theory was central to Governor Romney's own conception of the electorate, which also envisioned many fewer Democrats voting. Obama's base, disillusioned, would stay away from the polls. The winner, therefore, would be the candidate who won the independents—which Romney indeed managed to do, by five points, though in the end it didn't matter because he was overwhelmed by turnout among the decidedly undisillusioned Democratic base.[6]

This was not the only way that 2012 recalled Bush's close reelection in 2004, masterminded as it was by Karl Rove, then Bush's "political brain" and now the most powerful Super PAC Republican fund-raiser. Though it is not clear when exactly it dawned on the Romney-Ryan team that those actually turning out to vote on election day were not conforming to their models, Americans were able to witness, in real time, the astonishing moment when reality, staved off for months by models and self-serving predictions, finally swooped down and smacked Karl Rove on the top of his head.

The drama, which immediately went viral as "Karl Rove's Public Meltdown on Fox," began at 11:25 Eastern time, when Fox called Ohio for Obama and Rove, who had, said anchor Chris Wallace, "a rooting interest" in the decision—presumably the hundreds of millions he had raised to elect Mitt Romney and the calls he was even

5. See Dick Morris, "Why I Goofed! *Dick Morris TV: Lunch Alert!*" Dick Morris .com, November 7, 2012.

6. See John Dickerson, "Why Romney Never Saw It Coming," *Slate*, November 9, 2012.

then fielding from campaign officials—expressed strong skepticism. "Even if they have made [the prediction] on the basis of select precincts," said Rove, "I'd be very cautious about *intruding in this process....*"

And yet the polls had long since closed. Did Rove fear that an early prediction could shape a post-election political struggle (as Florida, prematurely called for Bush, had in 2000)? At Fox, whose broadcasters had for months been promoting a rock-hard certainty about a Romney victory, something very odd now unfolded:

Bret Baier (anchor): Karl Rove said we should figure out what the deal is with this decision desk....

Megyn Kelly: ... We'll do a little interrogation and see if they stand by their call, notwithstanding the doubts that Karl is attempting to place....

With cameras in tow, Kelly walked down bare hallways where several eager number crunchers awaited her:

Kelly: Is this possibly an exit poll thing ... ?

Arnon Mishkin: What we're looking at is actual raw vote, by county by county, city by city, and what we're seeing is sufficient vote in Ohio on the Democratic side to mean that Ohio will go for Obama.

Kelly: Percent certainty?

Mishkin: 99.95 percent....

The camera moves back to the desk where Baier is watching a furiously scribbling Rove:

Baier: . . . I've just called Karl back up from the, and he's coming back up here to the desk. He's crunching numbers, he's writing furiously, he's pointing at Bill Hemmer. A lot of things are going on right now. . . .

We're going to "tee" the graphic there. "Barack Obama Re-Elected President." That's our call. From the decision desk. As you saw, Megyn Kelly just walking down to talk to them. The White House, there is already a crowd in front of the White House . . . 1600 Pennsylvania Avenue. . . .

Fox, following NBC and MSNBC, calls the election for Obama. Rove, still scribbling, protests:

Rove: But again I just wonder when you're sitting there with . . . a difference [of] 49.19 to 49.17, if a little bit of caution might not be better until . . . I mean, if it's gonna happen let the votes begin to show it . . . and start to see some of that separation so you're *validating* it. . . . In terms of public perception, it looks a little odd for us to be making a call with 991 votes. . . .

Watching this extraordinary scene play out from Jacksonville, Florida—where the votes from the enormous turnout were still being counted and where the election would not be called for days—I heard the soft sound of a loop being pulled tight, as I recalled the most telling quotation of the entire Bush era, words about "creating reality" uttered in the months before the 2004 reelection of George W. Bush. They describe a dialogue between the reporter Ron Suskind and a then anonymous Bush "aide" who was none other than Karl Rove:

> The aide said that guys like me were "in what we call the reality-based community," which he defined as people who "believe that solutions emerge from your judicious study of discernible reality." I nodded and murmured something about enlightenment principles and empiricism. He cut me off. "That's not the way the world really works anymore," he continued. "We're an empire now, and when we act, we create our own reality. And while you're studying that reality—judiciously, as you will—we'll act again, creating other new realities, which you can study too, and that's how things will sort out. We're history's actors . . . and you, all of you, will be left to just study what we do."[7]

2.

History's actor, left scribbling and protesting on a Fox News set beneath a huge red, white, and blue graphic emblazoned BARACK OBAMA RE-ELECTED PRESIDENT, had been replaced. Obama and his campaign, in proving that the 2008 winning coalition led by blacks, Latinos, young people, and women was no excrescence, changed history. Dick Morris draws the stark conclusion that "this signals a permanent change in the American electorate." Morris goes on:

> This is not your father's United States. This is a United States with a permanently high turnout of blacks, Latinos, and young people.
>
> For many, many years the Republican Party has been a group of

7. Ron Suskind, "Faith, Certainty and the Presidency of George W. Bush," *The New York Times Magazine*, October 17, 2004.

committed conservatives who believe in limited government who live in a sea of people that don't really see it that way. And the Republicans have survived and stayed in power because the turnout of everybody else was lower and their turnout was higher.

Well, that finally caught up with us yesterday. And if Mitt Romney, a very good candidate, running a very good campaign—some flaws but very good—couldn't beat Obama, a dismal failure as president, in the middle of the worst recession since the Thirties, then no Republican can win in this electorate unless we make fundamental changes in the approach the Republican Party has to African-Americans, Latinos, and young people.... We can no longer skate by hoping for a reduced turnout among those groups.[8]

There is no way to know whether Barack Obama's reelection really does signal the advent of a "permanently high turnout of blacks, Latinos, and young people," which in any event is rather a caricature (leaving out, notably, educated suburbanites, and quite different electorates in New Hampshire, Iowa, and Wisconsin). Rove too thought he was building a "permanent majority" in shaping the coalition that reelected George W. Bush. He too depended on generating enormous turnout from among his party's base—by relentlessly targeting exurban conservatives—and battering the challenger ruthlessly with negative ads.

It was a delicious post-election moment when Rove complained that Obama had won reelection only by "suppressing the vote" with these ads, for in spending tens of millions in the summer of 2012 to destroy Mitt Romney's reputation as a competent businessman and

8. See Dick Morris, "Why I Goofed!"

paint him as a rapacious job-destroying plutocrat, David Axelrod was doing to Romney precisely what Rove had done to John Kerry in "swift-boating" him in the summer of 2004. Each identified early the challenger's perceived strength—military heroism and competence with Kerry, business and economic expertise with Romney—and attacked it directly, relentlessly, ruthlessly.[9] And it worked. Though after his victory in the first debate Romney saw his "positives" rise dramatically in nationwide polls, in the swing states, where the early negative advertising had been intense, they never recovered.[10]

On the positive side, Obama's campaign depended on an intensely modern and innovative organizing effort that proved stunningly effective in reaching sympathetic voters and getting them to the polls. At every rally a volunteer would mount the podium to instruct the crowd to "get out your cell phones" and tens of thousands of hands would dutifully hold up their phones to text, simultaneously, "Obama" and place themselves on the vast campaign organizing lists—and thus into a tenacious network that would track and coax them, and their family and friends, and millions of others, all the way to the voting booth.[11]

The administration supplemented this unprecedented "ground game" with election-year "constituency servicing" that would have been instantly recognizable to Franklin Roosevelt. Using an execu-

9. As of October 21, the Obama campaign and associated groups had spent $275 million on advertisements—only 14 percent of which were positive. Romney had spent $319 million on ads, 20 percent of them positive. See "The Ads Take Aim," *The Economist*, November 2, 2012.

10. See Charlie Cook, "Obama Can Thank Early Negative Ads for His Advantage," *National Journal*, November 1, 2012.

11. See, for example, Jim Rutenberg, "Secret of the Obama Victory? Rerun Watchers, for One Thing," *The New York Times*, November 12, 2012.

tive order, President Obama imposed key provisions of the stalled Dream Act and postponed deportation of Latinos (71 percent of whom voted for him). He repealed Don't Ask, Don't Tell and spoke out in support of marriage equality, expanded student loans while reducing interest rates, made it possible for young people to remain on their parents' health insurance until they are twenty-six, and guaranteed coverage for contraceptives and family planning—all policies popular among young voters and women (who favored him with their votes, respectively, by 60 and 55 percent).

In a bitter post-election conference call with his donors, Governor Romney denigrated these "gifts," complaining that Democrats were just following "the old playbook" and bribing voters:

> You can imagine for somebody making $25,000 or $30,000 or $35,000 a year, being told you're now going to get free health care... worth, what, $10,000 per family, in perpetuity—I mean, this is huge.[12]

The voice was that of the unforgiving plutocratic Romney who talked of "the 47 percent," but in fact he had a point: providing health care coverage to those who didn't have it *was* "huge." "Policies don't win elections," runs the old political maxim, "constituencies win elections." And from the White House Obama had done much to serve his constituencies. Whether this was bribery, as Romney would have it, or effective and responsive governance depends on your view of what the government should properly do—an issue on

12. See Ashley Parker, "Romney Blames Loss on 'Gifts' to Minorities and Young Voters," *The New York Times*, November 14, 2012.

which the candidates dramatically differed. As Obama never tired of repeating, the election was a choice between "two visions of America." In introducing Romney at a rally in Port St. Lucie, Florida representative Allen West, an African-American Republican congressman who had served as an army officer in Iraq, set out those visions starkly in what he called "the race for America":

> It is a race between what is simply called the opportunity society versus the dependency society.... We're talking about limited government. We're talking about fiscal responsibility. We're talking about your individual sovereignty. We're talking about the free market....
>
> The other side... they don't believe in that. They believe in taking over more of our production and you see that each and every day. They believe in creating and expanding a welfare nanny state and you see that with the unemployment, you see that with the food stamps, you see that with Americans in poverty.... They believe in taking more of your rights and freedom and your liberties. They don't believe in the free market. They believe in trickle-down government.... *That's not America!*

West's is an extreme and purified Tea Party version of the philosophy that came sweeping out of California in 1978, with the property tax limits of Proposition 13, and whose embodiment, Ronald Reagan, conquered the White House two years later, launching the current conservative era.

For West as for Governor Romney, Obama's policies, particularly his Affordable Care Act, represent yet another step down the road to the dependency society—and another patronage machine Democrats can use to buy votes. For them, the cheering thousands at the

Obama rallies, and the vast "turnout . . . in urban areas" on election day, came not least because these people were getting something from government—food stamps, student loans, health care, Social Security—and they wanted to ensure, by their votes, that they would keep on getting it. Romney, in limiting himself, as he ruefully told donors after his defeat, to "talking about big issues for the whole country: military strategy, foreign policy, a strong economy, creating jobs and so forth," was simply not able to compete with the array of glittering Christmas presents coming out of the White House.

Another way to say this is that President Obama, as he repeated constantly, really does believe that "America always does best when everybody gets a fair shot"—and that a majority of those who came out to vote, especially those who felt themselves excluded (and had been reminded of that by Mitt Romney's "47 percent" comments), agreed with him. Though Obama had been responsible for the greatest expansion of the welfare state since Lyndon Johnson, and though his speeches grew more populist as the voting approached—

> I ran because the voices of the American people—your voices—had been shut out of our democracy for way too long by lobbyists and special interests and politicians. . . . Over the last four years, the status quo in Washington has fought us every step of the way.

—he spoke mostly not about overcoming the status quo to enact new programs but about fighting it to hold on to the gains people had made. In Columbus that last day his message was clear: it was the "status quo" that was aggressive and threatening, that proposed to take things away, and it was he, Obama, who would be "the champion" to block that from happening:

> We've got to make sure that if the price of peace in Washington is cutting deals that are going to kick students off of financial aid, or get rid of funding for Planned Parenthood, or let insurance companies discriminate against people with preexisting conditions, or eliminate health care for millions on Medicaid who are poor or elderly or disabled, that's not a price I'm willing to pay.... That's surrender to the same status quo that's hurt middle-class families for way too long....
>
> The folks at the very top in this country, they don't need another champion in Washington....
>
> The laid-off worker who is having to go back and retrain at the age of 55 at a community college—she needs a champion.... The cooks and waiters and cleaning staff working overtime at a Columbus hotel, trying to save enough to buy a first home or send their kids to college—they need a champion.

These words bespeak a struggle that is in large part defensive, to conserve the gains of the social welfare state. And they speak to people who don't need to be called "the 47 percent" or "the society of dependency" to know that those gains are under fierce attack.

Obama's words, together with the vast get-out-the-vote effort engineered by the wizards in Chicago and Washington and embodied in the efforts of tens of thousands of volunteers, sent enough Americans surging to the polls to overcome voter suppression efforts in Florida and Ohio and Pennsylvania and return "the champion" to the White House. With no small help from ruthless gerrymandering, those same voters also returned a Republican Congress, ensuring that the representatives "of the status quo"—those who seek to dismantle the welfare state—will hold checkmate force in Washington.

Though major Tea Party figures, including Allen West, were defeated, enough were returned that the lineaments of our politics will likely look not dramatically different after the election than before it. But whether his reelection really signals, as Dick Morris insists, a "permanent change in the American electorate," it shows that Obama is no fluke. Republicans will have to work with him on a deal that will prune but largely protect major entitlement programs and draw more revenue from well-to-do Americans. Still, unless Obama can devise a way to attract his coalition to the polls to retake Congress in 2014, it is hard to see where he will find the huge infusion of money that he would need to set people to work rebuilding roads and bridges and schools, or to hire hundreds of thousands of teachers, or to make college "more affordable for everyone," all of which the president has pledged to do.

Obama's second term will likely be a hard slog "forward"(as his modest, one-word campaign slogan put it): capturing new revenue while protecting major entitlements in a budget deal, passing immigration reform, and gradually, as the various parts of the Affordable Care Act take effect, providing tens of millions more Americans with health insurance. That will be, however modest and halting and imperfect, real change. The gifts Barack Obama brings as a politician, his attraction for certain constituencies, may not be replicable; but for Democrats he has shown the way, and perhaps it is not too much to say that, with his reelection and the permanent imposition of national health care that it makes possible, the great wave of the conservative revolution that swept over the country's politics in 1980 and has dominated ever since may at last have reached its limit. Only with the next election—and those who, post-Obama, turn out to vote in it—will we see if that wave really has begun to recede, revealing not just struggles to be fought but new possibilities to be realized. That truly would be the reality-based community's revenge.

On the Election

November 10, 2016

All American elections tend to be touted as historic, for all American culture tends toward the condition of hype. Flummoxing, then, to be confronted with a struggle for political power in which, for once, all is at stake. We have long since forfeited the words to confront it, rendering superlatives threadbare, impotent. No accident that among so many other things Donald J. Trump is the Candidate of Dead Words, spewing "fantastic" and "amazing" and "huge" in all directions, clogging the airtime broadcasters have lavished upon him with a deadening rhetoric reminiscent of the raving man hunched beside you on the bar stool. "This country is a disaster." "We're in big trouble, folks." "Our leaders don't know what they're doing." Or his favorite declarative closer to those 140-character Twitter dispatches that form the campaign's anti-poetry, "Sad!" It is our loss that Mario Cuomo, who famously offered that "you campaign in poetry; you govern in prose," is no longer here to enlighten us about in what, if we campaign in tweets and dead superlatives, we are destined to govern.

We have no idea. While on one side we have a vague conception of what our future politics might be—a professedly progressive government of familiar faces and uncertain success, dogged to a greater or lesser degree by congressional opposition and revivified scandal—on the other we have terrifyingly little notion. For the animating element of the Trump campaign, beyond its self-propelling cycle of insult and crass entertainment, is not a positive political program—renegotiating trade deals or imposing a Muslim immigration ban or even building an "impenetrable and beautiful" Mexico wall—but a kind of furious and exasperated nihilism about government as it exists and the broader discredited elite from which it emanates: the corruption, the back-scratching, the self-dealing.

The most powerful emotion one feels at a Trump rally is a great bellowing lust to scrub thoroughly the Augean stables and to entertain raucously while shoveling out the shit.[1] *Throw them out!* And the "them," it should be emphasized, is proudly nonpartisan: the elite of the Republican Party counts as corrupt as that of the Democratic; longtime conservative newspapers are no less representatives of the "lamestream media" than the liberal *New York Times*.

Thus their candidate may declare that he might refuse to support NATO members in the Baltics or that he might offer nuclear weapons to the Japanese or South Koreans or apply waterboarding or something "a hell of a lot worse" to any captured terrorist. Whatever principle of the postwar *Pax Americana* he blithely shatters, and however many "national security leaders" from Republican administrations issue yet another condemnation of Trump and pledge to vote for Hillary, this will do little but reassure his supporters. That

1. See my report, "The Magic of Donald Trump," *The New York Review*, May 26, 2016.

their candidate offends, disgusts, appalls the elite and won't seriously apologize for it, that, as we have seen, he refuses to back down from the grossest violations of "politically correct" discourse in matters of race and sex, reaffirms that he, unlike all who have come before with their pallid pledges to "change Washington," might actually do it. The shocked, disgusted elite is not only an object of scorn and derision but an affirmation of his strength. And he is all about strength, a kind of embodied id.

It is this darkly echoing "no!" at the heart of the Trump campaign, joined to its permanent revolution of insult and entertainment, that makes the present moment so vertiginous. We have lived moments before in which the heretofore unquestioned political lineaments of our world seemed rendered suddenly unstable, fragile, mutable. But these were moments of sudden violence—the world-altering rifle shots of 1963 and 1968; the planes and towers of 2001—not a slow-motion reality freak show in which what we had believed to be the remaining sacrosanct conventions of our politics were thoroughly and methodically trampled underfoot like so many discarded banners and placards, so many punctured balloons...

What are these bedraggled balloons? Truth, say? Facts? An attention to qualifications? A respect for experience? An attending to... rationality? It is true that Trump appalls with the baroque flagrancy of his vanity and self-obsession, like those neurotics we sometimes meet whose obsessions are so self-assertive that we seem to be staring directly into their skulls: as with them, the forced intimacy of the encounter can border on the nauseating.

But perhaps this is all sanctimonious illusion. Perhaps we are seeing punctured here misconceptions long entertained, perpetuated through lack of challenge. Ronald Reagan, of whom Trump in some ways is a caricature,[2] maintained a decidedly capricious relationship with the truth. George W. Bush's self-styled imperial administration declared that "we're an empire now, and when we act, we create our own reality...." Is Trump simply thrusting full into our faces currents we have struggled to ignore? The "plunge of civilization into this abyss of blood and darkness," wrote Henry James at the outset of World War I,

> so gives away the whole long age during which we have supposed the world to be, with whatever abatement, gradually bettering, that to have to take it all now for what the treacherous years were all the while really making for and *meaning* is too tragic for any words.

Is Donald J. Trump really what the whole long age was gradually making for and *meaning*? That a reality television star and businessman con artist devoid of public office experience and proudly ignorant of public policy, of braggadocious and offensive and unstable character, given to the most bald-faced race-baiting and misogyny and demagoguery, could nonetheless be elected by our fellow citizens president of the United States?

It should be observed that this is not a question that will be answered by the election itself. If Donald J. Trump is not elected president of the United States on November 8, we will owe this not to some triumph of the superior American system or to the eloquent presentation of a progressive alternative but to the fact that this singularly offensive man offended too many voters, especially white,

2. See Frank Rich, "What The Donald Shares with The Ronald," *New York*, June 1, 2016.

college-educated women. It will not be because he was rendered unelectable by virtue of his lies and race-baiting and immigrant-bashing and demagoguery.

On the contrary. Trump embodies grisly aspects of our politics that are not new but that, on him, are starkly illuminated. What are these? That much of our politics in this increasingly diverse country pivots on the hateful fulcrum of race, of racial fear and xenophobia and antagonism toward the Other, and that this has only grown in power and ugliness since the rise of Barack Obama and his coalition. That in vital matters of gender and sexuality and marriage much of the politics of the presiding culture is furiously rejected by a significant minority of the country as a "politically correct" and immoral imposition. That in the aftermath of a severe economic crisis—and after decades of economic stagnation for most Americans—tens of millions of voters feel so abandoned by the system that they offer their full-throated cheers to a candidate pledging to wholly dismantle it and put "in jail" his opponent. That the electoral system as it has evolved over that time and especially in the wake of such decisions as *Citizens United* has become starkly, shabbily, and spectacularly corrupt. And finally that entertainment and money in the grossest sense play a far more important part in our politics than any attention to public policy, and that the commercial press, particularly the broadcast press, battens on that reality to an increasingly shameless degree.

In the wake of Donald Trump all these tendencies will persist and perhaps—during a Clinton presidency—flourish, awaiting the next opportunistic figure who demonstrates the ruthlessness and skill to exploit them, and the steady-handedness, perhaps, to avoid needlessly alienating quite so much of the electorate. It is a grim and echoing reality, and one that we ignore at our peril, that many of Trump's most egregious faults as a candidate are by no means intrinsic to his politics. He could be playing the ragged John the Baptist to a less outrageous and thus more dangerous savior to come.

Pondering the rise of the demagogue Cleon, Aristotle observed that he "was the first who shouted on the public platform, who used abusive language and who spoke with his cloak girt around him, while all the others used to speak in proper dress and manner." Trump has raised the cloak. Whoever becomes president, it is unlikely to be lowered again in our lifetimes.

The Con He Rode In On

October 21, 2020

AMID THE SENSORY SWIRL of the airplane hangar in Freeland, Michigan—the thousands of voices screaming, the red MAGA hats bobbing and shifting, the fifty-foot flags on cranes flapping and snapping, the long sleek blue-and-white bulk of Air Force One gleaming, the elbow-to-elbow crowd heaving and swelling (and, in my worried fancy, the predatory virus molecules dancing ominously amid the sea of tiny Trumps filling countless tiny cell phone screens)—the leader slow-walks toward us, fist pumping slowly, with that trademark ponderous tread of his (dating back at least to his boardroom entrances on *The Apprentice*), adjusts the mic, leans slightly sideways, and lances into it all with a stark declaration: "We brought you a lot of car plants, Michigan! We brought you *a lot* of car plants. You know that, right?"

Comes in prompt response the earsplitting roar of affirmation, clear as clear can be: *Yes, Mr. President, we know that!* A joyful knowledge, a knowledge to celebrate: all those jobs in all those car plants! But what exactly is it possible to know about those car plants? I could not have been the only one in that obstreperous crowd, made up overwhelmingly of Michiganders, to know the presumably important fact that, well . . . *those car plants didn't exist*. Any member in good standing of the ancient "reality-based community" could have told you that since the coming of Trump no new car plants had been built in Michigan, that since his ascension not less than three thousand Michiganders had lost jobs in the vital auto sector.[1]

Perhaps it wasn't Trump's fault, but it was a fact. But what was a fact exactly?

He had promised Michigan new car plants and within the chilly expanse of his own mind he had delivered. And the roar of worshipful approbation meant that he had carried these thousands of souls to that place with him. "Dang!" a sweatshirted middle-aged woman told me afterward as we waited in line to buy hot dogs and lemonade. "I had no idea he had done so much for the state! I mean, people hardly even *talk* about it . . ." She was a nurse, trained in anatomy, physiology, biology—science, that is to say. But to her the president's word was Truth; the idea that "people hardly even *talk* about" the car plants because they don't exist was not only heretical but inconceivable. She couldn't conceive it and neither could the thousands of others shouting around me.

Nor could they conceive—as could I, the timorous heretic hidden among them—the virus particles in every explosion of breath, every bit of spittle cast aloft on the gales of mass enthusiasm. The virus was a hoax. Was *the leader* afraid of the virus? (Asked the following

1. See Dave Boucher and Todd Spangler, "Trump Makes Wild Claims About Revitalizing Auto Industry at Michigan Rally," *Detroit Free Press*, September 10, 2020. Since the coming of Trump, at least three car plants have closed in Michigan and one "autonomous-vehicle-making plant" is planned to open.

week—before his own infection—if he was concerned about the virus spreading at his rallies, he responded with his customary laser focus: "I'm on a stage and it's very far away. And so I'm not at all concerned."[2]) So how could the virus threaten them, armored as they were in their Trump-as-Superman T-shirts and Trump flag pajamas?

So when he came before them, the leader's first words were a lie, one of the 20,000 and more that *The Washington Post* and other "enemies of the people" have presumed to track, catalog, and codify. To the reality-based community he would seem to embody as none before him the ancient Hollywood joke:

> How do you know he's lying?
> His lips are moving.

And yet to call this lie a lie makes little sense. These words constitute merely a single brushstroke on the vast canvas of a created world, full of car plants and steel plants and the millions of smokestacks making up "the greatest economy the world has ever seen." True, it was all imagined, but Trump's greatest gift had always been the imposition of his own imagination on the crowd. "I play to people's fantasies," he (or more probably his ghostwriter) had written back in 1987:

> People may not always think big themselves, but they can still get very excited by those who do. That's why a little hyperbole never

2. See Jonathan Chait, "A White House Aide Just Warned Us That Donald Trump Is a Sociopath," *New York*, September 18, 2020.

> hurts. People want to believe that something is the biggest and the greatest and the most spectacular.
>
> *I call it truthful hyperbole.* It's an innocent form of exaggeration—and a very effective form of promotion.[3] [my italics]

"Truthful hyperbole" because the details of that created world emerge from one central belief in the hero's mind, rooted directly in his gargantuan and fragile ego: *I have done an incredible job.* All those auto plants and steel plants become not lies or creations but exaggerations flowering decoratively from that a priori truth. Before the crowd of red-faced partisans chanting his name, he transformed from a snake-oil salesman, a great pattering con man in the Elmer Gantry tradition, a postmodern Willy Loman, to a masterful crafter and seller of dreams. They believed him and not their lyin' eyes because they wanted so desperately to believe.

In the imagination of the crowd Trump was an original but the lineaments of that imagination, its workings and its cravings, are anything but new. Those surrounding me were not poor (though poorer now than six months before); white working class, middle class, they could see clearly enough what they didn't have: power. What had become increasingly obvious over the decades of dwindling wages and pointless wars and now this endless pandemic was the extent of their own powerlessness. They needed not only someone to blame—immigrants, anarchists, affirmative action beneficiaries, Black Lives Matter protesters, a corrupt and devious elite who for its own self-interested reasons let them all have free run—but a

3. See Donald J. Trump with Tony Schwartz, *Trump: The Art of the Deal* (1987; Ballantine, 2015), p. 58.

voice to articulate it. The dynamic playing out before me was ancient: Already Nietzsche was calling it "*ressentiment*," and had he been transported to Freeland, Michigan, the German philologist would have recognized instantly what he was seeing enacted before him, a kind of Mummers' revolt of the powerless:

> The *ressentiment* of natures that are denied the true reaction, that of deeds, and compensate themselves with imaginary revenge.... This No is its creative deed.[4]

Trump, the tribune of the powerless, the unmasker of the powerful, the denouncer, the insulter, the despoiler of idols—Trump was their "imaginary revenge." He entertained them, flattered them, and from his strength they drew encouragement. Here before me, among those hooting and hollering at fanciful car plants and sacrificing themselves, maskless, to the leader's imagination was Nietzsche's futile "resentment of the lambs for the bird of prey," and it was on that soul-deep instinct that Trump played like a virtuoso.

He was the artist of grievance, for here was an emotion he understood intimately, as only an ambitious boy raised in Queens and never taken seriously in the sacred precincts of Manhattan power can understand it. "I have been treated very badly"—was this not his mantra, not only for his presidency but for all the decades before? What more appropriate phrase for workers who had fled the Democrats for Ronald Reagan but still saw their jobs shipped abroad, their cities and businesses despoiled of factories and downtowns?

4. See Friedrich Nietzsche, *On the Genealogy of Morals and Ecce Homo* (Vintage, 1989), p. 36.

The elite, the leader reminded them with offhand resentment, had spent the previous decades "offshoring Michigan's jobs, outsourcing Michigan's factories, throwing open your borders, dragging us into endless foreign wars, and surrendering our children's future to China and other faraway lands."

But, he told them, their aggrievement was his: the outsider, the one who would not rest in fighting for what was right against the machinations of the elite and the Deep State and the other agents of betrayal. Who fought even the diabolical child abductors and blood guzzlers around Hillary Clinton and the rest of the Democratic cabal (I counted the QAnon sweatshirts dotting the crowd, the magic-markered Q on a cheek here, on a forehead there) and stood against the torrent of abuse and for the innocence of childhood. He told them what they hated and he shared their hatred—but he could do something about it. And with every imaginary success he showcased the incompetence of the elite he'd supplanted. His followers took solace also in seeing that, despite the aggrievement he shared, the leader retained the plumage of the bird of prey—as had demagogues back to Cleon and Catiline and before—and they were proud of that, of his planes and houses and business chicanery (and even, were the truth admitted, of his porn stars and his Playboy Bunnies). For them in turn the leader offered his own peculiarly self-centered form of flattery and a reverie on their shared glory:

> You know, this is not the crowd of a person who comes in second place, you do know that? The same thing happened four years ago. It was election eve, but by the time I got here it was late. Some of you were in that audience, at one o'clock in the morning, now elec-

> tion day. We had 32,000 people show up, and the reason I went was that I heard that Crooked Hillary Clinton, Bill Clinton, and Barack *Hussein* Obama were traveling to Michigan because they heard they had problems. They were supposed to win Michigan but they did such a lousy job that they had to come and get some votes and they came and I heard about it. They said, "Sir, could you do it?" and I hopped in the plane. . . . Thirty-two thousand people. She had five hundred people. I said, "Why are we going to lose Michigan?" *And we didn't.*

They all knew by heart the climax of this epic: Trump with his late-night barnstorming had drawn to an inside straight and pulled out Michigan by a minuscule 10,704 votes—along with Wisconsin by 22,748 and Pennsylvania by 44,292. Those 77,744 people, in the face of Clinton's vast plurality of nearly 2.9 million Americans, had made Trump president. Barely twice the number that had been howling on the Freeland tarmac at one o'clock in the morning on election day four years before.

I felt an elbow jostle me, found myself crashing against a bearded man in a red hoodie: TRUMP 2020: NO BULLSHIT! We were packed shoulder to shoulder but no 32,000 now. By the next day the official estimate would be 5,500. How many were wearing masks? Two hundred? Maybe, at a stretch, five hundred? I felt vaguely self-conscious in my red TRUMP 2020 mask. Mostly I felt vertigo. It had been six months since I'd been in a crowd. And now the voices overwhelmed in the echoing hangar. Trump was insulting those ideologues among the elite whose greedy, blind belief in so-called free trade had pauperized the smokestack heart of the country. People laughed, hooted, rocked back and forth. "*Four more years! Four more years!*" He smiled benevolently at the crowd, drinking in the adulation. It seemed to make him grow in size. Easy to see why these events were necessary to him, why stopping them was like depriving an addict of his supply. What did a narcissist fantasize about?

But the crowd loved it, too. Above our heads floated still that constant glitter of cell phone screens with their little Trumps, tiny echoes of the man onstage, their bearers stretching and crouching and straining in that most contemporary pose of electronic prayer. The leader joked, sneered, laughed. "I love you!" came from the crowd. "Don't say that," Trump shot back. "I'll start to cry, and that wouldn't be good for my image." Huge chortles. Then back to the culpable elites.

He insulted, he ranted, he stabbed and hacked with his ridicule. With him, Nietzsche's "imaginary revenge" of the lambs on the birds of prey became vivid and entertaining—especially when it turned into the gold of elite outrage. "If you are a little different, or a little outrageous . . . the press is going to write about you," the young Manhattan developer had opined knowingly nearly four decades before, and how much truer now for a president? He would portion out the vitriol daily, just enough to dominate the news cycle, and for his followers this would be recycled as his "No," his "creative deed." Each wave of elite outrage bolstered his authenticity, made them love him more. From everyone else the outrage would bring that most valuable of contemporary commodities—eyeballs!—and Trump would rule the airwaves and the Twittersphere. Whether it was against Trump or for Trump, everyone everywhere was selling Trump Trump Trump. That was why, he explained to *The New York Times* with a knowing smirk, he was sure to be reelected:

> I'm going to win another four years... because newspapers, television, all forms of media will tank if I'm not there because without me, their ratings are going down the tubes. Without me, *The New York Times* will indeed be not the failing *New York Times*, but the failed *New York Times*. So they basically have to let me win.[5]

The joke was on the so-called commercial press, which had revealed itself decisively under Trump to be commercial first, press second. Was it $2 or $5 billion they had given him in free media in 2016? Had it not been this very cycle of outrage, and the eager selling of that outrage by his supposed political antagonists in the "lamestream media," that had made Trump president? Lenin would have been pleased. The elite had sold the rope to hang themselves with.

Of course no elites had been hanged. Trump had smeared and besmirched and traduced and denounced. The volume had been high, the outrage constant, the spinning news cycle exhausting. He had depopulated entire bureaucracies of the federal government. He had exchanged "love letters" with Kim Jong-un and long meaningful gazes with Vladimir Putin. He had schemed and plotted and obstructed. He had kept the white supremacists and the denizens of all sorts of armed and angry fever swamps locked and loaded. To Portland and other cities he had even sent the country's own version of Putin's "little green men," armed troops without insignia who tumbled random protesters into unmarked vans.

It had all been unprecedented. But there had been no revolution.

5. Interview with Michael S. Schmidt in *The New York Times*, December 28, 2017.

Amid all the disruption and furor and insanity there had been merely a right-wing Republican program of tax cuts for the rich and reactionary judges for the ideologues. Of populism, not so much—not even an infrastructure bill so the builder-leader could put his followers to work. Still, "we've already built 310 miles of border wall," he reminded us proudly, and as the chants echoed around me—"Build that wall! Build that wall!"—I was put in mind of a favorite bamboozling passage from *The Art of the Deal*:

> I called in my construction supervisor and told him that I wanted him to round up every bulldozer and dump truck he could possibly find, and put them to work on my site immediately. Over the next week, I said, I wanted him to transform my two acres of nearly vacant property into the most active construction site in the history of the world. What the bulldozers and dump trucks did wasn't important, I said, so long as they did a lot of it. . . .
>
> One week later, I accompanied top Holiday Inns [*sic*] executives and the entire board of directors out to the Boardwalk [in Atlantic City]. It looked as if we were in the midst of building the Grand Coulee Dam.[6]

Thus the southern border, where, in that strange, flickering anti-world of reality that seldom peeped through his words, Trump had built perhaps four miles of new wall. Here too the idea of the wall was what he had brought his followers, as real as those auto plants. It had begun as a Wall of the Imagination, and so it would remain.

6. *The Art of the Deal*, pp. 214–215.

The truth was that as president he had built little. The truth was he knew nothing of governing and was loath to learn. His ideas were cartoonish and shallow, and where his simple slogans had met with frustration—at the border, for example—he had imposed cruelty. Elsewhere his concerns had been mundane. He had fleeced the republic with amazing ease and embarrassing homeliness, charging his Secret Service detail more than $1 million to stay at his properties. He fired, craved loyalty, sought revenge. Every tempest a headline.

What astonished was not the leader's lack of respect for norms—had that not always been obvious?—but how ephemeral those norms proved to be. Before the will of Trump's henchman at the Department of Justice, the highly touted "rule of law" was revealed as one tiny step removed from "a country of men, not of laws." The widely cited *Wizard of Oz* comparison appeared truest when it came to the most cherished of the country's institutions, first and foremost its vaunted "separation of powers." What good are Congress's institutional prerogatives when those in the Senate majority want only their tax cuts and their judges and prove eager to close their eyes to the rest? Their brute reverence for political survival over all else was as mundane as it was shocking. Emoluments clause? Foreign countries are paying for rooms in Trump's hotel without even bothering to show up. "They *know* this guy," a friend in the Persian Gulf said of his own country's rich and autocratic leaders. He rubbed his thumb and index finger together. "With this guy, the only question you need to ask is: *What's it gonna take...?*"

Think of it all as a stress test for the country's institutions, one they badly failed. The reverence had been badly misplaced, or anyway badly dated. How much, with barely 80,000 votes and his own imagination, had he shown to be a façade? How many times might that Potemkin construction site be held up as metaphor?

Finally, it had taken nature, not man, in its embodiment as deadly virus to show the fatal limits of his imagination. We were "rounding the corner" on the virus, he assured us. And for these 5,500 mostly unmasked souls we were. They believed him, even those present who might well die of it. But elsewhere there were 220,000 dead and rising caseloads and kids were unable to go to school. Elsewhere people were wearing masks and staying home. Was that the reason we were 5,500 and not 32,000?

"You better vote for me, I got you so many damn car plants." Those car plants had become the leitmotif of the speech, but they had turned, slowly but inexorably, from a tone of triumph in his salutation to a blunt assertion and now at last to a kind of plea. The note in his voice was unmistakable. He had made the unforgivable error of the cartoon figure who has run out into space and dares to look down. He feared he might lose.

In his plea now I couldn't help but find a trace of poignancy. He had done so much damage, but had it not been true that we had let him? How much of my life of the last four years had been spent reading and watching and talking Trump Trump Trump? He had taken the adulation and the hatred, too, as a kind of drug, but so had we. And who were we to laugh at his self-estimation as "a very stable genius"? Had he not become president riding nothing but his own con? No, Mexico would not pay for the wall—but who else could have created, out of thin air, such an outlandish and lucrative bit of politics? The bearded TRUMP: NO BULLSHIT! red-sweatshirt man jostled me again and, looking at the slogan with the caricatured face above it, I recalled a wisp of a definition:

> For the bullshitter... is neither on the side of the true nor on the side of the false. His eye is not on the facts at all, as the eyes of the honest man and of the liar are, except insofar as they may be pertinent to his interest in getting away with what he says. He does not care whether the things he says describe reality correctly. He just picks them out, or makes them up, to suit his purpose.[7]

His original purpose, of course, had been to outrage, and to build his brand. That was his art, to capture the imagination—to capture the gaze—and he would go down in history for that. That he had shown the shambolic state of the country in its post–cold war embodiment was a vital consequence. A democracy that brings to office as president a man who receives three million fewer votes than his opponent. A country that preaches advancement based on hard work where median incomes have been nearly frozen for four decades. A nation whose political cleavages run so deep that the polity cannot even agree to wear masks during a deadly pandemic. A people struggling still to put into deed an end to the institutional racism that was meant to be banished by law a half-century ago. A population undergoing a painful shift to minority-majority rule where members of the coming white minority use every institutional advantage to cling to power.

After a twenty-year span that should have been a golden age and included instead a stolen election, a terrorist spectacular, disastrous wars of choice in far-off lands, two cataclysmic economic collapses, and a catastrophic pandemic, he had been a kind of cartoon leader

7. See Harry G. Frankfurt, "On Bullshit," in *The Importance of What We Care About: Philosophical Essays* (Cambridge University Press, 1998), p. 131.

shouting and gesticulating and illustrating with frenetic ferocity all we had taken for granted and all that had fallen into ruins. And we had followed every move with the fevered attention of the binge-watcher.

They had begun to leave, though the leader was still speaking. They had gotten what they'd come for, the people in their multifarious Trump paraphernalia. I saw not only the ubiquitous Trump-as-Superman T-shirt—here in red, white, and blue, there in rainbow colors—but Trump as motorcycle gang leader, Trump as Hulk, Trump as Rambo. I stopped someone, asked him if Trump would win. After the initial look of shock, he exclaimed, "Yeah, yeah, no question." A pause. "Course it depends on how much the other side cheats."

That was the consensus here. A Trump loss could mean only one thing: widespread and shameless cheating. The narrative was already laid down, elaborated, and well established: there would be an early claim of victory, then a stab-in-the-back narrative as those dubious mail-in ballots piled up.[8]

And why not? Trumpism was a movement of resistance, of grievance, of the creative No.

Win or lose, it would remain so—if or until those grievances began to be met. For some, perhaps, it was already too late for that. Walking in I had seen the pistols on hips, here and there an assault rifle. A few weeks later thirteen would be arrested in Michigan for plotting to kidnap, try, and execute Gretchen Whitmer, the Democratic governor. Had any of them been at this rally?

8. See Steven Rosenfeld, "Steve Bannon's Back: Ex-Adviser Says Trump Plans to Claim Victory Early," *Salon*, October 17, 2020.

Win or lose, the grievances would remain. They could no more be banished from this earth than the imaginary car plants. They would wait, as before, for the leader who would vow his imaginary revenge.

"Be Ready to Fight"

January 14, 2021

HARSH AND GRAY dawned the day of the Stupid Coup, with a lowering sky of dense dark clouds, slippery muddy grass underfoot, and a stiff, unforgiving wind that kept the STOP THE STEAL flags flapping. Face-painted and brightly festooned pilgrims bearing banners—snarling Trump straddling a tank, pumped-up Trump-as-Rambo brandishing a machine gun, grimacing Trump as motorcycle gang chieftain—milled about the archaic hulk of the Washington Monument looking like the remnants of a postapocalyptic cult, with beefy bearded men in camo pants and Harley jackets, and women wearing red, white, and blue sweatshirts and draped in red Make America Great Again flags like Roman togas. And everywhere on hats and helmets and sweatshirts and pants was that double-plosive syllable he had spent his life affixing to buildings and airplanes and "universities" and steaks and vodka: TRUMP: NO BULLSHIT! FIGHT FOR TRUMP! JESUS IS MY SAVIOR, TRUMP IS MY PRESIDENT.

As I advanced toward the White House and the booming, reverberating electronic voices, the crowd began to thicken and finally to coalesce. Before I knew it I had been pressed into a mass of bodies straining toward a faintly gesticulating figure hundreds of yards away, echoed by the crudely pixelated image of an amped-up Eric Trump, magnified a hundred times on the jumbotron, just glimpsable through the MAGA hats and flags. The crowd moved roughly as one, borne along by its rhythmic chants ("USA! USA! USA!" "Stop the Steal! Stop the Steal! Stop the Steal!"), and atop its messy bulk swayed the flags and the stretching hands clutching cell phones, on which the figure on the jumbotron (now the brass-voiced Evita of Trumpism, Kimberly Guilfoyle) was replicated a few thousand times as far as one could see. Pressing my elbows against the bodies beside me I struggled to keep my footing on the wet ground, swallowed the incipient claustrophobic panic, and breathed in the acrid smell of marijuana wafting over us. All we needed was a mosh pit.

"Oh, I *love* him!" "Yeah, he's *amazing*!" The dark-haired young women jostling against me from behind were struggling to hold a sight line to stare adoringly up at Don Jr., now kissing his girlfriend Kimberly. With his slicked-back hair, open-necked shirt, and gaping jacket, he looked for all the world like a just-past-his-prime used-car salesman. "This isn't *their* Republican Party anymore!" Don Jr. roared. "This is *Donald Trump's* Republican Party!" Preening like a rock star, he extended his hand-mic to the crowd to catch the answering roar. Did the Republicans now gathering at the Capitol hear it? Did Vice President Mike Pence, presiding over the electoral vote certification, hear it? For Don Jr. was shouting out a simple truth that for all its undeniability many in the party had never quite believed or managed to grasp in all its implications. Trump *owned* them. And as his owner's prerogative he imposed an unstinting and singular loyalty: not loyalty *mostly* to him, with some prudently reserved for the Constitution and the law. No. Loyalty *entirely* to him. Today would be the day of choosing.

It is a testament to the powers of ambition and self-delusion that the thousands of garishly costumed people around me could see this clearly even while the sophisticated members of Congress and the media and intelligentsia could not. Moments before, as the royal family chatted in a tent in front of the White House and prepared to come out on stage, a broadly smiling Guilfoyle, clad in a smart black cape and shimmying briefly for the camera, said she hoped Pence would have "the courage or brains to do the right thing" and block the certification of Joe Biden's election. Guilfoyle, a former Fox News anchor, is a lawyer who worked as a federal prosecutor and an assistant district attorney in California, and here she was, in a video later posted by Don Jr., professing to believe that the vice-president would soon be turning the 2020 election over to the loser. Trump himself had been explicitly pressuring and then threatening Pence for days, both on Twitter and especially at the rally in Dalton, Georgia, two nights before, on the eve of the state's two Senate runoff elections, where he mused that Pence "is a great guy. Of course, if he doesn't come through, I won't like him quite as much."

Shortly after Rudolph Giuliani appeared ("Rudy! Rudy! Rudy!") to propose that the election be settled by "trial by combat," Trump himself slowly sauntered onstage to the strains of Lee Greenwood's "Proud to Be an American." After admiring the crowd and praising the grandeur of the Washington Monument, he laid out in laborious and disordered detail all the ways the unprecedented landslide "we" had won had been stolen—a litany he had recited two days before in Georgia and the week before that during his hour-long cajoling and whining and threatening telephone call with Georgia secretary of state Brad Raffensperger. And after he had read out once more all the discredited claims about all the dark doings in inner-city Detroit and Philadelphia and Atlanta—adding ruefully that the wily Georgians had now succeeded in *stealing the election again*—the president came to the point of what lay before us this day:

> We're going to have to fight much harder. And Mike Pence is going to have to come through for us. And if he doesn't that will be a sad day for our country.... We're going to walk down, and I'll be there with you, we're going to walk down to the Capitol and we're going to cheer on our brave senators and congressmen and women, and we're probably not going to be cheering so much for some of them. Because you'll never take back our country with weakness. You have to show strength and you have to be strong. We have come to demand that Congress do the right thing.... We fight. We fight like hell, and if you don't fight like hell, you're not going to have a country anymore.

Deafening paroxysms of jubilation and rage greeted this doctrinal statement of Trumpism, for who could better summarize the philosophy, such as it was, in fewer words? Trump as Rambo, as tank commander, motorcycle gang leader, and on and on. The imagery of Trumpism is about strength and cruelty and dominance even as the rhetoric is about loss and grievance and victimization: about what was taken and what must be seized back by strength. And *we* would have to bring that strength, for certain it was that the politicians would turn out to be traitors, just like all the rest. From that fateful ride down the gilt staircase in the pink-marbled lobby of

Trump Tower five years before—Trumpism's March on Rome—it had been about this: "Taking back the country." Taking it back from the rapists and the killers, the undocumented and the illegitimate, the Black and the brown from "shithole countries" who should go back "where they came from." Now it had all come down to this.

"*Fight for Trump! Fight for Trump!*" Above my head a tall homemade flag on a jointed metal pole flapped and waved and finally extended out fully for a moment, and I could read the words that had been printed in black type: LEAD US ACROSS THE RUBICON! And on the other side: THE DIE IS CAST! I managed to nudge with my elbow the clean-cut, thirtyish young man gently waving the pole. "I like your flag," I said. He turned his head back at me and smiled: finally, one who understood. "Yes," he said. "It's time."

To the strains of "Tiny Dancer" and then "YMCA," the mass began to loosen and separate. I slowly followed my new friend's flag at a distance, my shoes wet and caked with mud, my feet near frozen. Caesar had led his soldiers across the Rubicon: the river had been the unwritten boundary beyond which a general was not permitted to bring his forces into Republican Rome. And yet the parallel had much to recommend it. Could his legions have been more loyal to their commander than these were to theirs? Was not our republic, too, beset with maladies its feckless leaders had proved powerless to remedy? Infestations of grasping and illegitimate foreigners. Obscene inequalities of wealth and power. Long-stagnant incomes. Senseless and unending foreign wars. Dispossessed and desperate veterans. And most of all a corrupt political class that had lost the confidence of the people. What was preserving the republic worth when set against such mortal ills? What was that supposedly noble cause but an excuse to maintain the rotting status quo?

In our dense procession we marched up Constitution Avenue. All the museums were shuttered, all the buildings closed. Washington had been shut down, first by the pandemic, now by us. Shops and hotels had covered their plate glass in plywood. The side streets were near deserted, except for the black-and-white police cars blocking the corners with their flashing blue strobes. This day would set a record in pandemic deaths and the next day would set another, surmounting for the first time four thousand dead. We were marching in a time of plague, and I felt vulnerable in my mask. Self-conscious, too: not one marcher in ten wore them. "They're *locking us down*, taking away our freedom and our country, too!" someone exclaimed. Were the words meant for my ears? Few masks, yes, but fine makeshift costuming: we were a parade in motley, a dense Children's Crusade of Trumpsters, with our flags pointed half forward now, as if we were advancing full-tilt on Jerusalem.

Lined up against the wall of a museum, men in tactical gear stood with backs turned, pissing. A woman in a kind of red, white, and blue pajama suit gazed down at her phone and shouted, "Pence just threw Trump under the bus!" A blond-haired woman in a woolly Trump hat said to no one in particular, "The courts won't help. The Supreme Court won't help. The only one left is us..."

Far ahead and to my right I could see rise into view the National Gallery East Building, I. M. Pei's masterpiece. From this vantage in the street, the building suddenly looked cold and vaguely threatening, standing for an elite and distant world of unapproachable privilege.

It was an illusion, of course. Its doors would one day open again, and to everyone. And the lines here were not about class, or not only about that, but about allegiance and about institutions. My friend with the flag had told me, "It's time to sweep them all away. All of them. And you see we can't do it by voting." Trump had run for office against government, but unlike Reagan and even Goldwater before him, he had also *governed* against government—against the Deep State and "the administrative state" and the permanent swamp that all these fine closed-off marble buildings represented. And now its denizens were snatching power back from him by blatantly stealing the election in broad daylight in that white-domed building looming up ahead.

If it all seems too fantastical, you might consider: How do you know the election wasn't stolen? In part it is because you trust institutions: the governors who preside over the elections, the secretaries of state who administer them, the courts that adjudicate the claims of fraud. When you see the news that the courts threw out the suits brought by Trump's lawyers you believe it proves the election was fair. But what if you hated and distrusted those institutions and believed instead what your duly elected president told you? That he had won in a great landslide, that corrupt elected officials were trying to steal it from him, that it was all happening in plain sight?

Up ahead gleamed the Capitol dome, looking otherworldly, as overphotographed buildings tend to do. The thousands of crusaders were pouring from Pennsylvania and Constitution Avenues and coursing freely, like blood from an open wound, onto the unobstructed Capitol grounds. Screaming protesters, some shooting pepper spray or bear spray or thrusting their flags like spears, had been facing off against the outnumbered and under-armed Capitol Police since before Trump had finished speaking. Already the flimsy line of metal barriers had been breached, the crowd had pushed past the base of the steps, the single line of police, broken and bedraggled, struggled to keep them out of the building. Within, Pence, whose four years of ardent obsequiousness would not save him from what was to come, was presiding. At what point had it finally dawned on him, with perhaps even now a sick-to-the-stomach recognition, that the president was *serious*—that he actually expected him, Michael R. Pence, former congressman, former governor of Indiana, aspiring president, to "reject fraudulently chosen electors," as Trump had tweeted two nights before? How much effort had he put into studying whether it could actually be done? How excruciating had it been to sign yesterday's letter, in which Pence confessed that he did "not believe that the Founders of our country intended to invest the Vice President with unilateral authority to decide which electoral votes should be counted"?

One need not speculate about how Trump received these words. Founders? Authority? Law? Preponderant evidence suggests that Trump sees the law the way a crooked real estate developer does, as a flimsy, malleable thing you pay lawyers to manipulate and circumvent. The law bends to audacity and to power. The law is something you have to have "the courage or brains" to overcome or to master. In a midafternoon tweet, Trump made this explicit:

> Mike Pence didn't have the courage to do what should have been done to protect our Country and our Constitution, giving States a chance to certify a corrected set of facts . . . USA demands the truth!

By then, the marauders had arrived to demand it themselves. Before thousands of chanting spectators—"USA! USA! USA!"—they were pushing against the doors and smashing the windows. Protesters were scaling the scaffolding and walls and pushing onto the balconies. Inside, the vice-president of the United States had been hustled by his security detail off the floor of the "world's greatest deliberative body" and into "an undisclosed location," just ahead of looters in the rotunda bellowing "Hang Mike Pence! Hang Mike Pence!" A wooden gallows stood outside the Capitol, festooned with a noose of thick orange rope.

Out on the grounds, where the sun had begun to peep through the bare branches, people strolled hand in hand, pushed carriages, chatted, laughed, snacked on sandwiches, waved a DON'T TREAD ON ME flag and multifarious Trump banners, and joined the occasional chant. Some boasted full Trumpian regalia, with face paint, hats, and sweatshirts, but many others could have been average citizens on a midwinter walk in the park. As you neared the grand domed building, crossing the litter of metal barricades, the crowds grew denser and roiling and you could smell the gas, some still in wisps and swirls of nauseous yellow or acid green. Above, bodies pushed against bodies, chants gave way to scattered shouts and screams and groans.

Inside was proceeding a peculiarly contemporary coup. Some attackers wielded pipes or hockey sticks or flagpoles, some wore helmets or gas masks or bandanas, but in this "second 1776" cell phones and cameras were the vital weapon in every revolutionary's hand. "Needing to have reality confirmed and experience enhanced by photographs," as Susan Sontag observed, "is an aesthetic consumerism to which everyone is now addicted." January 6 seems likely to be the most photographed coup in history. Amid the awful violence, what still more awful things might have been done if more revolutionary image junkies had spent their time to some purpose other than selfie-taking, videoing, and live-streaming?

Which raises the obvious question of what precisely the intent was this day. "Taking back our country"—but how? Pressuring Pence to "come through for us." Amid those milling about in wonder, those smashing windows, beating up policemen or crushing them against doors, waving American flags and posing in Camp Auschwitz sweatshirts, stealing podiums, rifling laptops, purloining mail, smearing excrement, making declamations, and documenting every moment of the intrusion—"This is my house," bellowed a bearded Trumpisto in the rotunda, "and I'm here to take it back!"—could be glimpsed various men of quiet purpose in tactical gear, at least two of whom came equipped with bunches of flex cuffs or "zip ties." Somewhere, secreted within the trashing and looting and destroying and photographing, was perhaps a more elaborated plan to capture and "try" the vice-president and chosen senators and representatives. Or perhaps to hold the building hostage and to make political demands—accepting "alternate" slates of electors? agreeing to a "revote" in certain states?—in exchange for relinquishing the sacred political space.

What is certain is that a rabble of hundreds of Trumpistos draped in outlandish *Mad Max* garb and armed with makeshift weapons managed to violently invade and conquer the Capitol of the United States and occupy it for nearly six hours. One rioter in carpenter jeans paraded a Confederate flag, a noxious intrusion of treason and frank racism not seen even during the Civil War. Later in the rotunda, one exhausted and battered Black policeman yelled out, "I got called a nigger 15 times today.... I cried for about 15 minutes and I just let it out," *BuzzFeed* reported.

Ahead of the clashes, the country's elected representatives and senators and its second-highest executive officer were forced to flee for their lives into ignominious hiding. That the day was coming had hardly been a secret. Not only had President Trump repeatedly and publicly summoned his supporters to Washington to "Save America!" on a day he promised would be "wild," but in a report only the day before the FBI had quoted explicit online "calls for violence" and "war," including this prophetic passage:

> Be ready to fight. Congress needs to hear glass breaking, doors being kicked in, and blood from their BLM and Pantifa slave soldiers being spilled. Get violent. Stop calling this a march, or rally, or a protest. Go there ready for war. We get our President or we die.

Despite these warnings, Capitol Police leaders failed to request or assign a single extra police officer to duty that day, and few who were on duty were in riot gear. Mutual sympathies between police and Trump marchers are well known—"Back the Blue!" is a frequent chant at his rallies—and there were clearly many police and military among the marchers. "These guys.... A lot of them were former military," the officer told *BuzzFeed*. "You have the nerve to be holding a Blue Lives Matter flag, and you are out there fucking us up. [One guy] pulled out his badge and he said, 'We're doing this for you.'" It is hard not to suspect that the shocking lack of preparation in the face of a widely anticipated assault is owed not only to complacency but at some level to complicity.

Trump reportedly had to be dissuaded from personally leading the march to the Capitol. Instead, he sat in the White House "enjoying the spectacle" he had unleashed unfold on television. Unnamed sources described the president as "bemused" but also, according to *The Washington Post*, mildly "turned off by what he considered the 'low-class' spectacle of people in ragtag costumes." Still, he resisted desperate pleas to call his supporters off or to order in the National Guard. "It took him a while," his friend Senator Lindsey Graham allowed, "to appreciate the gravity of the situation." In fact there is little sign he ever did. At 6:00 PM, with protesters still in the Capitol, he posted this on his Twitter account, before it was suspended:

> These are the things and the events that happen when a sacred landslide election victory is so unceremoniously & viciously stripped away from great patriots who have been badly & unfairly treated for so long. Go home with love & in peace. Remember this day forever!

By refusing calls to intervene, he prolonged and protected the coup he had incited. Thankfully, Trump's disordered, erratic mind has never been given to systematic planning. That he finally lost his bet on the sycophantic unscrupulousness of his vice-president had more to do with a handful of votes in the House of Representatives than with the vaunted truism that ours is "a country of laws, not of men." Had the Republicans held a bare majority in the House, it is alarmingly easy to imagine the results of the presidential election being overturned.

As it is, the overwhelming majority of House Republicans, even after an attempted coup forced them to scurry abjectly for their lives—and left five people, including a police officer, dead—voted for exactly that, as did eight Republican senators. With his up-thrust fist, young Josh Hawley of Missouri will remain the poster boy of the coup. Both Hawley and Ted Cruz of Texas, highly credentialed lawyers out of Yale and Harvard respectively, like Pence discovered only belatedly that Trump was *serious*. Like the lowly innkeeper and everyone around him indulging Don Quixote's conviction that he had arrived at a magical castle, they all humored the president about his chances to overturn the election. After all, as one "senior Republican official" asked a week after the vote, "What is the downside for humoring him for this little bit of time? No one seriously thinks the results will change." For Hawley and Cruz, voting to overturn an election was merely a way to buff up their political résumés. What could be the downside?

Donald Trump is not Caesar, but he has a will to power and a malignancy that our degraded institutions and corrupted politicians have been wholly unable to contain. His army of millions will not melt away. They will remain as a lurking poison in the political bloodstream, politicized and angry, ready to be activated, and their nihilistic rejection of the country's institutions and laws will only grow more venomous. Millions of them are armed. Those who died in the coup will become the movement's martyrs. Those arrested will become its heroes.

On the afternoon of January 13, in an eerily deserted Washington, with the Capitol surrounded by thousands of National Guard troops, 222 Democrats and ten Republicans voted to impeach President Donald J. Trump for the second time, charging him in a single article with "incitement of insurrection." A handful of Republicans in the Senate have let it be known that they might consider, perhaps, voting in support. Today it remains uncertain whether the seventeen Republican senators necessary to convict will dare come forward—even after the president has committed the very definition of a "High Crime." And in order to ban Trump from holding future political office, which seems the only way to begin to protect the country from him and his supporters, he must first be convicted. In full view of the world, the sovereign committed a grave crime against the state. The Romans would have well understood the threat. The Republicans, fully embracing the nihilism of a nihilistic president, as yet do not.

Our future Suetonius will have work to do, describing these several decades in the life of the "indispensable" nation. The genocides of the 1990s, the "Supreme Court election" of 2000, the attacks of September 11, the war of choice in Iraq, the torture and endless drone assassinations of the "war on terror," the economic collapse of 2008, the election of Donald Trump, the hundreds of thousands of dead in the Great Pandemic—and, finally, the Stupid Coup. Will Trump seem as striking and unusual to our historian as he does to us? Will he make more sense when viewed against the March on Rome or the Beer Hall Putsch? Or will Trump be seen as the beginning of something and not its ending?

Those thousands gathered in their postapocalyptic costumes certainly see him thus. So do his 74 million voters, few of whom are likely to grow more trusting of American institutions under an "illegitimate" President Biden. Trump has been banned from Twitter, but his family will continue to grift off these events, putting millions in their own pockets. As for the move to impeach him for "incitement of insurrection," a wholly unrepentant Trump pronounced it "a continuation of the greatest witch-hunt in the history of politics!"

He was speaking outside the White House, six days after he had sent his ragged army marching on the Capitol. Talk of impeaching him "is causing tremendous anger," he declared. And then: "I think it's causing tremendous danger to our country." Hearing Trump utter those dark and threatening words, I thought of the charges of complicity some in Congress had made against their colleagues who had allegedly conducted, the day before the coup, "reconnaissance tours" of the building for some of the rioters. I thought of the representative who refused to go through the newly installed magnetometer, presumably because she insisted on bringing her handgun into the Capitol. And I thought of watching the tumult and the flags and the savage fighting at the wounded Capitol that day and the words that had several times come unbidden into my mind there—that unctuous phrase that has come to describe America and our era: "This is not who we are." And yet, I thought, it is what we do.

“Reality Rebellion”

June 3, 2021

1.

Workmen have stripped the barbed wire from around the Capitol. The shattered windows have been replaced. The blood has been scrubbed away. And from the halls of the grand white-domed building the National Guard troops have at last departed.

The coup that did not succeed in overturning the election goes unpunished. More than four hundred of its foot soldiers have been arrested but its instigator remains at large. The former president golfs at his country clubs and receives visits of tribute from the leaders of his party. Nearly half of Republicans tell pollsters Trump was “called by God to lead.” Seven in ten say the election was stolen and the current president is illegitimate.

The attempted coup of January 6 destroyed two cardinal principles of American politics. The first says that we choose who holds power not through violence but through elections. The second says that when one party wins an election, the other accepts the result and forms a “loyal opposition” while it awaits its chance to win the next time. Today we have in office a restorationist administration that behaves as if proving that "government works" will somehow restore these two principles. It will not.

These principles have been decisively severed once before in American history. That led to the Civil War, the climax of a long political crisis that only abated a decade after the North's victory. In order to claim the presidency after the deadlocked election of 1876, Republicans agreed to withdraw federal troops from the defeated South and in effect to end Reconstruction. It was a dark bargain, and it debased the country immeasurably by making possible a brutal and thoroughgoing segregation and disenfranchisement.

A century later an authoritarian-leaning president perverted the institutions of government and violated laws to keep himself in power. He won reelection in a landslide, but his crimes led to a scandal and investigations that eventually forced him to resign. In retrospect the unfolding of Watergate in the press and the courts and Congress is our American *Oresteia*. In a kind of democratic pageant the country's civil institutions uncovered corruption and lawbreaking, ousted the lawbreakers, and restored the institutions they had damaged. The press revealed. Congress investigated. The courts expiated. And this revelation, investigation, and expiation not only purged the political system but reaffirmed its legitimacy before the public.

At the time it seemed that this mechanism had been built into the system as a necessary corrective. "In a democracy," Jonathan Schell wrote nearly fifty years ago,

> we are not permitted to seek out the truth about our affairs and then to ignore what we learn. When evidence of murder comes to light, indictments must be brought and a trial held. Our system is arranged

> to make such action reflexive.... Truth and justice... are rooted as powerful forces in the heart of our political system. They have shaped and determined the fundamental structures of our institutions. Thus, the system of justice is the mechanism whereby certain forms of truth compel us to act. In a democracy, we are free to do many things, but we are not free to ignore the truth.[1]

In the case of the Capitol coup we have thus far ignored the truth. The coup was a crime against the state, and because it unfolded live on television as a grand public spectacle, Americans believe they know the truth about it. But we do not. We do not know what kind of planning preceded the assault and who was involved. We do not know why Pentagon officials for several hours refused to send troops to the Capitol. We do not know what the president was doing as the violence he unleashed was unfolding on Americans' television screens. And much more. We do not know because there has been no thorough public investigation of what happened. Supporters of the former president within the political system have thus far worked hard to block such an investigation.

What we have had is the impeachment managers' presentation during the president's Senate trial in January. Their most striking evidence was a thirteen-minute film setting out the events of the day. It was powerful and shocking, but it was widely perceived to be as deeply partisan as the trial itself. The cycle of revelation, investigation, and expiation is meant to offer the country as convincing and objective a picture of events as possible. The Watergate hearings were able to achieve that in part because so many prominent Republicans

1. "Blowing the Whistle on Watergate," *The New Yorker*, May 5, 1973.

accepted the stories shaped by the congressional committees in their methodical taking of testimony. The presentation of the impeachment managers included no testimony, and while it may have convinced one or two Republican senators to cast their votes to convict the president, it did not persuade most of his supporters to abandon their overwhelmingly partisan version of events.

The result is a metastasizing corruption at the heart of the polity. About the Capitol coup there is no shared reality. Nor is there a shared reality about the integrity of the election or of the legitimacy of the president it produced. To millions of Americans the legitimate president remains Donald Trump. A quarter-millennium of American history offers no precedent for this.

2.

As I stood crushed amid the masses of flag-waving Trump supporters gathered before the White House on that frigid, windy January 6, I noticed one flag in particular. LEAD US ACROSS THE RUBICON! it implored the president. On the other side: THE DIE IS CAST! The words imagined Trump as Julius Caesar and demanded that he march his troops into Rome and destroy the corruption and dysfunction of the old Republic. "It's time to sweep them all away," the young man waving the flag told me. "And you see we can't do it by voting."

Since the election had been stolen, other means must be found. He and the people around him believed they had been forced to turn to them because all other "legitimate" pathways had been blocked.

To him and millions like him, those pathways remain blocked

today, even as an illegitimate president has begun to change the country in dramatic ways. To them every new regulation smacks of tyranny. Every new tax is an illegal taking. Any new executive order limiting the purchase of firearms will be the beginning of the totalitarian regime they know is coming. And any move to alter the filibuster will be the clearest sign that a leader who gained the White House through fraud will stop at nothing to crush those who oppose him. Not every one of Trump's voters feels this way, but what we know through polling and reporting suggests that most of them do.

An ambitious government and an opposition that considers that government illegitimate make for an explosive mixture. To millions of Americans the coup of January 6 represented direct and justified action. It was not successful in keeping their leader in the White House, but many of them believe that the Constitution, in its provision for citizens "to keep and bear arms," provides for precisely this kind of violent rebellion against a tyrannical government.

To millions of others the era of Trump seems an aberration in American history increasingly distant in time. The former president's social media accounts have been blocked. His dominance of the news cycle has ended. The new president has led quietly and efficiently, seeing to a nationwide vaccination program and passing trillions of dollars of aid to Americans who have suffered during the pandemic. The old era of scandal and conflict and bluster has receded. We appear to have returned to a kind of normalcy.

The appearance is misleading. The Republican Party is now the party of Trump. For many that means the party of "Burn it down!" The essential political dynamism of Trump lay not in his faux populism or even in his racism but in his calls to destroy the old and corrupt order. As the former CIA analyst Martin Gurri writes in

The Revolt of the Public and the Crisis of Authority in the New Millennium (2018):

> A candidate that innocent of qualifications and political direction can be elected only as a gesture of supreme repudiation, by the electorate, of the governing class. From start to finish, the 2016 presidential race can best be understood as the political assertion of an unhappy and highly mobilized public. In the end, Trump was chosen precisely because of, not despite, his apparent shortcomings. He is the visible effect, not the cause, of the public's surly and mutinous mood. . . .
>
> The right level of analysis on Trump isn't Trump at all, but the public that endowed him with a radical direction and temper, and the decadent institutions that proved too weak to stand in his way. . . . Trump is in the style of our moment: a man from nowhere, with no stake in the system, ignorant of history, incurious about our political habits and traditions, but happy to bash and to break old and precious things in exchange for a little attention.

This decadence of the old elite and the institutions they built is a worldwide phenomenon. It encompasses the collapse of mainstream parties in France and Germany, Great Britain's Brexit and the other fault lines yawning in the European Union, the emergence of new autocracies in Hungary and Poland and the Philippines, even the rise of the Islamic State. "The current elite class," writes Gurri, "having lost its monopoly over information, has been stripped, probably forever, of the authorizing magic of legitimacy." The success of Trump's politics of grievance must be understood not as a movement for Trump himself but as a movement against the current order.

He must be understood, as Gurri points out, not as an old-fashioned autocrat but as an embodiment-as-leader of the online troll:

> Trump has mastered the nihilist style of the web.... He speaks in rant. He attacks, insults, condemns, doubles down on misstatements, never takes a step back, never apologizes.... This is American politics portrayed as the last circle of hell: treachery by the people, from the people, against the people. Taken literally, it would mean that not a single pillar of our institutions deserves to be left standing. Coming from a president, it has the feel of the state devouring itself.

Trump not only ran against the established order. He governed against it. In office he railed against the elites. Every day his supporters saw their president battling valiantly against the Deep State. From the White House he ran for reelection against the elite. His railing against the system animated his rallies and inspired the crowds who invaded the Capitol: "We fight like hell," he told them that morning at the Ellipse. "And if you don't fight like hell you're not going to have a country anymore." To his cheering followers—or at least those who go beyond the sheer performative nihilism of "Burn it down!"—the stolen election represented the last gasp of the old order, which only proved its ruthlessness and its desperation. The only sure way to fight back is to use whatever means are necessary to destroy that elite and its institutions. Lead us across the Rubicon!

3.

He golfs, receives supplicants, issues the occasional statement. To his supporters he is not the former president but "the rightful leader of the country." They say that the current occupant of the White House is there as a result of "the outcome," not "the election." For the election was stolen.

Trump controls the fervent allegiance of those tens of millions and because of this he controls the Republican Party. The occasional prominent defection is nothing more than the exception that proves the rule. Weeks after the insurrection, three in four Republicans agreed with the statement "Trump is a true patriot." This followed his second impeachment. After a brief shiver of doubt among Republican elites—ten House votes to impeach, seven Senate votes to convict—the apostates were duly punished. They have been censured and soon they will be primaried and purged. Senator Lindsey Graham of South Carolina proclaimed Trump "a cross between Jesse Helms, Ronald Reagan, and P. T. Barnum" who has "a dark side" and is also capable of "magic." "What I'm trying to do," the senator explained,

> is just harness the magic. He could make the Republican Party something that nobody else I know can make it. He can make it bigger. He can make it stronger. He can make it more diverse. And he also could destroy it.

He could destroy it by starting a third party, and from time to time he hints that he might do just that. Those hints swiftly pull the wavering party elite—including Senate Minority Leader Mitch McConnell, who denounced him after voting to acquit him—scurrying back into line.

But his power comes not only from this threat of destruction. His support in the country has never exceeded 50 percent, and there is evidence that he grows less popular by the day, imprisoning his party in a deadly downward spiral.[2]

To replace the well-educated suburban professionals whom Trump's politics of grievance drove away, the party will need to dip deeper into the well of white working-class and middle-class resentment. Who else but the supreme artist of hate and fear can find those voters and lure them with his dark hymn? The pollster Stanley Greenberg, who decades ago coined the term "Reagan Democrats," notes that it was Trump who in 2016 and 2020 gathered to the Republican Party new voters who were animated by "white nationalism and racial resentment, and whose overwhelming motivation is a deep worry that Black people and immigrants will control the country."[3]

In effect the Republicans have cast their lot with what Greenberg calls this "whole new set of voters brought in by Trump." Only he can bring them—or anywhere near enough of them—to the polls. But the more he courts them, the more alienated suburban Republicans become. The more these "Biden Republicans" stay home or even vote for Democrats, the more the party is forced to depend on Trump. The party belongs to him.

2. According to internal Republican polling in April, "Trump's unfavorable ratings were 15 points higher than his favorable ones in the core districts.... Nearly twice as many voters had a strongly unfavorable view of the former president as had a strongly favorable one." See Michael Scherer, Josh Dawsey, and Dan Lamothe, "Liz Cheney's Months-Long Effort to Turn Republicans from Trump Threatens Her Reelection and Ambitions. She Says It's Only Beginning," *The Washington Post*, May 8, 2021.

3. See Zack Stanton, "The Rise of the Biden Republicans," *Politico Magazine*, March 4, 2021.

4.

Trump's Republican Party is radicalizing. Across the country, Republican elites, frightened by and pandering to their base, are feeding its resentment and grievance by doubling down on Trump's Big Lie that the election was stolen. Even as they weaponize the Big Lie—using it as a rationale to pass legislation that will make it harder for certain overwhelmingly Democratic constituencies to cast ballots—they are bolstering it through widely covered "pseudo-events" like the Arizona vote "audit" and other spurious recounts to come. The former FBI special agent and terrorism expert Clinton Watts calls these kinds of political events "reality rebellion," which he defines as

> essentially trying to create an entire atmosphere, a complete show, and they have inculcated their audience in such a bubble at this point that they start to shape their perceptions and belief, and it leads to things like January 6. It leads to the nonsensical vote recount that they're trying to do in Arizona.... Because if you create an action in the physical world it makes it seem all the more legitimate to use violence and to strike out... based on that violent rhetoric that's coming out of this forty percent of Americans that think they are justified in rising up based on some creation, some fiction.[4]

This "complete show" based on lies and myths produces "an action in the physical world," like the Arizona recount, which further mobilizes the base, making the party's most faithful voters ever angrier and more radical. We need to think of this radicalization in

4. See *Deadline: White House*, MSNBC, May 21, 2021.

ways more familiar from developing countries. "For the next four years," as the terrorism expert Malcolm Nance put it after the coup, Trump "is going to lead a political insurgency that will have a paramilitary insurgent element."

The "insurgent element" is the violent vanguard of those Trump voters animated by "white nationalism and racial resentment." Many of the eight hundred or so shock troops who invaded the Capitol were drawn from their ranks. Of the half who have been arrested, at least some will be tried and can be expected to make the case that they were in fact "invited in" to the Capitol by "their president" and that no federal "deep state" has the right to prosecute them. They will argue for the legitimacy of their actions. These trials might take their place alongside the election audits as pseudo-events supporting the Big Lie. Will at least some jury members take such arguments to heart, effectively nullifying the trials?

Such outcomes are possible because the country remains intensely divided over the election and the events at the Capitol. Like the election audits, trials of the rioters would bring out and deepen these divisions, further radicalizing the Republican base. So too would acts of violence. The Oath Keepers and the Proud Boys and the Boogaloo Bois are just a few of the better-known paramilitary organizations that acted violently on January 6. There are many others. Some are national and many are local. Some are well known and many remain covert. Now that the election has been stolen and the thief responsible has begun to propose dramatic changes to the country—and now that the Deep State has proven that voting is useless in blocking them—how will members of these organizations and their sympathizers respond?

It seems plausible that at least some will respond with violence.

The intelligence analyst Katrina Mulligan noted shortly after the Capitol attack that the country had just witnessed "violence with a political goal in mind: Preventing the lawful certification of presidential election results to disrupt the peaceful transition of power":

> There are troubling indicators, such as a shared grievance, a strong group identity, and recruitment and training, that America could be in the early days of a violent political movement that will endure after President Donald Trump leaves office. This movement... brings together conservatives, Christian nationalists, Nazi sympathizers, white supremacists, and ultranationalist groups such as the Proud Boys. While these groups united around Trump, they also have shared racial grievances that will continue to unite them even after Trump leaves office.[5]

Members of these violent groups see a political dispensation gaining force under an illegitimate president that privileges minorities and immigrants, which they understand as part of an elite plot to "replace" them as central participants in the country's politics.[6] Even before the Capitol attack a number of terrorism researchers saw the

5. Katrina Mulligan, "The United States Could Be in the Early Days of a Domestic Insurgency," Center for American Progress, January 19, 2021.

6. Among those arrested after the Capitol coup, writes the political scientist Robert A. Pape, "one driver overwhelmingly stood out: fear of the 'Great Replacement.' Great Replacement theory has achieved iconic status with white nationalists and holds that minorities are progressively replacing White populations due to mass immigration policies and low birthrates. Extensive social media exposure is the second-biggest driver of this view, our surveys found." Robert A. Pape, "What an Analysis of 377 Americans Americans Arrested or Charged in the Capitol Insurrection Tells Us," *The Washington Post*, April 6, 2021.

conditions for "incipient insurgency" emerging in the United States. David Kilcullen, an elite combat soldier who helped shape strategy in Iraq and Afghanistan, wrote that "the main long-term impact" of the violence launched against the Black Lives Matter protests last May and June might "be its radicalizing effect on a tiny minority of participants who join more violent groups as a result":

> It is commonplace in insurgencies for guerrilla talent spotters to identify recruits through street violence, inducting them into armed, organized groups over time....
>
> One possible interpretation is that America may be in what the CIA *Guide to the Analysis of Insurgency* calls "incipient insurgency."... It may involve inchoate action by a range of groups, followed by organization, training, acquisition of resources, and building external and public support, then increasingly frequent antigovernment incidents displaying improved organization and forethought.[7]

Kilcullen wrote those words six months before the armed assault on the Capitol. The country's main counterterrorism officials agree with him. "January 6 was not an isolated event," FBI director Christopher Wray told Congress on March 2. "The problem of domestic terrorism has been metastasizing across the country for a long time now and it's not going away anytime soon."

After the Trump presidency, such domestic terrorism should be conceived not as a separable "problem" but rather as the leading edge of a broader movement intended to delegitimize American

7. David Kilcullen, "America in 2020: 'Insurrection' or 'Incipient Insurgency'?," Foundation for Defense of Democracies, June 23, 2020.

institutions. Violent acts would be the means not only to draw attention to the illegitimacy of American elections and the current administration but to radicalize those already enraged by what they see as its overreaching. The morning after the Capitol coup a reporter for PBS's *Frontline* interviewed Mike Dunn, a Virginia leader of a Boogaloo Bois group. Dunn professed himself much encouraged by the day's events. "We realized," he said, "that we're a lot closer to a revolution":

> Our recruiting and interest went right through the roof as well. They're beginning to understand that the only answer is revolution. . . . I think that people are learning and adapting. I think we're definitely looking at armed insurrection. Many of us in this movement, myself and a lot of other young people like me, have come to grips with the fact that death is a reality. It's coming. We just want ours to count.[8]

How many such dedicated armed revolutionaries are there now in the country? Surely they number in the hundreds, if not the thousands. If they want to "make their deaths count," what will they do? Will they stage attacks in groups? Or will they pursue "lone wolf" operations? No doubt they will follow a path of decentralized "leaderless resistance," which is the American right's most striking contribution to the theory and practice of terrorism.[9]

Whatever they might do—kidnapping or assassinating public

8. See *American Insurrection*, a 2021 PBS *Frontline* documentary directed by Richard Rowley.

9. See Louis Beam, "Leaderless Resistance" (1983), available at *The Seditionist*, February 1992.

figures, staging bombings or mass shootings—it would take the efforts of only a handful of determined violent actors to overturn the politics of the country. Such actions would be intended to provoke the security organs of the Deep State to overreact and make widespread arrests, thereby revealing its repressive character and encouraging more sympathy for the terrorists' cause. This dynamic would further radicalize those whose anger has already been stoked by the delegitimizing rhetoric of the Republican Party. Potential terrorists, perhaps for the first time in this country, have what is vital to make violent actions politically successful: a pool of millions of willing sympathizers.[10]

One need not be an expert in the history of terrorism and insurgency to see that the United States is ripe for such a dynamic. The violence, if it comes, will feed the radicalization of Republican policy in a fervid feedback loop. Already the party's national strategy draws its lifeblood from the Big Lie. Because Democrats stole the 2020 election, Republicans in state legislatures are moving urgently to "make the vote secure" by "reforming" their voting laws—not only in states that Trump did not win, like Georgia and Arizona, but in others, like Texas and Florida, that he did. These new laws will curtail access to the polls for minority voters and in many cases will make way for Republican-controlled legislatures to wield more power to

10. In late May a national poll showed that 28 percent of Republicans agreed that "things have gotten so off track, true American patriots may have to resort to violence in order to save our country." The same number—nearly three in ten Republicans—agreed that "there is a storm coming soon that will sweep away the elites in power and restore the rightful leaders." See Karen Tumulty, "The Really Scary Reason Republicans Don't Want to Face the Truth About Jan. 6," *The Washington Post*, May 28, 2021.

award a state's electoral votes.[11] Already this has been made easier in Georgia, and it soon likely will be in Arizona. By transferring the ultimate power to appoint electors from the voters to the politicians, Republicans are pursuing a strategy to convert their control of state legislatures into control of the White House. "The core power imbalance in America," Ezra Klein observed,

> is that Democrats win more people, Republicans win more places. In 2020, Joe Biden won 551 counties and 81 million votes. Donald Trump won 2,588 counties and 74 million votes. The Democrats' advantage among people was enough to win power nationally, but the Republicans' advantage in counties gave them control of more states.... There are 23 states where Republicans hold the lower house, the Senate and the governorship—a governing trifecta that eases the passage of highly partisan bills—but only 15 states where Democrats do the same.[12]

If in close elections Republicans can place the effective power to award a state's electoral votes in the state legislature, they will have gone far toward establishing a permanent grip on the White House. In this way, the voter suppression laws that are being imposed across the country will put the final brick into a minoritarian wall that a shrinking Republican population increasingly relies on to hold power. Before our eyes, calls to "stop the steal" of 2020 are evolving,

11. See Jonathan V. Last, "Reading the Republican Autopsy: It's Real, and It's Spectacular," *The Bulwark*, April 13, 2021.

12. Ezra Klein, "Joe Manchin and Stacey Abrams Can Meet on Common Ground," *The New York Times*, March 11, 2021.

with the help of Republican-controlled legislatures in crucial states, into a movement to in effect "steal back" the presidency in 2024.

At the United States Capitol, after more than four months, the National Guardsmen have finally packed up and gone. Members of Congress come and go as always. But now they pass through magnetometers to make sure they are not bringing weapons onto the floor of the House or the Senate. Beyond the looming white building, the country has few magnetometers and a growing surge of political bitterness. In late April the president announced to Congress, rather poignantly, that a critical part of his program is "to prove that democracy still works—that our government still works and we can deliver for our people." Perhaps he will succeed and perhaps one day the Capitol coup and its aftermath will be remembered as a low point and not as the gateway to something worse. But that this rather modest goal is so central to our elected leader shows how late the hour is, and how much Americans need to be assured that it is true. "Can our democracy," the president implored Congress, "overcome the lies, anger, hate, and fears that have pulled us apart?" The plain answer is that there is as yet no sign that it can. All around us are signs that our angry politics are likely to grow angrier—and perhaps more violent still.

The Slow-Motion Coup

October 6, 2022

Today is not the end. It's just the beginning.

—DONALD TRUMP, January 6, 2021

1.

Our political End Times glitter with surreal scenes—the green-tinted shock and awe unleashed over Baghdad, the "Brooks Brothers warriors" rioting at the Miami election recount, the jetliner piercing the Manhattan skyscraper—and beneath the unearthly beauty of the Capitol dome that frigid January day, I gazed in wonder at the latest of them: the heaving bodies in their winter clothes, the dark-uniformed, club-wielding police falling back before the phalanx of fists and bicycle racks and flagpoles, and, floating over the straining limbs, the swirls and eddies of bear spray and tear gas in nauseous yellow and green. Was it all a grotesque mirage? *Is this what revolution really looks like?* And yet we know now that from this phantasmagoric tableau a vital piece was missing: *he* was meant to be there.

Donald J. Trump's essential advantage is to be always underestimated: treated as a narcissistic fop, a deranged and ignorant bull in the china shop of American governance. True, he knows little and refuses to learn more because he is certain he knows all. True, he flaunts his narcissism and mythomania with petulant and unflagging pride. But for all that, he is a connoisseur of grievance and resentment and outrage, and a master at shaping from these lucrative political emotions a creative and motivating message. Could anyone accuse him of failing to comprehend the politics of spectacle? Could anyone doubt that he would have known how to shape this fantastic scene of "the people" seizing back their government into a full-fledged camera-ready extravaganza?

Scarcely an hour before and a couple miles away—just as I was shuffling off the Ellipse with my half-frozen, flag-wielding fellows to march up Constitution Avenue toward the Capitol, where, the ranting president had vowed to us, "I'll be there with you!"—Trump was climbing into the Beast, the presidential limousine. When the driver took the wheel to return his precious cargo to the White House, Trump grew instantly irate. "I'm the *fucking president*!" he screamed to his Secret Service protectors. "Take me up to the Capitol now!"

They had refused, of course, and went on refusing, even after the enraged president seized one of the agents at the throat. Or so White House aide Cassidy Hutchinson recounted to the January 6 committee, unleashing a cascade of furious denials. Did the president really respond to this thwarting of his will with violence? Perhaps the better question to have explored was: What would the president have done had those Secret Service agents obeyed? How would that day have unfolded? For it is clear that he had some plan, clear that what was intended to seem an impromptu visit to the Capitol had been well thought out, at least for Trump. "Cass, are you excited for the sixth?" Rudy Giuliani had asked Hutchinson as they left the White House four days before. "It's going to be a great day." Why? she asked. "We're going to the Capitol. It's going to be great. The president is going to be there. He's going to look powerful. He's going to be with the members. He's going to be with the senators."

He's going to look powerful. In his mind's eye, did Trump see himself descending from the Beast amid the welter of bodies outside the Capitol, to the wild cheers of the beefy men pummeling the police—and turning from their violent work to howl and slam their gloved hands together or raise their fists—and to the shouts of noncombatants arrayed in their Trumpian finery milling about the Capitol lawn? There in his chic black overcoat he would have waved, smiled, thrust his fist in the air as the tens of thousands of his faithful, far and near, raised their voices in a bloodcurdling roar. And finally, after shaking scores of hands, taking a few selfies, and perhaps offering an inspiring word or two through a megaphone, he would have led the crowd up the steps, as the cheers rose deafeningly and the little screens of the cell phones held aloft conveyed him making his triumphant way up to the domed temple in thousands of miniature images.

For had the president chosen to stride up those steps, who would have dared stop him? His followers would have fallen in behind him and the Capitol police would have fallen away before him and he would have breached the doors himself, his gold-orange hair shining beneath the mythic white dome in the crisp cold sunlight of that historic January day.

Is that how Donald John Trump, forty-fifth president of the United States, had imagined it? And if so, what did he then intend? Would he have led his chanting, flag-waving followers through the ceremonial doors, past the looming statues, down the marble hallways, and into the Senate chamber, there to face squarely his white-haired, stalwart vice-president, poised in frozen shock on the dais? With his Senate supporters gathered around their victorious leader, shaking his hand, pounding him on the back, would President Trump have smiled up at Mike Pence, held out his famously small hand, and demanded the certificates certifying the electoral votes of the "stolen" election? And would Pence, a man who had shown himself until this very day to be one of the most obsequious public officials in American history, have dared refuse? And then perhaps, in a dramatic gesture for his rowdy minions and the senators and the congressmen and the television cameras and the whole world watching, Donald Trump with his own two hands would have torn those tokens of legitimacy asunder.

We may well never know, of course, what exactly Trump had planned for his momentous visit to the Capitol that day. We do know that this dramatic visitation was to be the last in a series of attempts—involving false declarations on election night, forged electoral certificates, insinuating telephone calls with state legislators and secretaries of state, consultations with marginally unbalanced conservative lawyers, and endless, merciless pressure on the hapless vice-president ("You can either go down in history as a patriot or you can go down in history as a pussy")—to overthrow the results of the election. Eight weeks after election day, after his vice-president's betrayal, the final betrayal of all the Deep State betrayals of his four years in office ("He's thrown the president under the bus!" a red, white, and blue–clad woman, eyes glued to her phone as we marched up Constitution Avenue, shouted out to us), Trump found himself with no choice but to seize power personally, at the head of thousands of rabid followers, some of them armed. ("They're not here to hurt me," he had shouted before his speech, when he learned that those bearing weapons were being stopped at the gates. "Let my people in!") It would be beautiful, unforgettable. It would be a true and decisive victory over the Deep State. It would be his March on Rome.

Or perhaps his Beer Hall Putsch. Who can say? Would Pence, however surprisingly firm he had held to the Constitution those last few days, have dared oppose the president and his merry band in the Senate chamber? And if Pence had not managed to perform his "ministerial" role, could the election have been certified for Joseph R. Biden that appointed day of January 6? And if the election couldn't be certified, would the matter have been thrown into the House of Representatives, where Democrats held a majority of seats but Republicans, crucially, controlled a majority of the state delegations, which the Founders in their wisdom had decided would be the deciding measure? If all the Republican-controlled delegations voted for Trump, the House would have chosen him as the country's next president. Biden could have appealed to the Supreme Court, but could the Court, with six Republican votes, have been depended upon to render dispassionate justice, any more than it had managed to do twenty years before?

It is shockingly easy to imagine how the events of January 6, with just a tiny detail altered—a Secret Service agent, say, who was not quite so determined in opposing a screaming commander in chief—could have worked out quite differently and produced a reelected President Trump and furious Democrats marching in the streets. Would the triumphant president have called out the military to quell those crowds, as he had tried to do the previous spring during the Black Lives Matter protests? Would the senior officers—as "non-political" as they pride themselves on being—have dared to disobey?

All counterfactuals, of course, are submerged beneath the relentless forward march of what actually happened. Still, however much we want to relegate the events of January 6 to the realm of the near-missed catastrophe, our politics remain imprisoned in a series of events unfolding from that day. The coup did not end on January 6 or even in the early hours of January 7, when Congress finally certified the election of the new president. Today this unfinished chain of cause and effect—call it a slow-motion coup—continues to unfold before the country. The coup drives news coverage. The coup elects candidates. And the coup has already gone far toward leaching from our democracy the one element indispensable for a peaceful politics: the legitimacy of our means of conferring power. By launching and leading his slow-motion coup, Donald Trump has led the country into an unfamiliar and darker world. We don't know how, or if, we will emerge.

2.

Thanks to Trump, election past is election future. To think about the 2020 election is to think about the 2024 election. To look back at the attempted steal is to ponder the steal to come. To tens of millions of Americans "the Steal" is what the former president tried and failed to achieve. To tens of millions of other Americans "the Steal" is what the current president did achieve. Whatever it is, the Steal is a living myth that actively shapes our world. Across the country more than a hundred Republican candidates are running on it—at least fifty-seven of them were present at the Capitol that day—and some of them will likely win. Conceived in the fertile and aggrieved mind of Donald Trump, the Steal has captured the imagination of tens of millions and threatens to attain a kind of perfect reversed reality the next time we go to the polls to choose a president.

It is in the nature of the Big Man that he imposes his mind upon the people. His obsessions are not private. The former president's obsession that he won the 2020 election in a landslide and that his victory was stolen from him is now the obsession of millions. That there is little or no evidence for it makes no difference. That he may not believe it himself does not matter. What matters is the Big Man's performative certainty, which has become his followers' certainty. Their certainty makes it a political fact.

Because of the Big Man's certainty, states are passing laws restricting who can vote and changing who has the power to judge which votes count. Because of it, millions of those who voted in 2020 will find it harder to vote in 2022. Because of it, candidates who deny the legitimacy of the last election—and, by extension, of the system itself—are winning the nominations of their party for governor and secretary of state and representative and senator, and if they are raised to power they will act accordingly during the election to come. And all these historic changes began not with evidence or with facts but with a living, growing obsession in the Big Man's mind.

Between the Big Man's mind and his mind-melded supporters cower the Republican political elite. "What is the downside for humoring him for this little bit of time?" an unnamed "senior Republican official" inquired of *Washington Post* reporters shortly after the 2020 election. "He went golfing this weekend. It's not like he's plotting how to prevent Joe Biden from taking power on

Jan. 20."[1] Perilous as it is to evoke certain political eras, one must go back to Paul von Hindenburg and other titans of the late Weimar Republic to find an elite that so perfectly embodies fecklessness, cowardice, and folly. In one of the unintentionally funny passages in *Landslide: The Final Days of the Trump Presidency*, Michael Wolff tells us that Senator Mitch McConnell's "view of Trump was as virulent as the most virulent liberal's view":

> Trump was ignorant, corrupt, incompetent, unstable. Worse, he called into question the value and seriousness of every aspect of McConnell's Machiavellian achievement—what good was power if you had to share it with people who had no respect for it?

Share? McConnell voted to acquit Trump in his second impeachment trial, even as he denounced him from the Senate floor, then weeks later—after the polls were in—slavishly pledged to support "the president" if he ran again in 2024. The majority leader saw his dearest political ambitions founder when the "ignorant, corrupt, incompetent, unstable" president, whom McConnell and his cronies had "humored" for nearly two months, preferred to rave to Georgia voters about his stolen presidency rather than urge them to come out to vote for their Republican Senate candidates, thereby losing the Senate runoffs on January 5 and unceremoniously demoting the crafty Machiavellian to minority leader. Had Trump's coup the next day seemed to be succeeding, can anyone imagine that *McConnell*

1. Amy Gardner, Ashley Parker, Josh Dawsey, and Emma Brown, "Top Republicans Back Trump's Efforts to Challenge Election Results," *The Washington Post*, November 9, 2020.

would have stood against him? Who is humoring whom?

*

McConnell and his fellow Republican officials and donors fear Trump because they fear his voters, particularly the mobilized base that worships him. While many of these elites act out of rank opportunism, the more strategic-minded profess to believe that Trump is essential if the Republicans are to have a chance at regaining power in their present incarnation: a white-nationalist populist party with a rich business-class appendage, which increasingly finds itself holding its nose at the stench of the white unwashed. The donor class may be embarrassed by the canaille—and by Trump himself—but it knows the party could not win without their voices and their votes. Senator Lindsey Graham, who in slithering his way from savagely denouncing Trump in 2016 to shamelessly currying favor with him since has marked out a path many Republican leaders have followed, is one of the few willing to say this forthrightly:

> Can we move forward without President Trump? The answer is no. I've always liked Liz Cheney, but she's made a determination that the Republican Party can't grow with President Trump. I've determined we can't grow without him.

Though the statement is characteristically misleading—Cheney has made it clear she believes Trump threatens the country and the Constitution—Graham is saying the quiet part out loud: only Trump can guarantee to maintain or hope to increase the party's appeal to lower-middle-class and working-class whites, and in so doing, Graham went on, "make the Republican Party something that nobody else I know can make it. He can make it bigger. He can make it stronger. He can make it more diverse. And he also could destroy it."

That last point is crucial. But better to say: He could destroy *us*. For Graham's voice here is that of the Republican elite, whom Trump delights in making tremble with his every derisive shout of *RINO!* (Republican in Name Only). There is personal fear of Trump's violent supporters but also an acknowledgment of and even attraction to the harsh male dominance he embodies, so critical to the successful autocrat. "You know what I liked about Trump?" Graham asked a crowd of laughing, nodding Republicans. "Everybody was afraid of him, including me.... But here's one thing I can tell you about him. Don't cross him. Don't you miss that?"

By virtue of his iron hold on the base, Trump represents both an unparalleled opportunity and an existential threat to the Republican Party. His power is in part a negative one: he can *prevent* the party from winning. And if crossed he has made it clear he would have no compunction about doing exactly that. He reminds traditional Republican leaders of that power and his willingness to use it not only by his frank and unapologetic narcissism but by enacting and reenacting rituals of vengeance, most recently upon those Republicans—including Cheney—who dared vote to impeach him. By performing these public blood sacrifices, and by issuing revitalizing endorsements to those who are obsequious enough in seeking them, he reminds the party of his dominance and keeps all but the most heroic and reckless would-be dissenters firmly in line.

3.

That the Steal came fully formed from the president's mind and grew thanks to the fear and negligence of the politicians who thought they could "humor" him, that such a demonstrably false idea is now, as a firmly held belief of half the American electorate, a dominating strain in American history—that these astonishing events could come to disfigure the public life of the United States testifies to the decadence of the country's traditional hierarchies of power and information. It testifies also to the sheer animal spirits of the media beast Donald Trump, who still effortlessly dominates the news cycle, seizing the spotlight from his successor even as President Biden manages to pass historic legislation. By virtue of Trump's embodied grievance, his shamelessness, and his daring and skill at shaping a narrative—and then, when it is debunked, shaping another—Trump proves himself victorious, again and again, in attracting and holding eyeballs, which are the golden currency of our age. That American politics was destined to be absorbed by television and the communication and entertainment media it spawned could be foreseen as far back as John F. Kennedy, but the "reality star" Donald Trump is this new world's first grand apotheosis.

The question, as I write, is whether, having absorbed politics and one of our two parties, the Trump Reality Show can absorb the legal system as well. Eighteen months after launching the only coup d'état in the nation's quarter-millennium history, Trump remains the odds-on favorite to become the Republican nominee in 2024. Yes, the indictments and court cases are coming. But are they destined to be transformed into new and ever more enthralling episodes? Will they bolster his popularity and the resonance of his anti–Deep State message even as he faces the country from the dock? Will he undermine the rule of law with the same ease as he undermined the legitimacy of the government?

For all its garish effectiveness, much of the show's script is not new. In *The Steal: The Attempt to Overturn the 2020 Election and the People Who Stopped It*, Mark Bowden and Matthew Teague quote the candidate at a rally in Colorado in 2016:

> They even want to try and rig the election at the polling booths, where so many cities are corrupt. And you see that.... And voter fraud is all too common. And then they criticize us for saying that.... Take a look at Philadelphia ... take a look at Chicago, take a look at Saint Louis. Take a look at some of these cities where you see things happening that are horrendous.

The Steal, like so many of Trump's more resonant master-fables, vibrates with all the most potent elements of his politics of resentment. The system is rigged. Everywhere you look the "others"—blacks, immigrants, city dwellers—pillage and usurp and steal. And no matter how plain and obvious these facts are, "political correctness" means that no one dares say them out loud. *Except me*, that is.

Small wonder that when defenders of "the system" argue the case with facts—You claim the election was stolen? Show us the evidence!—they get nowhere. Bowden and Teague point to one study of fraud in American voting, by the very conservative Heritage Foundation, that over the last thirty years "listed only widely scattered instances committed by members of both political parties, capable of influencing—and even then only in rare instances—local elections results." Since November 2020, all the recounts, audits, and court cases—more than sixty of the latter—have found the same: the election was sound. More than sound: given the pandemic, it was a kind of miracle. It doesn't matter. Even in 2016, write Bowden and Teague, Trump's charge

> resonated with those who feared big government, the growing number and power of minorities, the whole modern drift of American society. Drawing on antiquated stereotypes from the era of Tammany Hall, Trump especially stressed corruption in big cities, where Democrats ruled and the population was heavy with African Americans.

Which is to say that the Steal is a perfect microcosm of Trump's politics of resentment: The very system is corrupt. With the help of minorities and illegal immigrants, the swamp and the Deep State rule. Beneath the elaborate façade constructed with endless inventive mendacity by the mainstream media lies a tangle of political and sexual conspiracies that account for the mystifying collapse during the last three or four decades of the world of the white working and lower-middle classes: the stagnation of wages, the emptying out of midwestern manufacturing, the outsourcing of jobs to China and elsewhere, the financial and housing collapse of 2008, the opioid crisis, the rise of the tech and Wall Street billionaires.

Add to that any number of deeply fraught "cultural issues," among them the state recognizing same-sex marriages, schools teaching children frankly about gay and trans people, and colleges opening women's sports to trans athletes. The Steal of 2020 is only the latest example of the rigged, corrupt, perverse system ruthlessly rising up to defend itself against the attack waged upon it by that fearless and solitary warrior, Donald J. Trump. The Steal, like all his keystone narratives, validates the legitimacy and destiny of Trump himself.

If the reality show candidate and his media magic seem new, the deep grievances and societal dislocations that make his populism so effective most assuredly are not. Four decades of nearly stagnant wages and the wildly disproportionate distribution of the fruits of the country's growth are plain for all to see. So is the vast and unpunished corruption exposed by the financial collapse of 2008. History has shown how populism feeds on corruption and unaddressed grievance. "A longing for money and power took hold of citizens," Josiah Osgood remarks in *How to Stop a Conspiracy*, his new edition of the Roman historian Sallust's *The War with Catiline* (circa 42 BC), "and the moral inversion began."

> Greed taught arrogance and cruelty; ambition made men deceitful. . . . The powerful "few" felt more than ever that the state was theirs to dominate. In desperation, the ordinary citizens, oppressed with debt, were willing to embrace a dubious champion like Catiline.

Nor is Trump the first American leader who has schemed to manipulate the aggrieved populace to gain permanent power. Osgood quotes Alexander Hamilton's appraisal of Aaron Burr, the brilliant, unscrupulous rogue and would-be American emperor who came within a whisker of the presidency. Burr's "private character," Hamilton wrote,

> is not defended by his most partial friends. He is bankrupt beyond redemption except by the plunder of his country. His public principles

> have no other spring or aim than his own aggrandizement. . . . If he can he will certainly disturb our institutions to secure himself *permanent power* and with it *wealth.* He is truly the Catiline of America.

This American Cataline, of course, went on to murder Hamilton.

The struggle between the force of individual personality, however disreputable, and the limiting power of institutions fascinated Hamilton and his colleagues. Among other things, alas, these last years have taught Americans the shortcomings of the Founders' attempt to shape institutions impervious to aspiring dictators. Perhaps the effort is destined to fail in any political system designed for fallible human beings. Sallust offers in his *Catiline* an unforgettable portrait of the deranged and almost irresistible schemer, corrupt, alluring, concupiscent, indefatigable, his complexion pale, his eyes bloodshot. This electric blend of attraction and repulsion rings uncomfortably familiar, as does the tale of the leader's troubling traits disrupting the institutions of the country he rules. "So strong was the disturbance within him," Osgood tells us, "that it could not be contained. It spilled out and engulfed the whole Republic."

4.

It is the conviction of his followers that they know Trump well—that they know him personally. At his raucous rallies it is hard not to feel that he is showing you his true self, for not only his wit and his anecdotes but his aberrant personality—his narcissism, his mendacity, his endless preening—are on full and unbridled display. He flaunts his neuroses. They are what make him entertaining. Because of this, reading the memoirs of those who have worked for him can be an oddly disjointed experience. Each begins by hoping the real Trump will be different. And day by day each gradually and reluctantly comes to know someone *we* already do. The real Trump is the Trump all can see, and his neuroses are what now drive our history. The most important of these, of course, is the deep and obsessive anxiety about losing. William P. Barr, his last attorney general, tells us in his memoir *One Damn Thing After Another* that he "doubted the President could ever admit to himself that he lost the election," because

> in his cosmos, a "loser" was the lowest form of life. Shortly after the election he was already persuading himself, and his followers, that the election had been stolen. The Internet was awash with unsupported conspiracy theories and outright falsehoods, which the President was all too ready to repeat. His ever-hovering circle of outside advisers—experts in telling him what he wanted to hear—were feeding him a steady diet of sensational fraud allegations. These were presented to the President, and publicly, in such detail and with such certitude as to sound—at first—very convincing and troubling.

The Steal was born not of evidence but of a neurotic inability to accept defeat. Even the most casual viewer of one of Trump's rallies can't fail to notice how central this inability is to how he views the world. Mary L. Trump, a clinical psychologist and niece of the former president, attributes this obsession and much else in his strange personality to the influence of his "high-functioning sociopath" father, Fred Trump, the self-made real estate tycoon from Queens who in effect raised—or, in her view, failed to raise—Donald after his mother fell ill:

> Fred's fundamental beliefs about how the world worked—in life, there can be only one winner and everybody else is a loser (an idea that essentially precluded the ability to share) and kindness is weakness—were clear. Donald knew, because he had seen it with [his older brother] Freddy, that failure to comply with his father's rules was punished by severe and often public humiliation, so he continued to adhere to them even outside his father's purview. Not surprisingly, his understanding of "right" and "wrong" would clash with the lessons taught in most elementary schools.

Unmanageable in his private school, Trump was eventually sent to the New York Military Academy, where discipline was harsh. He thrived there, for

> life at NYMA reinforced one of Fred's lessons: the person with the power (no matter how arbitrarily that power was conferred or attained) got to decide what was right and wrong. *Anything that helped you maintain power was by definition right*, even if it wasn't always fair. [Emphasis added]

In Mary Trump's analysis, Donald had been intentionally shaped to succeed in this harsh world by Fred, who, having destroyed his first-born son—Mary's father, who died of alcoholism at age forty-two—resolved to encourage "the killer" in his second:

> [Donald] took what he wanted without asking for permission not because he was brave but because he was afraid not to. Whether Donald understood the underlying message or not, Fred did: in family, as in life, there could be only one winner; everybody else had

to lose. Freddy kept trying and failing to do the right thing; Donald began to realize that there was nothing he could do wrong, so he stopped trying to do anything "right." He became bolder and more aggressive because he was rarely challenged or held to account by the only person in the world who mattered—his father. Fred liked his killer attitude, even if it manifested as bad behavior.

Every one of Donald's transgressions became an audition for his father's favor, as if he were saying, "See, Dad, I'm the tough one. I'm the killer." He kept piling on because there wasn't any resistance—until there was.

A loser cannot also be a killer. Trump's conviction on this matter is no secret. That he would refuse to acknowledge his loss and resist leaving office voluntarily was prophesied by Michael Cohen, his ex–fixer and lawyer, among others who know him well. What was less easy to predict were the complex mechanisms of fecklessness and ambition that led most of the leaders and officeholders of one of America's two major political parties to humor the president in his fantasy about the Steal—and that led tens of millions of voters to believe it in turn, and to elect politicians who profess to believe it as well. It is a tale that would be marvelous, if it didn't pose so grave a threat to the country and its institutions.

Central to the tale is a peculiar kind of court politics. In every administration the courtiers rise and fall according to the favor of the sovereign. The principles animating this vary from one administration to the next, but Trump's staffing was unprecedented in its volatility—unheard-of numbers of officials at senior and middle levels were hired and fired—and its personalism. A courtier rose by pleasing Trump and pleased him by giving him what he wanted, which was almost always something that pushed against the government's customary practices and often against the country's laws.

Against the tireless will of Trump, the so-called Deep State—the permanent bureaucracy and its allies among political appointees—pushed back. Those officials who helped Trump push back against it in his turn drew his favor and advanced. Those who acted too blatantly to restrain him—like the famous "adults in the room," two of them prominent generals, who surrounded him at the start of his administration—were one by one defenestrated. Over time, the process gradually exhausted and winnowed out those willing to oppose the president in defense of normal practices, principles, and laws.

Because of its inherent dynamic (Trump —thoroughly uninterested in learning how to be "presidential"—remained Trump), those willing to serve him in high positions had to develop complicated survival strategies, both to avoid giving the president what he wanted in the most egregious cases and to justify their compliance when they felt they had to act in a way they knew they shouldn't. Much of Barr's book, like many of the Trump memoirs, offers a kind of extended aria on this theme.

Following the 2020 election, this process accelerated. Only a bedraggled group of compliant survivors remained in the White House, and their numbers diminished by the day. And even they were increasingly ignored by a president who began to take most of his counsel from "outside advisers"—Barr's despised "clown show" of Giuliani, Sidney Powell, Jenna Ellis, and John Eastman. At the best of times Trump was difficult to "manage." "It was hard to hold

Trump's attention," Wolff remarks, "when he wasn't the one talking." Barr writes:

> It had always been difficult to keep him on track—you had to put up with endless bitching and exercise a superhuman level of patience, but it could be done. After the election, though, he was beyond restraint. He would only listen to a few sycophants who told him what he wanted to hear. Reasoning with him was hopeless.

By this relentless process of elimination, Trump gradually constructed around himself a circle of "advisers" who increasingly reflected back to him his own views, however outlandish. To "agree" with him in the cause of preventing some larger harm to come was perilous. Those who believed there was "no harm" in "humoring" Trump were treading a well-worn track traversed by hundreds throughout his life. Wolff, who has spent a career reporting on dominating personalities and their handlers in the worlds of money and the media, is deft in describing these moments, with a satirical touch that nearly makes one forget the gravity of it all:

> But the president suddenly went from sourness to delight. And inspiration!... They could just use Covid as a reason to delay the election. "People can't get to the polls. It's a national emergency. Right?" He looked around to everybody for their assent—and for congratulations on his great idea.
>
> There was often a small moment of silence and a collective intake of breath whenever Trump, with alarming frequency, went where no one wanted to go or would have dreamed of going. The reaction now was somewhere between gauging Trump's being Trump, with

> everybody understanding that nine-tenths of what came out of his mouth was blah-blah and recognizing that here might be a hinge moment in history and that he really might be thinking he could delay the election. If the latter, then there was the urgent question of who needed now, *right now*, to go into the breach?
>
> A reluctant [Chief of Staff Mark] Meadows did: "Mr. President, there isn't any procedure for that. There would be no constitutional precedent or mechanism. The date is fixed. The first Tuesday..." Meadows's sugary North Carolinian voice was tinged with panic.
>
> "Uh-uh. But what about—?"
>
> "I'm afraid—no, you can't. We can't."
>
> "I'm sure there might be a way, but... well..."

Trump, as so often, did not give up on the idea. He simply looked for more agreeable interlocutors—Chris Christie, for example, the former governor of New Jersey, whom he saw at a debate prep session the next week:

> "I'm thinking about calling it off," said Trump, as though without much thought.
>
> "The prep?" said Christie.
>
> "No, the election—too much virus."
>
> "Well, you can't do that, man," said Christie, a former US attorney, half chuckling. "You do know, you can't declare martial law." Christie followed up: "You do know that, right?"
>
> It was both alarming and awkward that he might not.

On the afternoon of January 6, Chief of Staff Mark Meadows sat outside the White House dining room, scrolling desultorily through the texts on his phone, while Pat Cipollone, the White House counsel, desperately pushed him to get up and confront Trump. The president of the United States had returned from his speech at the Ellipse and, having failed in his attempt to get to the Capitol—for quite awhile he refused to take off his overcoat, convinced he would still persuade his Secret Service detail to take him on his triumphant mission—now sat glued to the television, watching as thousands of his followers sacked the seat of Congress. Transfixed by the scenes of carnage, the commander in chief refused to pick up the phone.

"We need to go down and see the president now," shouted Cipollone, according to Cassidy Hutchinson.

"He doesn't want to *do anything*, Pat," a beaten-down Meadows replied.

"*Something* needs to be done," Cipollone shouted, "or people are going to die and the blood is going to be on *your* fucking hands. . . . They're literally calling for the vice-president to be fucking hung."

"You *heard* him, Pat," Meadows said. "He thinks Mike deserves it."

What could be the harm in humoring Donald Trump?

5.

In our nation's 246-year history, there has never been an individual who is a greater threat to our republic than Donald Trump.

—DICK CHENEY, August 4, 2022

The former vice-president's blunt assessment comes as a shock, and yet it needs only a minute or two of pondering to realize that

Dick Cheney, a man who, whatever you think of him, knows as much about power and its exercise as any contemporary American, speaks a stark truth. By engineering a half-dozen or so plots and conspiracies between the election and Biden's inauguration, Trump committed a grave crime against the state. He plotted to overthrow the government, and he very nearly succeeded. And after committing this crime in full view of the country—the crime for which Cicero and his fellow Roman senators executed five of Catiline's co-conspirators and meant to execute Catiline—Trump not only walks free but remains the undisputed leader of the Republican Party with a chance, whether he is under indictment or not, to retake the presidency.

Is that likely to happen? No. But it is possible it will happen. And that it remains a possibility is deeply disquieting. Trump has done his fellow Americans the service of showing them how vulnerable their vaunted system of government really is. For all their concern about tyranny, the Founders put in place a mechanism to remove a criminal president that has proved, in the face of strong party loyalties, to be laughably impotent. And in a country supposedly of laws, not of men, the laws' workings have shown themselves to be, in the face of a genuine emergency, ponderously slow, allowing a leader who tried illicitly to seize power to prepare quite openly to take power again. History offers notable examples of dictators who have come to power through elections, but it is hard to think of one who attempted to cling to power through a coup and failed—and to whom the polity, in its blithe unconcern, offered the chance to try again.

The Grievance Artist

October 5, 2023

1.

I need one more indictment to ensure my election!

—DONALD TRUMP, August 3, 2023

BEHOLD, IN OUR SWIRLING VIRTUAL AGE, with what sickening speed the unprecedented becomes the commonplace. See, for the first time, a president's second impeachment! See an ex-president's first-ever indictment! See his second, third, and fourth! See him judged a sexual abuser! See his golden businesses declared a fraud! Pull up a chair and watch: We have reached the final melding of politics and popular culture promised six decades ago in the visage of JFK. We are living in the Age of Trump.

Trump's politics are that of public display. His art form is his own behavior. What outrageous act will he next perform? What historical norm will he shatter? What shocking mendacity will emerge from that sneering mouth? Trump commands the true currency of our time: the public gaze. Millions of Americans worship him like a god. An equal number hate him with a fervency unequaled in our history. But no one can help looking at him.

Twice impeached, four times indicted, he stands on the verge of running away with his third successive Republican presidential nomination. He launched a coup d'état against a system of government that has survived a quarter-millennium, and he did it on national television. Now, after dominating our attention for nearly a decade and coming within a hair's breadth of pulling the entire system down around him, he stands a fair chance both of being sentenced to prison and of regaining the White House.

Can we struggle through our Trump Fatigue to recognize this as the astonishing reality it is? It is a sign not only of Trump's energy and cunning but of the vulnerability of our system that it has been unable to protect itself from him. He committed his grand public crime against the state nearly three years ago and the state has managed to bring him to court only now—awarding him the chance to use his trials to promote his victimhood and grievance and to champion them as his cause. Already his trials *are* his presidential campaign. In June he told a cheering crowd in Georgia:

> For seven years we've been engaged in an epic struggle to rescue our country from the sinister forces within who hate it.... And on November 5, 2024, we're going to stand up to the corrupt political establishment. We're going to evict a totally corrupt president, Joe Biden, from the White House. And we're going to finish the job that we started....
>
> Now the Marxist left is once again using the same corrupt [Department of Justice] and the same corrupt FBI, and the attorney general and the local district attorneys to interfere.... They're cheat-

ing. They're crooked. They're corrupt. These criminals cannot be rewarded. They must be defeated. You have to defeat them.

That the system is so determined to hobble him with phony indictments and other such "election interference" testifies both to the truth of what he says and the seriousness of the threat he poses—and that his voters pose. "Every time the radical-left Democrats, Marxist, communists, and fascists indict me, I consider it a great badge of courage," he tells his crowds. "I'm being indicted for you, and I believe the *you* is more than 200 million people that love our country." And even more explicitly, "They're not coming after me, they're coming after you. And I'm just standing in their way."

If Trump has a genius, it is his ability to shape, often out of his own self-made follies and recklessness and crimes, a narrative that relentlessly reaffirms his grim story of an us-versus-them America. He is the strongman standing between the "sinister forces" and the millions of ordinary Americans who love their country. The audacity with which he shapes this narrative and the unerring accuracy with which he targets his followers' resentments and insecurities are unmatched in our politics. Trump is the grand artist of grievance. He has replaced the Republican nostrums of balanced budgets and tax cuts and military strength with paranoia and bitterness and white-hot anger. A party that once wanted little more than to cut rich people's taxes now wildly cheers gutting the FBI and the Department of Justice. This is Trump's Republican Party, brimming with working- and middle-class supporters only he could attract. Trump built this new party and he is determined to use it, energized with the ignominy of his prosecutions, to vault himself back into the White House. Regaining power is his only strategy, his only plan; and his very freedom, perhaps his life, depend on it.

It is absurd, of course. How could a politician indicted on ninety-one felony counts in New York and Washington, Miami and Atlanta, dare to hope to be elected to the highest office in the land? Absurd—almost as absurd as the idea that a reality-show loudmouth and failed businessman with not a whit of government or military experience could have reached the White House in the first place. And indeed, once again the smart money says it's impossible: Trump, with help from the Supreme Court justices he appointed who struck down *Roe* v. *Wade*, has lost the moderates in the suburbs and the independents, and not enough right-wing "base" voters exist to return him to office.

Perhaps this will prove true. Or perhaps Trump will manage to persuade legions of nonvoters on the right to come to the polls to save their hero. Perhaps he will be able to seize on a hung jury or even an acquittal to energize even more supporters. Whatever the results, Trump will use—is already using—the election campaign to carry forward a "slow-motion coup" that began with his political career and that has succeeded in undermining the legitimacy of the political system for nearly half the population. If he loses, it can only be because of the election interference he daily denounces, and this "second steal" will stand for his supporters as the final proof that the system is irredeemably corrupt. And if he wins, he promises to transform the presidency and the system in ways that will make them unrecognizable. Whether the man finishes by sitting in the White House or a federal penitentiary, this undermining, this destruction of faith in the country's political institutions and in particular in its ways of transferring power, will stand as Trumpism's toxic legacy.

2.

Already nearly half the country views America's political institutions as illegitimate: for them the vast precincts of government, the huge bureaucracies in distant Washington, are controlled and dominated by the Deep State, the corrupt dark underbelly of power, and it is the Deep State that exposes and reaffirms its dirty cunning grip with every Trump indictment. The Deep State and the corruption it nourishes explain not only the war directed against Trump but also the American carnage he highlights: the heartland's economic stagnation, outsourcing, unemployment, all those sicknesses that have plagued American capitalism and kept the wages of his voters virtually unchanged since the late 1970s. The Deep State also explains why Trump's populist policy proposals, which offer puerile "solutions" to complicated problems—*Build a wall and have Mexico pay for it! Repeal Obamacare and give good insurance to everyone!*—never come to fruition. Its insidious obstructions are central to the Trumpian mythos.

Deep within this dark mythology, one comes across more than a grain of truth. Indeed, Trump's claims about these sinister forces opposing him from within are confirmed by nearly every memoirist who tells tales about their time working in his administration. Writer after writer, whether they served as lofty cabinet secretaries or lowly staffers, rushes to confirm exactly what Trump charges: that his or her proudest achievement was brilliantly managing to prevent the unlikely president from doing the crazy things he wanted to do. There is here a strong element of the self-serving. For many writers, these successes are thought to wipe away at least in part the moral opprobrium that came from serving in the Trump administration. If they hadn't served, after all, things—no matter how bad they looked—would have been immeasurably worse.

Every cult has its apostates, but with Trumpism the matter is far more complicated. First, the supposed Deep State officials blocking Trump who tell their stories in most of these volumes—including Miles Taylor (better known, if one can so put it, as "Anonymous"[1]) in *Blowback* and the former Clinton administration official David Rothkopf's interviewees in the tellingly titled *American Resistance*—belonged not to the Deep State at all but rather to the "shallow state." Though Trump "often complained about the 'deep state' of career civil servants who, he asserted, were determined to undermine his presidency," the political scientist James P. Pfiffner points out, "it was his own presidential appointees who most visibly resisted his directives. . . . to an extent unprecedented in the modern presidency."[2]

The plotline here makes for an inherently satisfying story (evil leader has terrible and deeply illegal idea; heroic retainer strives and strives and finally prevents its execution), but at bottom the rationale

1. In September 2018, while he was serving as a senior official in Trump's Department of Homeland Security, Taylor—writing as "Anonymous"—published an op-ed in *The New York Times* in which he wrote that Trump's "dilemma—which he does not fully grasp—is that many of the senior officials in his own administration are working diligently from within to frustrate parts of his agenda and his worst inclinations. I would know. I am one of them." See also Taylor's subsequent book, Anonymous, *A Warning* (Twelve, 2019).

2. James P. Pfiffner, "President Trump and the Shallow State: Disloyalty at the Highest Levels," *Presidential Studies Quarterly*, Vol. 52, No. 3 (September 2022).

was not overly complicated: Trump's simple ideas to solve complicated problems tended to be outlandish, unworkable, and—where the limit was reached for more than one appointee—illegal. And his manifest inability to take in information meant that he raised these ideas and insisted on them again and again and again, with mounting stubbornness and petulance and anger. Taylor, a senior official in the Department of Homeland Security, tells us that a few months after Trump's election,

> word came down from the White House... to stop providing the president with lengthy documents. If there was a staple in it, the briefing paper was probably too long and needed to be cut. Fifteen-page updates on complex issues were chopped down to one. Bold fonts. *Simple words.* BIG pictures. Know your audience, they say, and the "audience of one" (as we called the president) had the temperament of a child, albeit a child with a finger lingering over the nuclear button.

How to explain that the border and its influx of undocumented immigrants is a bitingly complex problem, springing from global economic realities and the impositions of American and international law and the bitter bottlenecks of domestic politics, to someone who simply is unable to absorb it? Who seems able to listen only to himself? Taylor describes these encounters vividly:

> The president went back to his greatest hits—"a big, big border wall!" "cut off the cash!" "screw the Mexicans!"—and we sat there listening to the diatribe that had begun to sound like a Broadway sing-a-long from hell. We left without any clear direction....
>
> Two days later, on March 19, he did the song and dance for us

> again. The Oval Office meeting was supposed to be about combating opioid addiction . . . [but] Trump steered the briefing to his favorite subject. He ran through his list of cruelly imaginative immigration policies once more.

Between meetings, Taylor and administration colleagues compare notes about the "pretty crazy shit" Trump had just spouted, speculating darkly on the president's mental health. But he always manages to top the last performance, as in this phone call Taylor sat in on with Homeland Security Secretary Kirstjen Nielsen:

> "Kiiiirstjen," he said in his distinctive New York accent. "I can't believe what I am seeing at the border." The president . . . wanted to talk about creative options. . . .
>
> He had an idea: "a big, deep moat."
>
> She muted the line. "Did he just say what I think he said?"
>
> "I want you to figure out how deep you can dig it, okay Kirstjen?" Trump proposed filling the moat with "snakes and alligators" to eat people alive if they fell into it. "How much would this cost, honey?"
>
> She unmuted. "We'll look into it, Mr. President." He kept pressing the point until she assured him again we'd get back to the White House.
>
> He wasn't joking, and we weren't laughing anymore. The call derailed the morning as DHS cobbled together a back-of-the-envelope estimate for digging a border-long ditch and filling it with snakes and alligators.

Informing the commander in chief that "a two-thousand-mile reptile-filled moat would cost tens of billions of dollars" staved off the idea for another day at least, but Nielsen's fate, like that of so many of her colleagues, was already sealed. Like them, she had been doomed by her allegiance to reality: "He was sick of her saying no. *No*, you can't seal the border. *No*, you can't deport anybody you want. *No*, you can't gas and electrocute migrants. The insubordination was intolerable."

Nielsen was soon gone. Appointees who did not do what Trump wanted—who drew the line, say, at outright illegality—came and went, as the president, clinging to his idées fixes, fired and hired, fired and hired. Firing and hiring were good, after all: tweeting each new defenestration provoked outrage in the press and thereby allowed him to dominate the news cycle, even as it dramatized him to his followers as a leader heroically battling the Deep State. And all the while the true believers in the White House were leading a high-profile search for true loyalists, men and women who would do Trump's bidding no matter what. Why *not* build a moat filled with alligators and snakes at the border? True, there might be good reasons—"operational" obstacles in building such a vast structure and in feeding thousands of reptiles, and (dare one say it?) laws against decreeing a grisly blanket death penalty for all migrants—but he had to be told them again and again. And he never did learn. He didn't want to.

3.

He never will, of course. But in a system of government built on dispersed power that can function only through compromise—in which a policy progresses through the bureaucracy by officials "working" a problem, not dictating a solution—Trump's authoritarian strain was repeatedly frustrated. He knew instinctively how to dominate the news cycle. But for all his self-promotion as a genius in "the art of the deal," his inability to focus or to lead meant that he never figured out how to convert that attention into power within the government that would help him put his policies, however ill-judged, into effect.

Instead he fought against the obstacles that the institutions and the laws represented. By all evidence, if he were to return to office, Trump would impose historic changes that would in effect make the government adapt to him, not the other way around. "Together, we are going to finish what we started," he declared to a cheering crowd in Waco, Texas, last spring.

> With you at my side, we will totally obliterate the Deep State, we will banish the warmongers from our government, we will drive out the globalists, and we will cast out the communists and Marxists, we will throw off the corrupt political class, we will beat the Democrats, we will rout the fake news media, we will stand up to the RINOS, and we will defeat Joe Biden and every single Democrat.[3]

An ambitious program, but what will it mean in practice? It's clear that many of these changes would be aimed at destroying the Deep State, though to confront that task he would have to take a quite different approach to the shallow state. Taylor predicts the specifics of these policies and lays them out with admirable concision:

> The next Trump will install only devout loyalists in top positions, while purging dissenters from the executive branch.

3. See Isaac Arnsdorf and Jeff Stein, "Trump Touts Authoritarian Vision for Second Term: 'I Am Your Justice,'" *The Washington Post*, April 21, 2023.

A future MAGA cabinet will be led by unapologetically un-confirmable figures and Trump look-alikes.

In addition to the cabinet, the second layer down in government will be packed with a "rising generation of assassins."

In the name of countering the Deep State, MAGA forces plan to take a hammer to the government's career civil service.

This plan was foreshadowed in Trump's last year in office, when he ordered John McEntee—his former "body man," or personal aide, whom he raised to be his director of the Office of Presidential Personnel—to lead an increasingly ruthless purge of the administration. Anyone who showed any independence was forced out; replacements were hired for their loyalty, not their talent or experience. Many senior officials, whose lack of qualifications made them unconfirmable, were hired in an "acting" capacity, letting the administration bypass Senate confirmation. "I sort of like 'acting,'" Trump said. "It gives me more flexibility." In other words, he could hire whom he liked, however unqualified. And he did indeed sign an executive order that would have made it possible to purge the civil service, though Biden rescinded it.

The divide between shallow-state independents and Trump loyalists is well illustrated in Rothkopf's account of the discussion over responses to the Black Lives Matter demonstrations after George Floyd's murder:

> Trump met with his team, including Secretary of Defense Mark Esper, Chairman of the Joint Chiefs of Staff Mark Milley, White House Chief of Staff Mark Meadows, [political adviser] Stephen Miller, and others in the Oval Office to discuss how to respond to

the protests. Leonnig and Rucker[4] report Stephen Miller said: "Mr. President, you have to show strength. They're burning the country down." Milley responded: "Stephen, shut the fuck up. They're not burning the fucking country down." Trump nonetheless pushed for military intervention. Milley argued it was not needed. In a subsequent meeting, Miller asserted the demonstrations were an insurrection warranting the use of troops. . . . Again, Milley pushed back. He and Esper were deeply unsettled by Trump's appetite to deploy troops to suppress citizens who were simply exercising their First Amendment rights.

On the morning of June 1, the president again reconvened his advisors. . . . Trump argued that the riots were making the United States look weak to foreign countries. He again raised the issue of deploying troops, maybe even the 82nd Airborne Division, to quiet the unrest in Washington. Defense Secretary Esper argued that this was a job for the police, for local law enforcement. Trump was furious at the pushback. . . . Milley raised the issue of the constitutional right to protest. Trump fulminated. . . . Esper, eager to do anything to keep active-duty forces off the streets, offered to see if he could encourage governors to mobilize the National Guard. . . . At a moment of crisis, over and over again through the Trump years, this was what managing Trump looked like: absorbing his blows, laying out the facts, side-stepping his most extreme and often illegal suggestions, and searching for ways to give him the semblance of a win, since that seemed to be the only way to placate him.

4. Rothkopf's account is a much-compressed version of a series of meetings fully reported in Carol Leonnig and Philip Rucker, *I Alone Can Fix It: Donald J. Trump's Catastrophic Final Year* (Penguin Press, 2021), pp. 156–157.

The 82nd Airborne was kept off the streets of Washington, but such "managing" of Trump had its limits. In the days after the election, Trump fired Esper and replaced him with a relative unknown, Christopher Miller, a retired special forces colonel, who had been running the National Counterterrorism Center. At the same time installing staunch loyalists in several other top positions at the Pentagon, including chief of staff. This abrupt turnover after losing—and contesting—an election was unprecedented. To many, it looked suspiciously like preparations for a military coup.[5] Critically, though, Trump did not dare to replace General Milley, who enjoyed widespread allegiance and respect and whom he himself had promoted. In *The Divider*, their elegant account of Trump's four years in office, Peter Baker and Susan Glasser describe Milley's reception of the Trump loyalists at the Pentagon:

> After Esper's firing, Milley called [Kash Patel, Miller's chief of staff, and Ezra Cohen, acting undersecretary of defense for intelligence] separately to his office to deliver stern lectures. Whatever machinations they were up to, he told each of them, "life looks really shitty from behind bars. And whether you want to realize it or not, there's going to be a president at exactly 1200 hours on the twentieth and his name is Joe Biden. And if you guys do anything that's illegal, I don't mind having you in prison."

5. For example, to the ten living former secretaries of defense, who published an op-ed in *The Washington Post* three days before the attack on the Capitol: Ashton Carter et al., "All 10 Living Former Defense Secretaries: Involving the Military in Election Disputes Would Cross into Dangerous Territory," *The Washington Post*, January 3, 2021.

He ended with a warning: They were being watched. "Don't do it, don't even try to do it. I can smell it. I can see it. And so can a lot of other people," Milley told them. "And by the way, the military will have no part of this shit."

Whether Milley's self-described lecture had any effect on the loyalists' actions on January 6 is unknown. He told Baker and Glasser that during the last weeks of the administration he feared either an external crisis—such as the president ordering an attack on Iran—that would be used to justify seizing power at home or "a manufactured internal crisis to justify ordering the military into the streets of America to prevent the transfer of power." To some at the Pentagon, the sacking of the Capitol by Trump's partisans and the calls for the military to intervene must have looked perilously close to just such a manufactured crisis. Might the fear of accidentally being drawn into a "Reichstag moment" have accounted for some or all of the three-hour-nineteen-minute delay in deploying the National Guard to the Capitol that afternoon? Milley claimed to Baker and Glasser that he had "roared into the defense secretary's office one flight up from his at 2:30 PM and began rattling off actions to be taken" and that he advised him to "immediately deploy the D.C. National Guard."

Still, even if this is true, Miller by his own account didn't order the National Guard to the Capitol until three o'clock—ninety minutes after they were requested—and they didn't arrive until nearly 5:30. It remains unclear, even after extensive reporting and reams of congressional testimony, what exactly accounted for the delay in the Pentagon approving the National Guard's deployment. We know that at least two senior officers reportedly expressed worries about "the optics" of deploying soldiers to the Capitol, and that at least one made mention of "peaceful protesters."[6] It is also unclear what Trump's loyalists, apart from Miller, were doing during this time. Miller's delay might be explained in part by what he told Congress were "concerns and hysteria" about "politicizing and inappropriately using the military," including the the letter from the former secretaries of defense. "Hysteria" or not, Miller did make plain that these "concerns . . . nonetheless factored into my decisions regarding the appropriate and limited use of our Armed Forces" in responding to the insurrection at the Capitol. Whether he worried about "optics" or really did fear the military might be "inappropriately used" he leaves unsaid.

What we do know is that the president, watching the siege of the Capitol in the private White House dining room, never reached for the telephone to call Miller or Milley. And yet, after the Secret Service's refusal to take him to the Capitol, where he had planned to speak to Congress and probably Vice-President Pence directly, and after Pence's refusal to send the slates of electors back to the states, Trump's only option to hold power was to invoke the Insurrection Act and send the military into the Capitol and into the streets to "restore order" and perhaps close the Capitol down. Why did he make no move to do it? Likely at least in part because he had learned in those previous discussions of the Black Lives Matter protests that certain critical "shallow state" officers, notably the chairman of the joint chiefs of staff, would almost certainly oppose calling out the military. If so, that particular exercise in "managing Trump" turns out to have been the most consequential of all. Judging by the

6. See Betsy Woodruff Swan and Meridith McGraw, "'Absolute Liars': Ex-D.C. Guard official says generals lied to Congress about Jan. 6," *Politico*, December 6, 2021.

candidate's dark vow on the campaign trail last March to "clean out all the corrupt actors in our national security and intelligence apparatus—and there are plenty of them!"—Trump is determined to face no such obstacles should he regain the White House.

4.

One needn't sign on to the melodrama or even the accuracy of Rothkopf's subtitle—"The Inside Story of How the Deep State Saved the Nation"—to be impressed with the military officers' dedication to the law and the government and the resourcefulness of many of the officials, whether shallow state or deep, confronted by the Trumpian onslaught on norms and laws. Of course, the Trump administration more often than not was the gang that couldn't shoot straight, with the president only the most vivid example. Much of the time they had little idea what they were doing. Taylor argues with missionary fervor that it will be different in a second Trump administration—or indeed any near-term Republican White House, which he believes will be dyed-in-the-wool MAGA, given Trump's wholesale transformation of the party. "MAGA forces are purging internal opposition with striking efficiency," he notes. "The takeover of the GOP apparatus is largely complete."

Whether this guarantees that if Trump somehow fails to gain the nomination a MAGA candidate would triumph in his stead seems less certain. True, Trump owns "the base." But he is such a singular figure that it is impossible to know who might gain the allegiance of his followers—or whether anyone could. "The conditions are right," writes Taylor, "for the Next Trump to emerge." Perhaps, but if so, where is he? And no matter who might take his place at the top of the ticket, it seems even harder to imagine Trump lending his support or even standing aside.

Still, whether it is Trump or a successor, the picture Taylor offers of a second MAGA term is plausible and horrendous. The justice system and investigative agencies will be corrupted. The president will prosecute his rivals and "weaponize the nation's domestic security apparatus to wage political warfare." The next administration will ignore and, when necessary, obstruct congressional oversight (as Trump's first administration increasingly did). When noncompliant judges rule against it, it will ignore those rulings and accelerate its program to pack the judiciary with ideologically sympathetic replacements. It will abandon Ukraine, embrace Putin, and doom the Western alliance. It will transform the immigration system, as Trump so often demanded, choking off the inflows from "shithole countries." And so on.[7]

It is striking how closely some of this program resembles the litany of charges Republicans in the House of Representatives daily unleash against the Biden administration. These are the politicians who have created a special committee to investigate "the weaponization of government." No doubt the lure of projection is very strong. But in truth many of these charges spring from long-standing grievances against the "administrative state" that Trump, however artfully he has exploited them, did not create. Post-Watergate Republicans strongly benefit from the energy of perpetual opposition. Even when they hold power, they are convinced, not entirely without reason, that the country's major institutions—not only the "permanent

7. Many reporters have offered predictions of a second Trump term, but still the strongest might be an early report by Jonathan Swan, "A Radical Plan for Trump's Second Term," *Axios*, July 22, 2022.

government" but most of the news media and the culture industry—continue to wage war ruthlessly against them. We can expect that a second Trump administration, the program for which is currently being painstakingly prepared at the Heritage Foundation and other right-wing Washington think tanks, will seek not to destroy the government but rather to neuter it a bit and then wield it as a weapon, as its cadres fervently believe the Democrats so fruitfully have done for the past half-century.

Taylor paints a picture of Trump (or a successor) installing a sort of "soft totalitarianism" without firing a shot. Anyone who doubts it could happen need only cast eyes on Viktor Orbán's Hungary, currently enjoying adulation on Fox News and other media of the right. Perhaps the most persuasive sign that Taylor's vision could soon come to be is not the polls, which, very early in the cycle, show Biden and Trump roughly tied, but the sheer fraying of belief in the country demonstrated so luridly on January 6. Biden has given conciliatory speeches, reached across the aisle to pass landmark legislation. But next to Trump, he appears a vanishingly small figure on the public stage—and for Trump supporters a pathetic and corrupt one they largely ignore.

For them, the Steal and what has come after, including the arrests and Trump's indictments, prove only that things were worse than they thought, and that the vaunted self-correcting mechanisms of our constitutional republic, atrophied by corruption, have ceased to function. This is what the January 6 rioters believed: If we couldn't make urgently needed changes to corrupt Washington by elections, what option was left but insurrection? One Trumper standing in front of me in the crowd at the Ellipse that day beseeched the president with his sign: "Lead Us Across the Rubicon!" For him as for his fellows, only a new Caesar could hope to confront the myriad corruptions of our present-day Rome.

This desperation with democracy, this hopelessness about achieving change through nonviolent means, this frustrated conviction that the whole rotten system must be swept away, rings vividly with the echoes of European politics. A century ago in Italy and Germany, a large part of the population believed that the entire rickety apparatus of government, stinking with corruption, had to be destroyed. For the tens of millions of Americans who believe this today, the indictments of Donald Trump only add to the unbearable stench. They do not see the prosecutions as a sign that no one is above the law or that justice will triumph. They see them as proof that the system is rigged and not only against their leader but against them. And if they ever begin to forget this, Trump will be there—everywhere—to remind them.

5.

As we approach the 2024 elections, the title of Luke Mogelson's remarkable account of the year 2020, from the Black Lives Matter demonstrations in Minneapolis to the January 6 insurrection, sounds a warning: *The Storm Is Here*. In his hands, January 6 seems somehow predetermined, a natural outgrowth of all that happened during that dreadful and remarkable year. Mogelson reports from the streets of Lansing, Minneapolis, and Portland, where we get to know Proud Boys, Black Lives Matter, Antifa, QAnon—activists of the right and left who appear and reappear in the accelerating political phantasmagoria. In part because of this thorough immersion in the violent politics of that year, Mogelson's account of January 6, in which he takes us into the Capitol and the Senate chamber, is unmatched for its clarity and vigor.

The insurrection, naturally, is the climax of his story. But will it be the climax of ours? My eye was drawn to an interview in the book's final pages, when Mogelson travels to a small town in Georgia to interview Chester Doles, a former KKK wizard who has decided to run for county commissioner because, he says, "I want to be in a position to be able to do something when this shit pops off. Because I do think it's gonna pop off. I really do. Whether we want it or not." Mogelson goes on:

> He envisioned a scenario in which some inevitable government affront would provoke a response, as Ruby Ridge and Waco had triggered the Oklahoma City bombing—except this time, a cascade of rebellion and reprisal would follow. "Timothy McVeigh was trying to spark a chain reaction of resistance," he said. "But the climate wasn't ready yet." The climate was changing. The lockdowns, the riots, Antifa, the election: "We'll have to be pushed into a corner, but we're definitely getting pushed there now."... When I asked whether Trump running for president in 2024—and losing—might set in motion something... he nodded. "That would be a breaking point. I think that America would balkanize." Doles paused, and then added, "But probably only after blood runs knee-high in the streets."

The image is apocalyptic, and it matches imagery evoked, a bit less vividly, by none other than Donald Trump, when he threatened last March, before his New York indictment, that "potential death & destruction in such a false charge could be catastrophic for our Country." None of that came to pass. Perhaps the arrests and convictions of hundreds of insurrectionists have quieted the fervor, or at least stanched the enthusiasm. Or perhaps the fever has broken.

It seems unlikely. Trump's campaign rhetoric so often flirts with incitements to violence that most of those comments scarcely even make the news. We are long accustomed to him denouncing his opponents or his judges or members of the news media as traitors. He must come up with something truly striking and original—for example, calling for the chairman of the joint chiefs to be executed for treason—to make us take notice. But those who hang on his every word—including those conspiracy-obsessed who are certain "the storm" will soon break—know what he's saying, and echo it.

Does Trump really long for blood to run in the streets? This remains unclear, likely even to him. What is clear is that the right bloodcurdling threat will dominate the news cycle—will *make us look*. Mogelson, who has reported from Iraq and Syria, remarks that every civil war he

> covered had been premised on real grievances, real oppression, real violation.... Were large-scale violence to erupt in the US, it would be something different: a war fueled not by injury but by delusion.

And yet, how surprising would that be? In the Age of Trump, when the public gaze is doggedly, relentlessly drawn back to him, delusions have become our daily bread.

How We Welcomed Him Back

July 26, 2026

1.

If you find yourself obsessively appalled by the dark signs and wonders coming out of Washington—the systematic corruption, the stunningly unqualified people elevated to high office, the wholesale deporting of hundreds of thousands of largely law-abiding people and the imprisonment of sixty thousand others, the catastrophic war of choice in the Middle East, the purposeful undermining of the country's alliances, the illegal tariffs, the blithe destruction of USAID, PBS, and the Kennedy Center, and on and on—you have a perfect right to be astonished but not surprised. This is the president, after all, who more than five years ago staged a violent coup against the state on national television, killing at least five people. In its wake the federal government managed to convict nearly 1,300 people who assaulted police, ransacked the Capitol, and halted the peaceful transfer of power. But those convicted felons—all of whom, thanks to Donald Trump's sweeping pardon, are now free—acted at the incitement of the forty-fifth president of the United States. Why was that government unable to prevent him from returning as the forty-seventh? How is it that the only president in history to mount a coup d'état was four years later ushered back into the White House? What does it say about the world's most powerful state that it was unable to defend itself from so incontrovertible a threat?

2.

Was it somnolence, or decadence, or a simple failure of imagination? In the bright cold early morning of January 6, I found myself wandering the otherworldly precincts of the Washington Monument. In the golden light it took me a moment before I realized I had stumbled into an armed camp. Bearded men in tactical vests. Guys in MAGA hats checking side arms on their hips. A man sighting an assault rifle. To the clueless tourist, they returned blankly hostile looks. Duty called for me to pose a question or two and yet these men were grim and unreachable, focused on their weapons, so I raised my hand in a limp wave and turned back toward the White House. I felt dazed. And yet had I not told friends, when they asked why I was flying to Washington, that I was "going to attend Trump's coup"? It was a joke but only barely. "Big protest in DC on January 6," the president had famously tweeted. "Be there, will be wild!" The evidence of what was to come was splashed all over the Internet. But confronted with the reality of it, I could not yet quite grok what I was seeing.

This inability to recognize the threat that was looming in front of our faces replicated itself throughout the vast national security bureaucracies designed to protect the country. Partly this was the unprecedented nature of what was happening. More precisely, it was the unparalleled ability of this most singular president of the United States, making dazzling use of contemporary communications and social media, to create almost entirely on his own an alternative reality. "Stop the Steal" began on Facebook the day after the election and grew exponentially, at one point taking on a hundred new members every ten seconds. (The group reached 320,000 before Facebook finally shut it down, leading "Stop the Steal" to migrate to Parler, Gab, and other sites.[1]) Within weeks of the election, the unfounded conviction that it had been stolen, nourished by Trump's televised assertions and his social media feed and reinforced on Fox and Newsmax and in various corners of the Internet, had taken firm root in the minds of tens of millions of people. On January 6, that conviction leapt the firebreak between cyberspace and our own and incarnated itself into brutal reality at the Capitol.

In the days before, one only needed eyes and a willingness to see to recognize the signs of "the storm" approaching. Calls to civil war, posts about the tunnels under the Capitol, appeals to bring assault rifles: much of it was duly gathered by the Capitol Police intelligence analysts but little made it into the "Special Event Assessments" issued to staff and other law enforcement agencies, leading to the conclusion on December 30 that there was "no information regarding specific disruptions or acts of civil disobedience targeting this function." Similarly, the FBI, though they had tips that the Proud Boys and their leader, Enrique Tarrio, were headed for Washington "to cause mass unrest, destruction and potentially kill many people in the streets of DC on January 6th," dismissed most of what they heard as "unsubstantiated" and asserted they did "not have any information to suggest these events will involve anything other than [First

1. See Dan Barry and Sheera Frenkel, "'Be There. Will Be Wild!': Trump All but Circled the Date," *The New York Times*, January 6, 2021.

Amendment] protected activities."[2] In *Storm at the Capitol*, her oral history of January 6, Mary Clare Jalonick retells this depressing tale of bureaucratic sleepwalking but includes a startlingly precise prophesy from a threat assessment of January 3:

> Supporters of the current president see January 6, 2021, as the last opportunity to overturn the results of the presidential election. This sense of desperation and disappointment may lead to more of an incentive to become violent. Unlike previous post-election protests, the targets of the pro-Trump supporters are not necessarily the counter-protesters as they were previously, but rather Congress itself is the target on the 6th. As outlined above, there has been a worrisome call for protesters to come to these events armed and there is the possibility that protests may be inclined to become violent.

Despite the clarity of these sentences, the summary of the report, Jalonick notes, "repeated language similar to that used in previous assessments, directly contradicting the blunt warning." The assessments of January 4, 5, and 6 omitted the warning altogether, concluding that civil disobedience was "remote" to "improbable." On January 5, protesters rallied on the east side of the Capitol and "they were talking about civil war, and they were talking about violence," a reporter tells Jalonick. Later that evening the president tweeted that "Washington is being inundated with people who don't want to see an election victory stolen by emboldened Radical Left Democrats. Our Country has had enough, they won't take it anymore!"

2. See Carol Leonnig and Aaron C. Davis, *Injustice: How Politics and Fear Vanquished America's Justice Department* (Penguin, 2025).

Meantime the Capitol Police chief's request for National Guard support—perhaps the one step that might have prevented the breach of the Capitol and even much of the violence—had not been approved. By the morning, the guns had come out: I saw them not only around the Washington Monument but on the hips of men who had climbed trees to get a better view of the president. Few coups in history can have been less secret.

3.

Thanks to national television, the brutality of that day was witnessed by tens of millions of people in real time and it is brought back to vivid life in *Storm at the Capitol.* "I can just remember my breath catching in my throat," recalls Capitol Police Officer Caroline Edwards, "because what I saw was just a war scene.... There were officers on the ground. You know, they were bleeding. They were throwing up. I saw friends with blood all over their faces. I was slipping in people's blood. I was catching people as they fell. It was carnage. It was chaos. I can't even describe what I saw."

What looked like bloody medieval chaos was in fact the public face of a uniquely postmodern coup d'état: loosely organized on the Internet with various highly adaptable moving parts, all orchestrated by the president of the United States. Tens of thousands of Trump foot soldiers came maniacally determined to "stop the steal." Mixed in with these loyalists, many of them armed, were more organized groups of paramilitaries, who were determined, as Oath Keepers leader Stewart Rhodes put it on January 4, to support "President Trump's fight to defeat the enemies foreign and domestic who are attempting a coup, through the massive vote fraud and related attacks on our Republic."[3] This "mirror language"—we must support the president (in fact, attempt a coup) to *prevent* a coup—is an increasingly unavoidable feature of our age that underlines the ongoing battle over legitimacy: Who exactly were the ones mounting the coup? The paramilitaries saw themselves as following in the footsteps of the revolutionary forces of old to prevent a coup by the Washington establishment against their rightful president. By early afternoon, as Jalonick notes, these paramilitaries "were headed toward the Capitol.... One group had equipped themselves with communication devices and reinforced vests, helmets, goggles, and other tactical gear. A second group, speeding toward the Capitol on golf carts, was not only wearing battle gear but also had hard-knuckle tactical gloves, ballistic goggles, radios, chemical sprays..."

The paramilitaries were a hard core of hundreds within the larger circles of thousands and they would be central to actually breaching the Capitol. At the precise center of all these whirling parts stood the forty-fifth president of the United States. Around midday he would address his foot soldiers, sending them toward the Capitol bellowing, "If you don't fight like hell you're not going to have a country anymore!" As they marched off he would remain in contact with them via the electronic filament that was his tweets. A second filament reached out to the paramilitary groups, the Oath Keepers, the Proud Boys, and others, both directly—"Proud Boys! Stand back and stand by!" the president had commanded in a televised debate that fall—and via his associates, including the old dirty trick-

3. Quoted in Chairman Bennie G. Thompson's subpoena letter to Elmer Stewart Rhodes, January 6th Committee, November 23, 2021.

ster Roger Stone, who spent time with Tarrio and Rhodes when they worked as his "security" and was in constant touch with them through his encrypted "Friends of Stone" chat network. A third filament reached out to congressional allies determined to delay the counting of the votes that day, both directly and via the president's main coconspirators, including his personal attorney Rudolph Giuliani and his strategist Steve Bannon—the president spoke to both by telephone before his speech at the Ellipse—as well as lesser players John Eastman and Bernard Kerik and other plotters working out of the coup's "War Room" in the Willard Hotel.

4.

The coup was free-form, improvisatory, adaptive—that is, very Trumpian. Plenty of evidence suggests that after his speech Trump was vaguely planning to drive to the Capitol, mount the steps, and confront his vice-president directly, persuading him by his own force of will to accept the slates of fake electors—which had been forged and signed in the six swing states over the past weeks—or at least to send the votes back to the state legislatures. When despite his angry insistence, Trump's Secret Service agents refused to take him there, the president set himself up alone before the television in the dining room off the Oval Office and, wielding his telephone and his tweets, actively directed his thousands of supporters. I recall vividly when, deep in the huge motley wave trooping toward the Capitol, a woman near me festooned in red, white, and blue American-flag garb bent over her phone and shrieked, "Pence has thrown us under the bus!" As Jalonick's witnesses describe the moment:

Jessica Watkins, US Army veteran and bar owner, Oath Keepers, Ohio: So before we left the Ellipse, like, the crowd was real, real thick. And then, like, everybody—like, literally everybody—just started pulling out their phones. They were like, "Pence betrayed us. Pence betrayed us." Like, we have to go....

Jason Dolan, former marine, Oath Keepers, Florida: I think you kind of felt a palpable feeling where the crowd went from being pretty—a pretty happy, joyful crowd to a pretty kind of pissed-off crowd.

At 2:24 p.m., Trump, perhaps finally conceding that his coaxing and threats had failed to persuade the vice-president to "do the right thing," tweeted his famous words, "Mike Pence didn't have the courage to do what should have been done ... !" and the crowd, hearing the words booming out through megaphones from the steps of the Capitol, turned very ugly. The shouts of "Hang Mike Pence!" began and the vice-president's security detail rushed him to a loading dock under the Capitol. Trump, watching the crowd's reaction on television, was informed by a panicked White House aide of the vice-president's peril. "So what?" the president responded.

With one phone call he could have ordered the Washington National Guard to the Capitol, and it has often been remarked that his refusal to do so constituted "dereliction of duty." (Though the Guard was equipped and loaded on buses, generals at the Pentagon, worried about "the optics" of troops at the Capitol, delayed approval —which meant it would take more than three hours to arrive and clear the Capitol.) But in what sense did the president have a duty to prevent the coup he himself was directing? Even as the crowd surged wildly shouting through the Capitol and the vice-president and the senators and representatives hunkered down in fear for their lives, the president was personally lobbying senators to delay certifying the election:

Sen. Mike Lee, R-UT: Moments after the proceedings in the Senate were halted by the Capitol Police my phone rang. The caller ID indicated that the call was coming from the White House....

Sen. Tommy Tuberville, R-AL: When he brought me the phone, it said "White House" on it. It was the president.

Sen. Mike Rounds, R-SD: And so I was sitting here, and Coach [Tuberville] is right next to me. And the conversation—I'm only hearing one side of it, but it is "No, we're not doing much right now. No. Well, there's, you know, we can hear stuff outside. It's—no, Mike [Pence], no, they just took him out. They've taken him out. No, well, I don't know."... And he says, "Well, Mr. President, I gotta go. I guess they're gonna get us out of here now." And I never forgot that. Because while we were in the room, and there was enough going on to where they were going to remove us, there was still a lobbying effort going on by the president of the United States to stop the ballot from moving forward.

Amid the overwhelming violence at the Capitol—shortly after this, a Capitol policeman would shoot demonstrator Ashli Babbitt as she tried to push through the broken window of the Speaker's Lobby—the president was pressing forward with the so-called Green Bay Sweep, lobbying individual senators to delay the proceedings long enough to exert pressure on legislators back in the swing states. Trump was still single-mindedly convinced that by his own persuasive powers and the force of foot soldiers, he could impose his will, triumph over the system—and a quarter millennium of history—and remain in office.

5.

What do you do with the author of a failed coup d'état who also happens to be the president? What do you do with a chief of state who commits a crime against the state? The framers were familiar with such cases from their classical educations. They knew of Catiline, he of the eponymous Conspiracy of 63 BC, who plotted to overthrow the Republic and whom the Romans killed in battle. Had he survived, Cicero—serving as consul at the time—certainly would have had him executed. And of course they knew well the story of Julius Caesar, whom a group of senators, in the belief they were defending the Republic, assassinated shortly after he'd named himself dictator. In both, a crime against the state meets the most severe sanction. In our own era, the little-known ex-corporal Adolf Hitler mounted a comic-opera Beer Hall Putsch against the Weimar Republic, served nine months in prison—he used them to dictate *Mein Kampf*—and a decade later was elected Chancellor of the Reich. In perhaps the closest parallel, Alberto Fujimori, who mounted what in Peru was christened an *autogolpe* (or "self-coup"), was eventually put in prison. (Peruvians recently elected his daughter president.) It is hard to think of a leader who mounted a failed coup going free and returning to power four years later.

In this as in so many other things Donald Trump is singular. His decade at the pinnacle of our political life has been a stress test for our constitutional system and has shown it to be badly wanting. His first election, in which he reached the White House having won three million fewer votes than his opponent, was itself an indictment of the anachronistic absurdities perpetuated by our founding document. If anything qualifies as the high crimes deserving of impeachment and conviction, it was his actions on January 6. And yet the senators, having borne witness to the crimes with their own eyes, came barely within ten votes of convicting him. Under the severe factionalism of our current party system, impeachment proved to be an impotent joke. We can expect, if the Democrats gain control of Congress in the 2026 midterm elections, that it will remain so.

Senator Mitch McConnell, at the time the majority leader, put the matter squarely to his colleagues and the country: "There is no question—none—that President Trump is practically and morally responsible for provoking the events of the day. No question about it. The people who stormed this building believed they were acting on the wishes and instructions of their president." Alas, McConnell then concluded, "We have no power to convict and disqualify a former office holder who is now a private citizen." (He neglected to mention that he himself was responsible for delaying the Senate trial until after Trump had left office.) Not to worry, McConnell went on: "President Trump is still liable for everything he did while in office as an ordinary citizen.... He didn't get away with anything yet. Yet. We still have a criminal justice system in this country."

Whether the majority leader was sincere in his professed belief that the Constitution forbade the conviction of a private citizen—or whether he merely sought to avoid the political retribution a vote for conviction would have brought from the tens of millions of Republicans who still worshipped Trump—he had in effect, by blocking Trump's conviction, handed the hot potato off to someone else. For that criminal justice system he praised so highly was now in the hands of President Joseph R. Biden.

Or rather in those of Biden's handpicked attorney general, Merrick B. Garland. The distinction is important, for the incoming Democratic administration, and Garland in particular, had pledged to "de-politicize" a Justice Department that was thought to have been badly corrupted. Trump had publicly excoriated his first attorney general for failing to "protect" him, had summarily fired the FBI director for investigating what Trump called "the Russia hoax," and had ordered that the special prosecutor then named to carry on that investigation be fired. These were all shocking departures from how business had been done in the Justice Department since its reconstruction after the abuses of the Nixon administration. For decades, write Carol Leonnig and Aaron C. Davis in their meticulous account, *Injustice: How Politics and Fear Vanquished America's Justice Department*, veterans would warn young prosecutors "of Justice's past failures to be transparent and impartial. Such violations risk undermining public confidence in the justice system." They go on:

> Through the passage of decades, Justice has become a living, breathing organism of dedicated public servants yoked together to uphold these shared values in Republican and Democratic administrations. They pledged to keep Justice blind and impartial—and independent from political influence. They agreed that the facts and the law should guide their decisions on whether to charge a suspect or drop a prosecution when the evidence warranted.

Admirable words but perhaps a touch high-minded: one needn't go back to Nixon to find persuasive instances of the Justice Department acting politically. The elusive borderline between legal and political is often precisely where the dispute lies. Still, there is no question that Garland, who had been a distinguished prosecutor and then a revered federal judge—and whom McConnell and his Republican majority refused a hearing in 2016 after Barack Obama had nominated him to the Supreme Court—believed strongly in these principles and prided himself on acting on them. "As everyone who watched yesterday's events now understands," Garland said, after the president-elect introduced him on January 7, "the rule of law is not just some lawyer's turn of phrase, it is the very foundation of our democracy." And coming into office after Trump, how could he not be painfully aware that the "department's political independence... was never protected under law, but instead flourished through American presidents' shared respect for this core precept"? After all, it was these very weak points in the governing structure—longtime practice dictated by norms, not laws—that the predatory Trump had been quick to sniff out and exploit. In doing so, he had left a Justice Department and FBI that were skittish and politically traumatized.

6.

By the time Garland was confirmed as attorney general in early March 2021, the Department of Justice was already fully engaged in a vast effort to prosecute the thousands who had breached the Capitol on January 6. Using cell phone data and video posted to the

Internet, hundreds of FBI agents and prosecutors identified and built cases against those who had bloodied police officers, smashed the Capitol doors and windows, and invaded the Senate and House chambers. Millions of Americans had witnessed these crimes.

Of course they had witnessed as well Trump's speech on the Ellipse that day and had read his inflammatory tweets. But this was different. As Garland had set out during his confirmation hearings, "We begin with the people on the ground, and we work our way up to those who are involved, and further involved, and we will pursue these leads wherever they take us." There would be, that is, no "leap-frogging" to more powerful figures who actually might have planned and directed what happened that day, or incited it in their ringing words to the crowd. The small fish would lead to the big fish, presuming of course that there were any of the latter.

Of course Garland was right that for many crimes this was standard law enforcement procedure: for drug trafficking, for example. But for a coup d'état? In which the perpetrator had acted publicly? To move against the planners and directors of the coup—including the former president of the United States—would be to expose Garland's beloved DOJ to charges that it was acting in the cause of political retribution. And did not the new attorney general, as he had said at his confirmation hearings, want "to turn down the volume on the way in which people view the department—that the Justice Department not be the center of partisan disagreement"? To investigate the former president for fomenting a coup d'état was not exactly the way to regain the DOJ's reputation for bipartisanship. And it was not simply Garland's determination to "right the ship at Justice." The new attorney general "had told a few friends," according to Leonnig and Davis, that he hoped that the country on January 6 "had burst a bubble of hyperpartisanship" and that in its aftermath the United States "was ready to pick up the pieces and move on, as it had after Watergate."

For a nonpartisan attorney general this would seem a remarkably political basis on which to decline to investigate directly the author of the greatest political crime in the country's history. Not only did the judgment itself prove to be strikingly ill-founded; it blithely assumed that any threat to the state had passed. Whatever the reason, because of his reluctance to have the DOJ seen to be acting "politically," Garland and his associates proved willing essentially to ignore clear evidence that Trump, Stone, Giuliani, and others had committed crimes in trying to overthrow the results of a national election—evidence that became impossible to deny once the January 6th Committee in the House began holding its hearings. And Garland was not alone. Leonnig and Davis describe how FBI investigators also proved reluctant, "a little gun-shy of tangoing with Trump again." Trump's relentless savage criticism of the FBI and the DOJ had had its effect. From the White House the former president had indefatigably "worked the refs" by denouncing the DOJ and the FBI over "the Russia hoax," among other things, and the refs were now showing themselves traumatized.

As for higher-level officials at the FBI, many "saw the Capitol attack investigation as a political minefield if they leapt to pursue a former president or his aides at this stage." Obviously they were right. But does it follow that the crime against the state and its perpetrators should go uninvestigated? Going forward with an investigation, of course, was certain to sharpen the department's own political divisions. *Injustice* is perhaps at its best when showing the internal political stresses as the various January 6 cases progressed. FBI agents in red states refused to interview witnesses or even execute arrest warrants. "On multiple occasions, prosecutors had groused that agents had even resisted investigative steps involving members of the Proud Boys." Agents questioned why "grandmothers and blue-collar dads who followed the mob" should be charged with any crime more serious than trespassing. Meantime Garland's reluctance to investigate those who had led the coup was attracting critics within the department, who "worried an obsession with safeguarding the perception of an apolitical DOJ was interfering with its core mission in a moment with little historical precedent. To them, the department couldn't uphold the rule of law without bringing the most senior people responsible for January 6 to justice."

From our vantage, two years into the second Trump administration, it all looks depressingly parochial. In the wake of a coup d'état, was anyone within the federal government concerned to protect the country from its perpetrator? Only officials long accustomed to taking for granted the United States' overwhelming power and stability could evidence such a blithe disregard for the evident threat to its security. And the threat was becoming unmistakable. Acquitted in the Senate, Trump had regained his grip on the Republican Party and had begun leading a campaign of retribution against members who had broken ranks to vote for his impeachment. Party leaders flocked to Mar-a-Lago to kiss the ring. The former president was growing more powerful by the day, with the same unmatched ability to command the news cycle at his pleasure or his whim. As the months went by it would become ever clearer that as a figure of national attention—a figure commanding the millions of "eyeballs" that were a critical currency of contemporary power—Trump was unmatched, by Biden or anyone else.

7.

Would the United States government ever have indicted the president who staged a coup against it had the Congress's January 6th Committee not blazoned, in the summer of 2022, the damning evidence of his crimes all over prime-time television? We can never know. What we do know is that Attorney General Garland finally let himself be forced to select a special counsel to investigate "whether any person or entity violated the law in connection with the lawful transfer of power following the 2020 presidential election" only on November 18, 2022—nearly two years after Trump had staged his coup to hold on to the White House and barely two days after he had declared his candidacy to retake it.

Which is to say that Garland and the Biden administration, by resisting until the last moment the effort to punish the authors of the coup, had contrived to let the story of Trump's struggle for freedom and the story of his effort to recapture the White House become *one story.* Would the former president become the first in history to be indicted? Would he become the first to be convicted? Would he be able to win his fight to delay his conviction until after the election? Would he spend his next years in the White House—or in the penitentiary? The heroic president was fighting not only for the office that was stolen from him but for his very freedom: What a story! "This is a vastly different kind of politics," observes Michael Wolff in *All or Nothing: How Trump Recaptured America*, "the man on the tightrope without a net. Who can take their eyes off him? As Trump's third presidential campaign came to life . . . and as the stakes for him became crystal clear, his proposition as a candidate playing both hero and martyr became utterly straightforward: Elect me or destroy me."

Perhaps Trump's greatest skill as a politician is his ability to tell stories and the Biden administration had just given him a momentous one: the story of his martyrdom. First, the powers that be had stolen the election and now they were trying to put him in jail. It was a tale of persecution and resentment and grievance—dark emotions that his supporters broadly shared. Had they too not suffered at the hands of the nefarious elite who had shipped their jobs to China? Had not the elites thrown open the border so illegal immigrants could steal the jobs that were left? Had not the usurper Democratic president brought murderous inflation that had stolen their savings and made their daily lives unaffordable? And was not Trump showing every day that he knew what it was to be unfairly harmed and hounded by the powers that be? He knew how they felt, he would tell his crowds, and the only way for him and them to fight back was to vote for Trump. "They have to go through me to get to you," he bellowed to his exultant crowds. "I am your retribution!" Or: "Our country is being destroyed and the only thing standing between you and its obliteration is me!"

Can any election in American history match 2024 in sheer unadulterated insanity? On a television debate stage in Atlanta, barely a hundred days before the vote, the incumbent Democratic president collapses into geriatric incoherence and in the days after is forced to give way to his little-known vice-president. The Republican challenger (and also a former president), meantime, is *indicted four times* on federal and state felony charges and convicted in New York of thirty-four felonies tied to covering up his affair with a porn star. His unrepentant mug shot from Atlanta becomes a treasured artifact of the campaign. So too does a Supreme Court decision, written by the chief justice, granting the president almost unqualified immunity for acts committed within the ambit of his official duties. The decision by the court to intervene, together with the government's two-year delay in investigating and indicting him, made it impossible to try Trump before the election. Would a jury of his peers have convicted him? Alas, we will never know because the American people in their wisdom went ahead and elected the defendant their forty-seventh president. The federal felony charges, however merited, were withdrawn.

There are many ways to understand the 2024 election but one begins with the perception that Trump was a former president who simply had the better story to tell. He dominated the news from what he denounced as his "Stalinist show trials," holding impromptu press conferences in the courthouse hallways. He lost many of these cases, of course, not only the porn star case but the E. Jean Carroll defamation and business fraud suits in New York, and often seemed to go out of the way to alienate the prosecutor and judge with his antics. Actually, though, Wolff reminds us, "for drama, his courtroom appearances were serving as a better debate replacement."

> He is hardly even playing the game at hand. He, and perhaps only he, is seeing a much larger game: The legal strategy is the media strategy, the media strategy is the legal strategy.
>
> The goal is not to hide or minimize the legal peril, but to bring it on. Combine everything: It's all part of one big witch hunt. It's all part

of one big election interference. The goal is to hammer DA's, judges, Jack Smith, and primary opponents—it's the system against him.

The recognition here is that every indictment juices his fund-raising and raises him up in the polls—and that "he wins this trial," as Wolff puts it, "whatever its outcome, if he wins this election." But it is a tightrope walk, and the point of view in this book is from some point on the rope itself. "Can you believe this shit?" Wolff quotes Trump. "They are literally trying to put me in jail. That's actually pretty cool. I'm like Nelson Mandela. I'm ready, I'll do fine, and you send me to jail, I'm guaranteed to be president." The indictments, the prosecutors, the courts: all of it is a dramatic media machine, allowing him to dominate every news cycle. It is the heroic martyr's struggle, enacted and reenacted. "Trumpian politics is an act of cruelty," Wolff writes. "He's a deranged comic with a rapt audience." The anger, the defiance, the aggression is constant, and for his aggrieved partisans both satisfying and cathartic. However much partisans of democracy resist admitting it, the more powerful appeal is often to voters' darker natures. "He rises," writes Wolff, "in his own mind as well as in the polls, as a function of how much he can trash his opponent." To discuss Trump in policy terms may explain some numbers but in the end it takes too literally what people tell pollsters, for Trump ran on few real policies. He is an entertainer, a celebrity, and, emotionally, an open wound. "Trump is often just a raw nerve, his own rage, resentments, and personal grievances churning in him and, at any given moment, expressed in his public performances—which is exactly what makes them so compelling and, for the campaign, unpredictable." The suspense of unpredictability, of course, is at the heart of much entertainment, and if Trump shows anything it is that much of politics, no matter how serious the stakes, begins with the sheer suspense of being unable to look away. All the way back to Cleon, the demagogue whom Aristotle condemns as the first to "speak coarsely from the rostrum and gather up his skirts about him," democracy has been prey to violent rhetoric and the brutal values of the public gaze. Could but the crowd's fascination be confined to what is benevolent and good we would have a very different country.

What is true of the campaign is true of the second presidency. More so, because that "raw nerve," as Trump ages, becomes steadily more visible—indeed, more intrusive. One is struck once again, in Wolff's very close portrait of Trump regaining the presidency, of how precisely unsuited the man is to occupy the office. He is an aberrant pile of instincts and impulses and it is largely these that help him command the fascinated or appalled stares of tens of millions. Such it was in the campaign and so it continues in his second stay in the White House: however nauseated and fatigued we are, we find ourselves compelled to look. "He is just a content machine," as Senator Chris Murphy put it. "He creates an episode every day you have to tune in to."[4] These episodes shape the public conversation, however rage-filled or erratic or inane and however little they have to do with the national interest. Meantime his waning popularity does not stop his grift or his corruption or much constrain his ability to dominate the supine and still largely terrified Republicans who control Congress. Sinking poll numbers or not, Trump remains, as Wolff writes, "the truly consummate huckster, unafraid that his misrepresentations might be revealed because he had, up

4. See Chris Hayes, *All In*, MSNBC, June 24, 2025.

his sleeve, endlessly more of them. Without humility, and with a taste—even a need—for constant battle, he never relented, never even came close to an admission, and hence a true, no less final reckoning always rolled into the future." Nearly two years later, that reckoning is rolling still.

A closely observed account of his final campaign, *All or Nothing* is in the end an intimate portrait of Trump himself and the grifters and fools who surround him, and it offers generous revelations for those seeking a clue to the wreckage of this presidency nearly halfway in:

> His calling card was as the consummate businessman, but in fact, he was in almost every sense anti-organization. He often seemed incapable of appreciating . . . everything that occurred outside the reach of his own voice or that he did not see on television. He ignored rather than delegated. He almost entirely lacked the ability to listen—sourly looking at anyone who tried to talk to him, before reflexively grabbing back the floor and resuming his own discursive stream of consciousness. He was neither cowed nor impressed by nor appreciative or even comprehending of anyone else's expertise. One result here was that there was no vetting and no basic standard or discernment, nor, often, even a reasonable explanation for the kind and the caliber of people who crowded into his orbit—a democracy of opportunists, grifters, and dunces. The cacophony around him of people trying to get his attention seemed to register, if he heard it all, as a low murmur. Everybody's voice was equal to the extent that they were mostly unheard.

Is such a man capable of making a reasoned decision about, for example, launching a war in the Middle East? If the catastrophic stupidity of the Iran War seems scarcely credible, the simple answer is that this president is incapable of listening to what he is told. Yet Wolff's account seems to focus and clarify a reality that we had long seen but hoped, in its intermittent blurriness, that we were not quite taking in. The truth is we have known him for a very long time. And we kept staring. We couldn't help ourselves.

If he had not before, Trump told us who he was on January 6. After the violent events of that day, no one could doubt that the man Americans had elected as the forty-fifth president was unfit to hold the office. But the political and legal mechanisms that existed to protect the country from him, beginning with impeachment and federal prosecution, were pushed aside, whether out of corrupt ambition within the Senate or a tone-deaf and irrelevant longing for an "apolitical" Justice Department. Those in a position to act to protect the country did not do so. It is painful to admit that Trump's ever-popular denunciations of the elite ring true precisely here, for it must tell us something vital about our democracy that when the stakes were highest those who are meant to devote their lives to protecting the country failed to do their jobs. That Trump was able to become the democratically chosen leader four years after his crimes against the state bespeaks a decadence in the country's ruling institutions and those who direct them. If he was right about anything, he was right about that. No one knows how deep the present darkness will become. For all its power the country may well not have the liberty to make such mistakes again.

Trump's Constitutional Dictatorship

July 22, 2026

AMID THE TUMULT and the bluster and the noise, what exactly makes our singular president tick? After revisiting in minute detail the innumerable outrages and atrocities of Donald Trump's second term we come upon, in the epilogue to *Regime Change*, the purported answer. The *New York Times* reporters Maggie Haberman and Jonathan Swan, having mostly completed their epic chronicle, arrive at the now-gilded Oval Office for their "fact-checking" interview. The president, in an expansive mood, greets them and guides them to their seats in front of the Resolute Desk. "No other president," he had recently declared with his customary eloquence, "could do some of the shit I'm doing."

Exactly what shit might he have had in mind? Sending masked ICE agents to seize and deport hundreds of thousands of largely law-abiding people and imprison 60,000 more? Overturning the eighty-year-old world trade system by imposing arbitrary tariffs? Launching a war of choice against Iran with nary a word to Congress or the American people? Firing hundreds of thousands of government workers and destroying USAID, PBS, and the Kennedy Center? Attacking law firms and universities and television networks?

One could go on, but the president wishes to make a broader point. A loyal-unto-death aide, Natalie Harp—known to her colleagues as "the human printer"—is dispatched to fetch a document, and the president begins to read from it,

> reciting the names of some of history's most powerful figures, explaining how each fell short of his own power as US President. Alexander the Great, the Caesars, William the Conqueror—"They didn't have airplanes, right? You couldn't travel around." Genghis Khan. Attila the Hun. Tamerlane. "Napoleon," he said with relish. "Hitler. Mao. Stalin."
>
> These leaders "maintained power through fear," he said. "Who would ever do a thing like that? Right?"
>
> Trump lingered on the document's central argument: that each leader, however fearsome in his day, had no global reach. Their power was local. But his was not.
>
> "I never thought of it in terms of that," Trump said. "It's very interesting, the power." Then he added: "But when I read it, I said, 'He's right.'"

And the "he" in question? The "historian" whose name had slipped the president's mind, Harp later texts them, was actually the golfer Gary Player's longtime caddy. No matter. "What was revealing," they write,

> was not really that Trump agreed with the thesis but the way he inhabited it: the evident pleasure he took in the company of Mao,

Hitler, and Stalin, masters of state control through murder, torture, and detention, and Napoleon—and the untroubled ease with which he accepted a place among men who had reshaped the world through conquest and fear. He drew no distinction between those who built and those who destroyed.

The scene is irresistible: the president of the United States sitting at the Resolute Desk and comparing himself blithely to Mao, Hitler, and Stalin. Still, what does it tell us? That a tireless and amoral will to power is deeply embedded in Donald Trump's narcissism and vanity is not exactly a revelation: anyone who has watched him perform a ninety-minute stand-up routine before a crowd of supporters—drinking in, with almost erotic delight, the fervent worship of thousands—cannot have failed to notice. And after the undermining of NATO, the destruction of USAID, and the calamity of the Iran war, Trump's name is more likely to appear on lists of leaders who have diminished their country's power than lists of those who have increased it. But that he has become one of the most powerful American presidents—that he has since his second inauguration "put on a demonstration of raw executive power the country had not seen since the presidency of FDR"—is well-nigh indisputable. One could go further and say that not only has Trump, like Roosevelt and Lincoln, successfully imposed on the world's first modern democracy a "constitutional dictatorship,"[1] he is the only president to have done so in the absence of a true emergency.

1. We owe this invaluable term to the historian and political scientist Clinton Rossiter. See his *Constitutional Dictatorship: Crisis Government in the Modern Democracies* (Princeton University Press, 1948).

*

How did he do it? Aggressively, brutally, relentlessly—weren't we all watching him? The more specific answer is that he did it by exploiting the chief executive's myriad emergency powers or, as Haberman and Swan rather politely phrase it, by "redefin[ing] the very concept of an 'emergency.'" Another way to put it is that Trump did what Trump does as easily as he breathes: he lied. Is the trade deficit, in uninterrupted existence for half a century, an emergency? Can a country leading the world in energy production be said to be undergoing an "energy emergency"? Can we consider that the southern border, where crossings dropped 77 percent after Joe Biden's executive order limiting entry, remains in the grip of a "border emergency"? The answer is no. But it doesn't matter. In issuing more than 140 executive orders in his first hundred days in office—Roosevelt issued ninety-nine—Trump declared that the country was beset by no fewer than ten separate emergencies.[2] And in the face of this supposedly unprecedented onslaught the president must have unprecedented powers to confront them.

This is what would-be autocrats do: declare an emergency and rule by decree. ("Sovereign is he who decides the exception," in the celebrated words of the Nazi legal theorist Carl Schmitt.) For a president thirsting for more power, this is the obvious path. But surely the Framers in their wisdom anticipated this danger? Of course they did, which is why Trump's true innovation as an Amer-

2. This is according to Karen Yourish and Charlie Smart, "How Trump Used 10 Emergency Declarations to Justify Hundreds of Actions," *The New York Times*, August 22, 2025. The Associated Press, using different criteria, puts the number at over forty.

ican authoritarian is not the profligate abuse of emergency powers but the full-on castration of a Congress that allowed him to do it. As we all learned in school, Congress, cantankerous and jealous of its powers, particularly the power of the purse, was meant to be the immediate bulwark against an unbound executive. But during his decade of dominance, Trump has wielded his charisma and his fury and his unquenchable taste for vengeance to systematically destroy any Republicans who would dare raise a voice against him. Though these days a few so-called YOLO—"You only live once"—Republicans, who are retiring or have lost primaries thanks to Trump, are nervously raising their heads from under a rock, since his reelection senators and congressmen have been only too happy to remain silent as he relentlessly increases his power by suborning theirs.

For anyone who has spent Trump's second term ranting about spineless Republicans and their lack of fealty to the country's founding principles, Haberman and Swan offer a useful course in the iron laws of Republican self-preservation. The president wields sticks, yes—we have all seen how the insufficiently "loyal" are wiped out by Trump-backed primary challengers—but even more he offers carrots, aggressively seducing those who show the least reluctance to comply. Power in Congress, having increasingly in recent years flowed upward to the leadership, now "flowed out of the Speaker's office directly into the Oval Office." And it was not just that Speaker Mike Johnson owed his job to Trump:

> Johnson understood the fear Trump inspired.... But it was not just about the threats. He knew also, as did his colleagues, that Trump had a more powerful connection with Republican voters than any of them. And he knew that his own members were seduced by Trump.

> Trump exploited those emotions. He understood that many Republican lawmakers related to him like starry-eyed fans rather than as elected representatives of a coequal branch of government. He offered more access than any modern president. Since 2017, he had handed out his cell phone number freely—even to the most junior members of Congress, who would never have dreamed of texting or calling the President. He invited them to play golf with him at his clubs, for dinner at Mar-a-Lago, and for flights on his private jet.

With these lavish perquisites on offer, unusual was the young congressman or senator who needed to be shown the stick. Trump had long since rooted out of Congress most of the Republicans who had voted to impeach him, but his memory is long and his vindictiveness unflagging. (Senator Bill Cassidy, who voted to convict him in 2021, was finally crushed in a primary in May.) So why risk it? Take the presidential phone calls and the plane rides—and the money.

And the money in the post–*Citizens United* age is staggering. By the day after the 2024 election, Haberman and Swan report, "Trump was already receiving phone calls from Fortune 500 CEOs, many of whom had criticized him in the past." They wanted to get back into the president-elect's good graces, but the cost

> would be high.... Trump would dictate the number—the exact dollar figure—he wanted [his fundraiser] to extract from each CEO. Within days, millions of dollars, and then tens and hundreds of millions, were pouring into Trump's various fundraising accounts.

The sums are truly fantastical: $1.9 billion raised from corporate donors. Trump's political apparatus, much more organized and efficient than it had been during his first term, made full "use [of these] outside groups as weapons to enforce compliance" with his agenda. Next to corporate resources, mere politicians are cheap: a couple billion buys a lot of compliance. And should the campaign cash and the phone calls fall short, there was always the social media army, a bevy of MAGA influencers "who had massive audiences and threatened any Republican who would consider voting against Trump's nominees." Senator Joni Ernst, a combat veteran who expressed doubts about Pete Hegseth's nomination as secretary of defense (for his part Hegseth, one of the dimmer of the dim bulbs among Trump's appointees, had doubts about whether women should even be in combat), found herself beset with a full-on social media campaign that included nasty details of her divorce. She voted for Hegseth.

And so even before his second term had commenced, Trump and his minions, who make up in loyalty and obedience what they lack in competence, were able very quickly to reduce the United States' three branches of government to two. Except for isolated cases like the Epstein files—Haberman and Swan offer an entertaining account of the full-on panic caused by that political scandal, including the president's alleged "nipple fetish," treated with great seriousness in the Situation Room—the conflict has been between the executive and the courts, which apart from the ideological deformations of the Supreme Court have generally performed ably, though they have not always been obeyed. But is anyone thinking of Tamerlane yet? Or Hitler? Stalin perhaps?

The comparisons seem absurd because although Trump as a politician certainly has elements of genius—his aggression and energy, his uncanny instinct for finding weakness in adversaries, his mastery in dominating the news cycle, his endlessly creative shaping and projecting of his own grievances, his sheer shameless willfulness in making his reality our own—he also remains an ignorant blowhard. He lies so much that he often forgets what the truth is. He doesn't read. He knows little or no history. And he is so captivated by the sound of his own voice that he almost entirely lacks the ability to listen. Finally, he is wholly in the grip of a decades-old set of beliefs—imposing tariffs will make the United States rich with other countries' money, American cities are so ravaged by criminal immigrants that only the military can restore order, alliances are simply the means by which freeloader countries "take advantage" of the United States, climate change is nothing more than a fallacious "green new scam"—that are demonstrably false.

What remains astonishing is that Trump, through his indefatigable showmanship, was able to ride his reality show fame to such power in the world's strongest country that he has been able to impose these aberrant views on nearly 350 million people, with consequences for billions more. As Haberman and Swan show, Trump in his second term has built a government that, but for a few important exceptions (Susie Wiles, Stephen Miller, Russell Vought), is made up of incompetent toadies who are wholly responsive to his wishes—a government that, forced to choose between his fantasies and reality, will choose the fantasies every time. The result is that our politics have seemed to turn the world on its head. Thousands are dying in unprecedented heat waves, and the American government is firing rafts of climate scientists, paying multinational corporations not to put up windmills that have already been paid for, and scrubbing the words "climate change" from government websites. Trump's patrimonialist administration has become a stark embodiment of his own ignorance and irrationality.

One result is that parts of Haberman and Swan's meticulously reported chronicle read like science fiction. Their account of the meetings about the president's vaunted Liberation Day, on the other hand, a week before the United States unilaterally dismantled the international trade system, sounds like something out of the Marx Brothers:

> "Nobody has fucking given me any numbers," Trump fumed. "Hard facts of how much China tariffs us, how much India tariffs us. You give me bullshit numbers."
>
> Commerce Secretary Howard Lutnick pulled out a folder, saying, "Here are the numbers. . . ."
>
> But Trump was convinced that the real numbers for India and China were much higher than Lutnick's printouts. "No, these are bullshit numbers," he said, giving Lutnick a hard look. "These are fucking bullshit."
>
> Harp, despite her best efforts, was not finding the numbers that didn't exist.
>
> "No, these *are* the real numbers!" Lutnick insisted. . . . Turning to the President's trade representative, Jamieson Greer, Lutnick pleaded, "Right, Jamieson? Jamieson, say these numbers are real. Jamieson, speak up."
>
> Greer, a trade lawyer who was not inclined to get into a spat with the President, just looked at Lutnick and said nothing.
>
> The President's global tariff program, set to launch on "Liberation Day," was just a week away, but the rates were still undecided. Trump wanted to set the rates using a formula he had been devising in his

> mind. No one was sure precisely how it was being calculated, and it would vary by the day, sometimes by the hour. But how could he make his calculations with these bullshit numbers from Lutnick?

A handful of very wealthy people who are way out of their depth are playing with the world's trade system, which was developed under the leadership of the United States in delicate negotiations by hundreds of experts over many decades, and they are about to shatter it with a single announcement, all because the president fervently and irrationally believes that the country has "been treated very unfairly" by its trading partners and that tariffs will make the country rich with their money.

In the event, Trump's announcement crashed the markets, with the S&P 500 losing $2 trillion in one day, and soon the bond market began to plunge as well. Finally, faced with financial Armageddon, Trump backed down, "pausing the tariffs" for ninety days:

> That afternoon, the markets surged nearly 10 percent on the news, and Trump surrogates rushed to the cameras to clean up the mess, claiming that pausing the tariffs was the plan all along. This was, they said, a genius negotiating strategy from the dealmaker of dealmakers.... The world had just witnessed a master class in economic brinkmanship, they would all say.
>
> But in fact, Trump had blinked. The collapsing bond markets left him no choice. Investors were losing faith that the United States would be able to make good on its debt.

One lived through these events, of course, but in reliving them through this inside account one feels a kind of terrible awe at the blithe incompetence and sheer irresponsibility on display. In service to his obsessions, the president is willing to take the country right up to the edge of catastrophe, and no one is willing to incur his ire by trying to stop him. Only the reality of the consequences of what he had done—the collapsing bond markets—persuaded him to reverse course. Perhaps it is not too much to hope that as this divergence between Trump's fantasyland and reality grows, reality increasingly will triumph. The trouble with this lunge for optimism is not only that thus far—with tariffs and the Iran war, for example—we have needed a catastrophe to mark the dividing line but that it fails to account for the damage already done, which is unquestionably very great indeed.

The catastrophe of Iran may reveal this country's decline no less than the Suez Crisis revealed Great Britain's. There is the same stunned realization abroad of having seen the limits of the late imperial mind. Haberman and Swan's account of the decision to attack Iran—a decision presidents have resisted for very good reasons since 1979—is a bravura piece of reporting and, for those who retain any faith in American power in the world, deeply saddening to read. As he has with previous presidents, the Israeli prime minister comes to the White House Situation Room with a war to sell, and he promises that regime change will follow and the nuclear threat will be removed forever. Trump will be a hero, doing what presidents before him have lacked the audacity to attempt. And although US intelligence analysts call the Israeli scenarios "farcical"—"In other words, it's bullshit," helpfully translates Secretary of State and National Security Adviser Marco Rubio—Trump decides to buy in anyway. The chairman of the Joint Chiefs mentions something about Iran closing the Strait of Hormuz—one of the principal reasons presidents have resisted similar Israeli importunings for decades—but Trump in his vast ignorance says not to worry, it'll all be over in a few days. And anyway what do we have to lose?

The account put me in mind of a phrase from an essay published early in this administration: "The Dumbest Imperial Collapse in History."[3] Today, because of Trump's blithe decision, nearly four thousand Iranians are dead, more than four thousand Lebanese are dead, and eighteen Americans are dead. The Strait of Hormuz, a critical economic choke point, is firmly in the hands of the Islamic Republic of Iran, and the aircraft carriers of the mighty US Fifth Fleet have been unable to keep it open in the face of Iran's speedboats, mines, and drones. "It's very interesting," as Trump mused to these reporters, "the power." It would be reassuring if those anodyne words bespoke some knowledge or wisdom instead of its simulacrum. In truth, military power—the power to blow things up—is less important than military authority: the ability to dictate terms without blowing things up. And Trump, for all his musings on Tamerlane and Stalin, has managed to reduce the United States' authority immeasurably, thanks to his own shallowness, vanity, and inability to listen.

The mummers' play of negotiations that led to the memorandum of understanding and the restart of the war that followed fall outside the ambit of Haberman and Swan's account. Had they not, the authors might have said that when it came to the absurd memorandum—in which the Americans agreed to pay the Iranians billions of dollars to restore the status quo ante—the rising inflation caused by the closing of the strait along with the rapidly approaching mid-

3. See Ryan Cooper, "Musk and Trump Are Causing the Dumbest Imperial Collapse in History," *The American Prospect*, February 19, 2025.

term elections "left him no choice" but to kowtow to the Iranians. But this is the weakness and danger of Trump's transactionalism: he has no enduring scale, beyond his own vanity, to judge what's important or what's right. And if some in his tiny circle of decision makers do, they lack the courage to tell him. In fact he himself set up an eventual war when he rashly tore up Barack Obama's nuclear agreement with Iran in 2018. Now, like some woeful tragic hero, he finds himself doomed by his own unknowing decisions and struggling to negotiate an agreement that can never be as good as his predecessor's. As drama, there is something right and satisfying about this. But we are all along for the ride as the Iran war and its aftermath turn into a terrible, decadent sham.

Trump, quickly bored, has moved on. He is presiding over other scandals—the algae-filled Reflecting Pool, among others—and other projects, like his splendid ballroom, larger than the White House itself, and his "Arc de Trump," which is to be nearly one hundred feet taller than its Napoleon-conceived model in Paris. Even as he muses on his power, his approval numbers have stabilized in the mid-thirties: two Americans in three disapprove of the job he is doing. He has long since lost the support of many of the independents, Latinos, and younger voters who brought him back to office. As the midterms approach he struggles to manipulate them through redistricting, rantings about voter fraud, and proposals to suppress voting. But in California and other states the Democrats have matched Republican gerrymandering, and the president's much-hyped SAVE America Act, which would impose burdensome identification requirements on voters, will not pass the Senate.

The signs are everywhere that the failed assault on Iran marked the high tide of his power. The Supreme Court ruled that he lacked the authority to impose his tariffs or to end birthright citizenship. Lower courts in dozens of decisions have blocked his more presumptuous emergency actions. His high-profile campaign of deportations in "blue cities" crashed on the shoals of Minneapolis's civic resistance, including that of the two protesters ICE agents shot and killed there. Confronted with a wave of bad press and plunging poll numbers, the administration backed down, ignoring the urgings of some within it (including Stephen Miller and, as Haberman and Swan reveal, Vice President J. D. Vance) that the president invoke the Insurrection Act and send troops into the city. Here, as with the tariffs and the war, faced with darkening reality he retreated, though his administration, working more quietly now, continues to deport tens of thousands.

What truly matters to Trump beyond his ballrooms and his reflecting pools and his arches? Does he lose sleep over immigrants "invading" the country? No doubt he has thrown into high relief the weaknesses of our governing system on its 250th birthday, beginning with his own coming to power after winning nearly three million fewer votes than his opponent. But he will bequeath no doctrine or philosophy. The norms he has shattered with his systematic corruption remain to be made into laws that will be stronger and more lasting. The nihilism he has exposed among voters disgusted by their powerlessness amid ever-rising inequality remains to be addressed by future leaders, but none seems likely to replace him as a ubiquitous social media troll. For two years more and counting, the incessant cacophony—the twenty-four-hour dominance of the news cycle with tweets and insults and scandals—will go on. He is a huckster, an Internet-age buffoon with endless resources to entertain and outrage us. However much we long to banish him from our consciousness, he will not be banished.

He will leave us having succeeded in putting an end to the country's imperial dominance and in closing borders that were once more welcoming to outsiders. He will have helped ensure that the rich grow ever richer and that millions with less will not have insurance when they get sick. He will have made the government weaker and less responsive and the society around it starkly more corrupt. He will have politicized many parts of the country's public life that were not politicized before.

But his pretended reflection on what he longed to acquire—"It's very interesting, the power"—is inert. He has a vast appetite for power only insofar as it satisfies his greed and directs the spotlight upon himself. But it is power merely as self-aggrandizement, and it ends with the sterile farce of his name plastered on arches and monuments. As I write, the courts have ordered that name removed from the Kennedy Center, and that humiliating operation, shaded from the eyes of the public behind a nondescript tarp, also marks a turning point. Would Tamerlane or Stalin have stood for such a disgrace? He has on occasion sent in the troops, but when the courts have pushed back he has loudly complained and quietly complied. For all his bluster about emergencies, he has not invoked the Insurrection Act, fearing that the political damage would far outweigh the gain. Unless he succeeds in blatantly subverting the coming elections—by sending troops into polling places, say, to seize ballots and thereby "protect" the vote, a fateful step that plainly tempts him—his power, however proudly he flaunts it, will continue inexorably to ebb.

Acknowledgments

ROBERT B. SILVERS, one of the founding editors of *The New York Review of Books*, commissioned the bulk of these writings. It was one of the delights of my life to call Bob from some noisy rally and provide him with a real-time dispatch from the field. From the moment he hired me, right out of college, Bob taught me more about thinking and writing than anyone else. I will remain forever grateful to him for his wisdom, his loyalty, and his faith.

Reverent gratitude also to the *Review*'s brilliant and impossibly charming coeditor, Barbara Epstein. Thinking about Bob and Barbara reminds me that my life has been singularly blessed with gifted mentors and that so many of those who taught me the lessons embodied here have passed on. I will always be grateful to Fouad Ajami, John Bennet, Joan Bingham, James Chace, Robert Gottlieb, John Homans, Peter Jennings, Frank Kermode, Tom Luddy, Czesław Miłosz, Susan Sontag, Theodore Draper, and Peter Tarnoff.

Emily Greenhouse, the current editor of the *Review*, and Michael Shae, her deputy, commissioned the pieces in the latter part of the book and saw them to press. My deep thanks to them and to their excellent staff. And thanks to Edwin Frank, the editorial director of New York Review Books, and to Muhua Yang and Sara Kramer, for editing this book and publishing it so well. I thank Joy Harris, my longtime agent and friend, for her brilliant reading and her unflagging encouragement.

For their friendship and their conversation, I am grateful to Michael Pollan, Don DeLillo, David Gelber, Lynn Glaser, Robert Hass, Thomas Laqueur, Adam Hochschild, Arlie Russell Hochschild, Gerald Marzorati, Daniel Sargent, Orville Schell, and Tamara Straus.

My father, Robert, early on taught me about politics and history, among so much else. I am formed by those discussions. My mother, Rosalyn, taught me how to write and how to laugh. I am grateful to my parents for so much, not least for living fruitful and very long lives, which allowed them to get to know my children and my children to know them. Grace and Truman live in a world where it is impossible not to be buffeted by politics, even at their tender ages. Building the new world falls to them. This book is for my parents and my children.

—M.D.D

MARK DANNER has been writing about foreign wars and American politics for more than three decades. Among his books are *The Massacre at El Mozote, Torture and Truth, Stripping Bare the Body*, and *Spiral: Trapped in the Forever War*. He was a staff writer at *The New Yorker* for many years and is a longtime contributor to *The New York Review of Books*. His work has received many honors, including a National Magazine Award, three Overseas Press Awards, a Guggenheim Fellowship, an Emmy, and a MacArthur Fellowship. He is currently Class of 1961 Distinguished Chair in Undergraduate Education at the University of California at Berkeley.